W9-AMX-222

Margaret Junkin Preston
A Biography

ALSO BY MARY PRICE COULLING

The Lee Girls

MARGARET JUNKIN PRESTON
A Biography

Mary Price Coulling

 JOHN F. BLAIR, PUBLISHER
Winston-Salem, North Carolina

This book is printed on acid-free paper.

DESIGNED BY DEBRA LONG HAMPTON
COMPOSED BY THE ROBERTS GROUP
PRINTED AND BOUND BY R.R. DONNELLEY & SONS

Library of Congress Cataloging-in-Publication Data
Coulling, Mary P.
    Margaret Junkin Preston : a biography / Mary Price Coulling.
        p.   cm.
    Includes bibliographical references and index.
    ISBN 0-89587-102-5 :
    1. Preston, Margaret Junkin, 1820–1897—Biography.   2. Women and
literature—United States—History—19th century.   3. Authors,
American—19th century—Biography.   4. Lexington (Va.)—Biography.
I. Title.
PS2663.C68   1993
811'.4—dc20
[B]   93-16256

This book is dedicated to

my family,

and to

Janet Cross Preston and the late Herbert Rush Preston,

grandchildren of Margaret Junkin Preston,

who provided unqualified use of original papers,

offered constant encouragement,

and gave me the gift of their friendship.

Contents

Acknowledgments

Many people have assisted in the preparation, revision, and completion of this biography. Librarians across the country have been untiring in their assistance, including: the staff of the Huntington Library, San Marino, California; M. N. Brown and others of the John Hay Library of Brown University, Providence, Rhode Island; Frances D. McClure with the Walter Havighurst Special Collections of the university library at Miami University, Oxford, Ohio; Dianne M. Gutscher, the curator of special collections at Bowdoin College, Brunswick, Maine; the curator of the West Virginia and Regional History Collection of the University of West Virginia at Morgantown; Charlotte Walter of the Northumberland County Historical Society, Sunbury, Pennsylvania; Barbara Bailey Bauer of the Easton (Pennsylvania) Area Public Library; Freda Cohen, curator at the McDonogh School, Baltimore, Maryland; William R. Erwin, Jr., senior reference librarian and others in the William R. Perkins Library, Duke

University, Durham, North Carolina; John E. White with the Southern Historical Collection, University of North Carolina at Chapel Hill; James J. Holmberg, curator of manuscripts, Filson Club, Louisville, Kentucky; Albert Gendebien and Diane Windham Shaw with the College Archives, Lafayette College, Easton, Pennsylvania; and Louise T. Jones of the Historical Society of Pennsylvania, Philadelphia.

Unusually helpful have been professionals at three institutions in Lexington, Virginia: Diane Jacob, curator, James Gaines, librarian, Wilma Davis, reference librarian, Keith Gibson, director of museums, and others at the Virginia Military Institute; Barbara Brown, librarian, Betsy Brittigan, Virginia Smyers, Betty Kondayan, Lisa McCown, and others at the university library at Washington and Lee University; Michael A. Lynn, director, Joanna Smith, and others at the Stonewall Jackson House.

Valuable research assistance came from Royster Lyle, Richard Hastings, Betty Munger, Richard Marks, Lad Sessions, and Taylor Sanders, Lexington, Virginia; E. D. Witherspoon, Jr. and Linda H. Zipper, Louisville, Kentucky; Anna Brooke Allan and Lynn Roundtree, Chapel Hill, North Carolina; Owen Robbins, Philadelphia, Pennsylvania; Agnes Junkin Peery, Tazewell, Virginia; Randy W. Hackenburg, Boiling Spring, Pennsylvania; Elisabeth Robinson, Palm Springs, Florida; Jean Vinson Urquhart, Rock Island, Illinois; Elizabeth Lapsley Pendergrast, Atlanta, Georgia; William C. Pollard, Staunton, Virginia; Paul Hagist, Dallas, Texas; and William W. Pusey, III of Lexington and Charlottesville, Virginia. Drs. Frank W. Price and John D. Harralson, both of Lexington, offered helpful medical insights. I am grateful to Denise Watts and Tom Raisbeck of Lexington for technical assistance. My special appreciation goes to W. Patrick Hinely, photographer of Washington and Lee, for photographs made in Lexington and in Baltimore, Maryland.

James I. Robertson, Jr. (Civil War Historian and Alumni Distinguished Professor at the Virginia Polytechnic Institute and State University) has been especially supportive. Rayburn S. Moore (professor emeritus at the University of Georgia and author of numerous books and articles about Paul Hamilton Hayne) encouraged me over the years as I struggled with research and writing. Both he and Michael A. Lynn read the entire manuscript and offered useful corrections and suggestions. My husband, Sidney M. B. Coulling, has given unfailing support and valuable editorial assistance. Special thanks must go also to the staff of the publishing company of John F. Blair, including Margaret Couch, Debra L. Hampton, and Carolyn Sakowski, and to my copy editor, Gail Lathey Warner.

Finally, this book would not have been possible without the use of family papers provided me, without restriction, by Margaret Junkin Preston's two grandchildren, Janet Cross Preston and the late Herbert Rush Preston, of Baltimore. Janet Preston also read the manuscript in its entirety. With the assistance and encouragement of so many individuals, I have enjoyed the happy privilege of learning to know well a remarkable woman of the nineteenth century—Margaret Junkin Preston.

Introduction

The small Virginia town of Lexington had never seen anything like it. Special excursion trains backed up to the local railway station, bringing hundreds of Confederate veterans. Thousands more arrived by coach and private buggy, traveling up and down the dusty Valley Pike, until the huge crowd of nearly 25,000 persons threatened to overwhelm the community.

The date was July 21, 1891, the occasion the dedication of a heroic statue of Stonewall Jackson that had been erected over his grave in the local cemetery. There were banners and bands, parades, commemorative poems, and ardent eulogies. Finally, in the afternoon, under a sky of "azure blue broken in many places with floating, fleecy clouds and gentle breezes,"[1] Jackson's two grandchildren pulled the cord, unveiling a handsome bronze likeness of the mighty Stonewall in Confederate uniform, standing with his field glasses in one hand, his long sword by his side.

In a house across the street from the graveyard there lived a woman who had been the general's close friend, a tiny seventy-one-year-old invalid whose memories of Jackson could not be erased by deafness, failing eyesight, or the debility caused by a serious stroke. Forty years earlier, she had been Jackson's opponent and then his friend. He had taught her Spanish, and, during the Federal occupation of Lexington, she had hidden his sword under her petticoats. In more recent years she had written poems about him, as well as a host of other topics, earning for herself the title "Poetess of the South."

The name of the frail invalid was Margaret Junkin Preston—and this is her story.

Margaret Junkin Preston
A Biography

Chapter 1

Scenes of Childhood
1820–1831

> For in the history of life,
> > Turn o'er the leaves, from youth to age—
> And find, mid lines of joy and grief,
> > That *Childhood* is its brightest page![1]

One spring afternoon in 1820, as the western sun slanted in through the windows of his small frame house, the Reverend George Junkin sat down at his desk to write a letter.

Selecting a large sheet of paper, he began: "Milton, May 20th, 1820, Saturday. My dear sister . . ."[2] On other Saturdays, when busy water traffic on the nearby Susquehanna River slackened at the approach of dusk, the young Presbyterian parson might have used the quiet and the lingering sunlight to refine his sermon for the morrow.

But today he had the more personal and pleasant task of writing to his sister-in-law about one of the most important events in his life to date—the birth of his first child. "Our dear little Margaret was ushered into the world yesterday afternoon," he wrote, "[at] 20 minutes before 2 o'clock." With relief, he reported that his wife had come safely through her ordeal and had endured "severe pains" with "uncommon fortitude." He himself had been the first to place the child in her mother's arms, where, he said, the baby had begun to "suck . . . powerfully," with "an excellent prospect for a good supply" of milk.[3]

Junkin had little to say about the baby's appearance, but instead wrote at length of his newfound sense of parental responsibility. Likening his new daughter to Moses, the God-chosen firstborn who was given into the care of Miriam, the young father prayed "that my dear wife & I may hear the Lord saying to us, 'take this child away & nurse it for me & I will give thee thy wages.'"[4] Using the biblical story from Exodus, George Junkin underscored his desire to forge a unique parental relationship with a very special child.

Although eight more children would be born to Julia and George Junkin, the father always retained a closeness to this diminutive, red-haired daughter that he felt toward none of the others. And Maggie, as the little girl was soon to be called, grew up to be the child most like her father—high-strung, scholarly, and, above all, gifted in language. Throughout his life, he communicated with the public in a torrent of sermons, books, lectures, church papers, and newspaper articles. His daughter would become a poet, book reviewer, and essayist. With their shared passion for words and symbols, they loved and supported each other in times of family need and professional crisis.

Many years later their lives would diverge sharply, but the

bonds of love and shared interests remained unbroken. When the Civil War tore them apart, Maggie understood better than anyone else her father's dramatic gesture of wiping Virginia dust from his wagon wheels, while she remained loyal to the cause of her Confederate husband and her brother-in-law, Stonewall Jackson. During the war, unable to correspond except through occasional smuggled letters, they continued their own writing far from each other, Dr. Junkin in long, rambling polemics and Maggie, by then Margaret Junkin Preston, in wartime poetry that touched the hearts of a defeated people and won her a place as "Poetess of the South."[5]

The small house in Milton, Pennsylvania, where Maggie was born has long since been torn down. The village, originally built around docks on the narrow west branch of the Susquehanna River, is today a placid farming and manufacturing town of some 7,000 persons, with only a handful of the early river houses still standing. Indeed, almost every aspect of life as Maggie Junkin experienced it has disappeared. However, by using her poetry and extant Junkin family letters, it is possible to reconstruct something of her early years and the influences that shaped her character—her attractive, energetic, God-fearing parents, the five siblings born during the years in Milton, her exposure to the classics, and the stern Calvinism that permeated her childhood.

The most important person in her young life was her father, an intense, active young man with a strong, rugged face and "keen black eye."[6] George Junkin was a powerful speaker who swayed audiences by his commanding presence, his forceful rhetoric, and his absolute conviction of the rightness of the causes to which he devoted himself. A man of boundless energy, he not only prepared sermons for two small churches each week, but also conducted Sunday schools in the area, organized a vigorous temperance movement within the community, started a small preparatory school, edited a biweekly newspaper called *The Reli-*

gious Farmer, and visited every family in his congregations once a year. Despite his busy schedule, he spent as much free time as he could with his daughter. And Maggie responded eagerly to his desire that she share his intellectual enthusiasm and single-minded search for God's truth. As a child, she happily accompanied him on pastoral calls in the community, and twice each Sunday she sat enthralled at his spellbinding sermons, attentive to "what most I loved to hear,/ *The sweetness* of a Father's tone."[7]

George Junkin had grown up less than a hundred miles from Milton, in New Kingston, Pennsylvania, the sixth child and fourth son of fourteen children born to a third-generation Scotch-Irish farming couple. True to their Calvinist heritage, the Junkins were devout members of the Associate Reformed Presbyterian Church, an offshoot of more traditional Presbyterianism that was characterized by rigid biblical doctrines, prohibitions against any hymn-singing but psalms, and exceedingly strict Sabbath observances. George's father, Joseph, had fought in the Revolutionary War and as a child had narrowly escaped capture by Indians on what was then the frontier. His early stories of the war for independence and encounters with Indians became part of the Junkin family folklore, reinforcing George Junkin's passionate belief in a divinely ordained American union, and weaving their way into little Maggie's consciousness. Among her earliest poems were eulogies to George Washington and verses about American Indians and captured white settlers.

After a sketchy education in a one-room school under teachers often "more drunk than sober," Maggie's father went on to spend several years at Jefferson College in Canonsburg, Pennsylvania, where he won distinction as "the best debater in his . . . class"[8] before graduating in 1813. Convinced that God had chosen him to be a minister, Junkin traveled east by horseback to Philadelphia, where he sold his horse at auction to pay for postgraduate education. In New York City he placed himself under the tutelage of Dr. John Mason, provost of Columbia College, who conducted a small theological class in his own home. After several years of study, the young man was ordained in 1817 by the Associate Reformed Presbytery of Philadelphia. He served an apprenticeship as an itinerant preacher in Pennsylvania, New York, and Maryland, and then in 1819 he undertook his first and only pastorate, ministering to two small A.R.P. congregations in Milton, fifty miles northwest of Harrisburg, Pennsylvania.*

Having grown up in a rural setting, the twenty-nine-year-old Junkin settled easily into the small, bustling river village, where farmers of German descent brought their produce for sale, itinerant merchants plied their trade to and from eastern counties, and a constant stream of Scotch-Irish immigrants passed through on their way to fertile farms in Ohio, Virginia, and the Carolinas. But the parson's bride, five years younger than her husband, found the transition to central Pennsylvania far more difficult.

Julia Rush Miller Junkin, one of four daughters of immigrant Scottish parents, had grown up in comparative luxury in Philadelphia. Her father was a well-to-do marble worker and stone mason whose friends and patrons included Benjamin Rush, the eminent physician and signer of the Declaration of Independence, and Rembrandt Peale, the noted portrait painter. Julia had been named for Dr. Rush's wife, and among Miller family treasures were six Peale portraits—of John Miller, his wife Margaret, and their four daughters—which the artist had painted as payment for marble mantels. When the Millers had arrived at the docks in Philadelphia, they had brought with them a certificate of commendation from their kirk in Scotland, an endorsement that

---

*When the A.R.P. synod of Philadelphia was dissolved in 1822, George Junkin led his congregation into the synod of Northumberland, a unit of the larger body of the Presbyterian Church U.S.A. He remained a loyal member of the conservative (Old School) wing of the mainline Presbyterian discipline for the rest of his life.

quickly led John Miller to become an influential member and later ruling elder in the Germantown Presbyterian church. Here, a few doors from the Miller home, George Junkin had first met the vivacious, sweet-faced, devout Julia. After a courtship of several years, the couple married in June of 1819 and set out at once for their new home, far away from all that the young woman had grown up with.

Julia quickly discovered that the house they had rented was only half built and located unpleasantly close to neighbors' pig-pens. "The kitchen is not yet finished," she wrote to her sister in Chester County, Pennsylvania, but she cheerfully anticipated that "it will be a very pleasant convenient one when it is finished," and she pronounced the house itself to be "altogether . . . very pleasant." Before winter, however, she found herself pregnant and overwhelmed by all that was expected of her, from serving tea to parishioners to milking the newly acquired cow and making butter. Still, despite weariness and the "distance from my dear friends," she was, she wrote, content with "a husband who does all in his power to make me happy."[9] Fortunately, she had brought with her from home a black servant named Hannah, a tangible connection with relatives at Germantown and a woman whose assistance proved invaluable when children began arriving in rapid succession.

The second child in the family was John, the eldest son, born when Maggie was two years old. He was to mature into a sandy-haired, mechanically minded youngster, not much inter-ested in books or studying. A year later a second son, Joseph, arrived, a lad whom Maggie described in one of her early poems as "the fairest . . . of all his father's sons." Then came Eleanor, born in 1825, a child "with hazel eyes—and sunny hair,"[10] followed in 1827 and 1829 by George, Jr. and Ebenezer.*

After Maggie's birth, George Junkin had written, "I feel myself relieved from every burden almost but the burden of gratitude."[11] But burdens in abundance were to overwhelm George and Julia Junkin between 1820 and 1831—an ever-enlarging family to support, serious illnesses, responsibilities that taxed their energies to the limit, and a constant need of money. Her husband's salary was paid mostly in "grain and other articles from the congregation," Julia wrote to her brother-in-law, Ebenezer Dickey, and consequently there was "precious little money." With faith in her husband and the Almighty, however, she tried to be optimistic. "I trust we will still get food to eat and clothes to wear. . . . We enjoy health and comfort in each other, and these are blessings that no money can buy."[12] In 1823, when the family had outgrown the small house on Water Street, Junkin moved them all to a farm in Turbut, a rural community northeast of Milton. Here he hoped they could feed themselves more economically and raise silkworms for profit, to augment his meager stipend.

As good Calvinists, the Junkins believed strongly in the Puritan work ethic, "for the Son of Man . . . gave . . . to every man his work"; "I must work the works of him that sent me, while it is day: the night cometh, when no man can work."† Indeed, there was plenty of hard work for them all to do. From the time they could walk, the Junkin children shared in the never-ending chores of a farm family, the boys working in the fields and barn, the two girls, Maggie and Ellie, helping their mother indoors with cook-

---

*All nine of the Junkin children were named for relatives: Margaret and John for their maternal grandparents, Eleanor and Joseph for their paternal grandparents, George for his father, and Ebenezer for his uncle Ebenezer Dickey. The youngest three children, born after the family moved east, included William, named for his uncle William Finney; David, named for George Junkin's youngest brother, David Xavier Junkin; and Julia, who was given her mother's name, Julia Rush.

†See Mark 13:34 and John 9:4.

ing, washing, and sewing. Years later Maggie recalled that "we made everything we wore . . . from our hand-embroidered collars and cuffs . . . to our gaiter-tops,"[13] and family letters contain numerous references to supplying handmade linen shirts for "Father" before every meeting of presbytery or synod.

Just as the brothers and sisters were given different tasks to perform, so too did they move along divergent educational paths. At first all the children were taught by their mother. But soon the boys began attending local schools, while Maggie and Ellie remained at home for further instruction from their parents. When she was only six, George Junkin taught Maggie the Greek alphabet and Latin grammar, perhaps in an attempt to provide the less-interested John with stimulating competition. But the girl quickly surpassed her brother and, reading by candlelight after the rest of the family had retired, soon acquired enough skill to study Greek and Latin texts in the original. In recognition of her precocious ability, Junkin presented her with a small, black, leather-bound Greek New Testament. On the flyleaf, in a childish hand, Maggie carefully wrote: "Margaret Junkin from her beloved Father."[14]

Like any normal youngsters, the children managed to find time for play once they had finished their work and study. In leisure hours they wandered together through the meadows around Turbut, picked wild flowers, hid in copses, built dams along small streams, and relished the beauty and freedom of the countryside in "that wild wood, so fair and green," that Maggie remembered years later as

> green-wood bowers,
> Where, in bright summer's sunny days,
> I've wandered, gathering sweet wild-flowers.[15]

Her earliest poems are filled with references to the scent and color of blossoms: "mignionette's [sic] sweet fragrance," "rose-buds . . . lilies . . . jassamine's [*sic*] glow," the columbine "swinging its little crimson-bell," and clumps of forget-me-not, "sweet gentle flower of azure."[16] Verses recall summer walks along shady paths and through the woods

> Where I and my young brothers oft
>   Were wont to stray in glee;
> To stand beneath the very shade
>   Of the old forest tree,
> Under whose leaves we sought relief
>   From the warm summer sun,
> And where we used to come and sit
>   At eve, when school was done![17]

Other poems describe spring afternoons with Ellie:

> Together have we played
>   Beside the murmuring stream,
> Or in the green tree's shade
>   Or 'neath the pale moon's beam—
> Together have we sought
>   The earliest flower that springs—
> Together homeward brought
>   Its richest blossomings.[18]

Living in the country, the youngsters had few friends outside their immediate family, relying upon each other for companionship. In spite of being five years apart in age, the two girls were especially close, dressing alike and sharing tasks around the house. Indeed, from their childhood until Ellie's death in 1854, the sisters were extraordinarily interdependent, Maggie serving as mentor and guide while the lively, mischievous Ellie provided warm support for her more studious sister.

Though their children enjoyed generally good health, George and Julia Junkin were always aware of the dangers of serious illness, even sudden death, within their family. Epidemics were frequent, sometimes wiping out whole families within a few hours. Knowledge of hygiene and of medical treatment was limited, with bleeding the standard remedy for most ailments. Many of Julia's letters written from Milton referred to smallpox and typhoid fever, to the deaths of friends and members of her husband's congregations, and to constant concerns about childbirth. After the safe arrival of each of her own children, she always recorded her relief and gratitude when the new babies flourished. She regularly took "bark" (quinine) to prevent malaria, and she was deeply concerned about the poor health of Hannah, the black servant, who "appears to be far gone in consumption."[19]*

The children contracted the usual childhood diseases—chicken pox, whooping cough, and "the French measles," maladies that frequently came when George Junkin was out of town on church business and Julia was forced to cope, not only with housekeeping and farm chores, but with the nursing of a half-dozen small, unhappy youngsters. In most cases the children recovered without incident. An illness of far greater consequence was Maggie's serious case of regular, or "red," measles that left her with residual ocular strain. The ten-year-old girl, who had already placed stress on her eyes by reading poorly printed books at night by the light of a candle, came away from this illness with the potential for grave eye problems.

Ellie suffered a more dramatic physical mishap during the same year of 1830. It occurred while the older boys were working in the barn and presumably keeping an eye on little Eleanor, aged five, and their three-year-old brother, George. Unfortunately, the pair, wandering into the "gig house," discovered a straw

---

*It is remarkable that of them all, only Joseph contracted tuberculosis, many years later.

cutter recently sharpened by their father. "They were engaged in cutting straw with the axe," George Junkin later wrote to Ebenezer Dickey, Ellie "laying & I suppose holding it on a large block & he chopping it off," when the ax slipped and cut off portions of the two fingers of Ellie's right hand. Within fifteen minutes a hastily summoned physician had sewed the severed pieces in place, while the little girl lay in her mother's lap, sobbing that "now I cant [*sic*] sew or do anything." Not surprisingly, the surgery did not hold and the rotting tissues had to be cut away. Still, her father wrote philosophically, "we have reason for much gratitude. . . . The wounds will be healed over in a few days & she will never know much inconvenience. And as for the looks—that is a small matter. . . . We thank God it is not worse." [20] The maiming of Ellie's hand may well have made Maggie especially solicitous of her younger sister. Years later her fierce protectiveness culminated in her jealous opposition to Eleanor's marriage.

The parents, too, had their share of physical trouble. Julia often took months to recover completely from her many pregnancies, and George Junkin was taken dangerously ill in the fall of 1825 "with a high grade of billious [*sic*] fever . . . nigh to the gates of death." [21] Too sick to conduct prayers but still determined that worship around the family table should continue, Junkin sent for one of the carpenters working on the place with the request that the young man substitute for him. Matthew Laird was so eloquent in his prayers that, upon his recovery, Junkin immediately set about educating the laborer for the ministry. His brush with death and the impression made upon him by his unlettered laborer's simple faith stimulated George Junkin to modify his vocational direction and eventually to change it altogether.

As soon as he had recuperated sufficiently, he began taking many of his workmen into his home, offering them not only room and board but also instruction in theology and the classics. Julia Junkin quickly discovered that the extra boarders added considerably to her labors and to family expenses, but for Maggie, dinner conversations now became exciting educational sessions. The little girl, already more proficient in Latin and Greek than the lads twice her age, was enormously stimulated by arguments and comments that nourished her as much as did her porridge and potatoes.

Not surprisingly, as the daughter of a minister, Maggie learned Bible stories, psalms, and catechisms before she could read. Calvinism permeated every area of her young life, for in addition to hearing her father preach twice every Sabbath, she attended Sunday school classes, prayer meetings during the week, and daily devotions around the family table. When she was only four, her mother taught her portions of the Westminster Confession of Faith. George Junkin wrote to his brother-in-law on February 16, 1824, that "just this minute Margt, who lies *sleeping* beside her brother in her little blue bed, gave a twist around & cried out, 'Christ the king & head of his church' & sleeps on. Such are some of the fruits of a pious & faithful mother's attentions. She can repeat all her little questions."[22]

Maggie's extensive knowledge of the Bible provided her with ready material for later dramatic poems, including verses about such obscure Old Testament figures as Michal and Barzillai.* In letters Maggie often resorted to biblical language, as when she apologized for not writing "a tithe as often as I think of you," or hoped that a relative might rely upon "Israel's gentle Shepherd . . . [as] her never failing support."[23] Even more important for the nascent poet was her absorption of biblical phraseology and the parallelism of the metrical psalms she sang at church every Sunday. By today's standards, her use of archaic speech seems

---

*Michal, daughter of Saul, became the first wife of David (1 Samuel 18:20–27). Barzillai was a Gileadite (a member of a non-Israelite tribe in Canaan) who befriended David. David offered him a place to live in Jerusalem, but the eighty-year-old Barzillai demurred, saying he was too old to move and preferred to remain near his own people and be buried with them (2 Samuel 19:31–39).

affected:

> Never may thy bosom know
>   E'en a throb of anguish
> Never may the pangs of woe,
>   Bid thee darkly languish.[24]

But she was simply using language she was comfortable with, garnered from the King James version of the Bible. The first lines of one of her earliest poems, "The Two Stars," is similar in rhyme scheme and meter to Isaac Watts's famous hymn, "Our God, Our Help in Ages Past"* and to the 1650 *Scottish Psalter*'s paraphrase of Psalm 23:

> The sun had set in glory. Now,
>   His last bright tints were gone;
> The stars that deck Night's sable brow,
>   Were rising one by one—[25]

George Junkin had announced in 1820 his intention to supervise Maggie's upbringing with special care. By the end of the decade he and his wife must have felt considerable satisfaction in their eldest daughter, who gave every appearance of being a happy child, conscientious in assisting her mother and caring for her brothers and sister, eager to learn and unusually gifted in the study of classical languages. If she sometimes seemed high-strung, it was because she felt that she could never measure up to the high standards of scholarship her father expected of her. Fortunately, her mother was a far less demanding and more serene parent whose strong faith survived the harshest trials. The girl

---

*This is the first line of Watts's famous hymn, which was later changed by John Wesley to read "O, God, Our Help. . . ." Wesley's version is the one that appears in most modern hymnbooks.

must have read at least some of Julia Rush Junkin's letters to relatives in the East, letters in which the young mother slipped almost imperceptibly from descriptions of family problems to biblical quotations of resignation. She once wrote, "Mysterious often to us, are the dealings of Providence; and when he lays his rod upon us, we find it hard, to say 'thy will be done.' . . . how constantly are we receiving warnings of our mortality, but like the deaf adder we stop our ears."[26] Though she was not aware of the magnitude of the financial struggle her parents faced during the years at Milton, Maggie often commented years later on her mother's faith and fortitude.

What neither her parents nor her siblings knew was that during the time she lived in Milton, Maggie experienced two emotional shocks that scarred her deeply. If she had been able to share the episodes with her family, their effects might have been less traumatic. Instead, she brooded over them in silence, rethinking their meaning again and again within herself.

The first incident occurred when, at the impressionable age of six, she was invited by her father to accompany him on a pastoral call. Unaware of the nature of the visit, she enjoyed his companionship during the "drive of a mile or two through a lovely pasture-land" until the carriage "stopped before the house of a neighbor. I was a very shy child," Maggie wrote many years later, "and was frightened to see the shady front yard filled with people. . . . When we entered the house, I was still more alarmed to find it darkened." In the shadowy room, her father "lifted me up in his arms, took my unwilling hand . . . and laid it upon the dead face" of a boy lying in "what I afterwards knew to be a coffin." It was the face of a fifteen-year-old lad she had seen only a few days before, skipping along the path in front of her home on his way to school. "In one awful moment," she wrote, "the fearful idea of death was borne into my soul; and as I heard the creak of the coffin screws, I received my first idea of the King of

Terrors."[27]

Her father seemed unaware of her alarm, "little dreaming how he was terrifying me." And she was "too shy to tell him of the unspeakable fear that had taken hold of my mind." That night she lay awake in her small bed, "staring and trembling till the morning," afraid to close her eyes for fear that if she went to sleep she too might die. Years later, when she described the incident in a long article, "Giving Children Right Impressions of Death," Maggie exonerated her father of blame. He "never knew," she said, "what an impression he was giving" her, nor did he comprehend "how unprepared she was for such a sudden introduction to the awful mystery of death." For her part, Maggie was too filled with "shy reserve" to confide in either parent, hiding "the torturing memory" within herself. Her natural diffidence, coupled with an inability to communicate her fears to her parents, drove her to articulate her "deepest feelings" only through poetry and prose.[28] From that memorable day on, she was terrified of death, of coffins, and of lonely graves in desolate cemeteries. Of the seventy poems she wrote between 1837 and 1840, one-fifth concerned some aspect of death, a surprising concentration for a teenaged girl even in the first part of the nineteenth century, when death was seen to be as much a part of human existence as birth.*

She refused to attend funerals or visit graveyards, as if by visiting them she might hasten her own demise:

> That burial-place is lonely,
> Oh! do not lay *me* there,
> Where wild grass bendeth only,

---

*Many years later, Maggie commented on this inability to communicate her concern to others. "It is very strange," she wrote, "how children make *caches* for themselves, carefully concealing their anxiety about what they really have an intense desire to know. They do not forget their *cache*, but in thought continually return to it, never imparting to any one a suspicion of its existence" (MJP, *Monographs*, 62).

Beneath the summer air![29]

Maggie never forgot the sight of the young boy's face or the sound of the coffin screws. The memory of his white, motionless face heightened her personal apprehensions for family members during the Civil War, and her sense of the terrible anonymity of death sharpened the poignancy of her war poems about lonely, unmarked graves. "As long as she lived . . . [Maggie] could never again bring herself to look upon the face of the dead, not even her best beloved."[30]

The second experience was less dramatic, but its overtones of personal sin and future salvation affected her even more deeply than had her first sight of a dead body. While she was playing outdoors one Sunday afternoon, an overzealous theological student caught her up, carried her indoors to a "darkened room," and began to query her "about the safety of her soul." Confused and frightened, she answered the young man as best she could, but it was not enough to satisfy him. He solemnly "told her that he was very much afraid her soul was going to be lost."[31] Now she grew fearful, not only of death itself, but also of what lay beyond death. This experience, too, she carefully hid from parents and siblings, revealing her fears obliquely through self-deprecating letters to relatives. She questioned why her older cousin Helen should "*deign* to correspond with *such a little thing as I. . . a selfish creature.*"[32] At the same time, she yearned for proof of Helen's appreciation: "I prize more than any tongue can tell, the affection of those whom I love, yet I own . . . that I am too selfish to deserve that fierce deep affection I so much covet."[33]

To be sure, she spoke of reconciliation in heaven. But she never quite achieved her parents' confident reliance upon God's ultimate grace and the hope of eternal bliss:

There are who tell me I should be

> So firm of faith, so void of fear,
> So buoyed by calm, courageous cheer,
> (Assured, through Christ's security,
> There is a place prepared,) that I
> Should dare not be afraid to die.[34]

"No faith, no hope, no promise," her stepdaughter wrote years later, "was able to banish from her life the haunting, nameless dread of its inevitable end."[35]

Because she was never convinced of heavenly forgiveness, Maggie struggled for years with a sense of her own unworthiness and an eagerness to please those she cared most about. This lack of self-confidence adversely affected her poetry, stimulating her on occasion to write in a style she thought others desired.

———

Five years after his severe illness, in 1830, George Junkin made the decision to leave the pastoral ministry altogether. In Germantown, near Philadelphia, a group of earnest Presbyterian laymen were attempting to maintain a four-year-old Manual School, combining vocational education and ministerial studies, just the kind of endeavor that George Junkin had been pursuing on his own in Milton. When he learned that the school was seeking a new principal, he believed the opportunity represented heavenly guidance, despite the institution's considerable debt and the small enrollment of twenty-three students.

Julia Junkin was clearly less enthusiastic about the move. "So it seems we are to go to Germantown," she wrote to her brother-in-law. "When I think of the care & responsibility, my heart almost fails me, but the promise is, 'As thy day is, so shall thy strength be'; this is all my dependence."[36] After sending "a couple of the children" ahead, and holding a "vendue" to sell off unnecessary possessions,[37] she and her husband, along with the other three children and two young men from Milton (recruited to be teachers), journeyed east in June to take up their new abode in an old three-storied brick building in Germantown, located on forty-two acres of land.

At once Mr. Junkin set about with his usual energy and enthusiasm to expand the student body, upgrade the curriculum, and pay off some of the school's debt. He increased the enroll-ment from twenty-three to forty-eight, and his newly recruited instructors from Milton began teaching agriculture and cabinetmaking, while he himself taught Greek and Latin. Unfor-tunately, however, items made in the school could not compete in price with other manufactured goods, and Junkin was forced to use his own money—and some from his wife's dowry—to purchase supplies, pay his tutors, and help settle the academy's obligations.

Yet despite the Manual School's lack of success, the family thrived in Germantown during their two years of residence. For Maggie, in particular, the years of 1830 and 1831 remained "red-letter days" that she cherished the rest of her life.[38] Here in a metropolitan environment, she discovered art galleries, libraries, and other cultural facilities that were within easy access. She already knew and appreciated the Peale portraits of her mother, aunts, and grandparents, and she had spent many long hours poring over a book of engravings that belonged to her parents.*
But now her horizons broadened to include landscape paintings and the plastic arts. She haunted Philadelphia's museums, stimu-lated by the design, color, and form of the paintings. With new enthusiasm, she taught herself to sketch and even began giving

---

*Among the many engravings, she wrote years later, was "an unusually fine one of the approach to the city of Antwerp." It seems a curious landscape for a little girl to be so taken with, but she reported that "this picture fascinated my gaze above all others. . . . I was magnetized by its rare beauty, and fancied that this Antwerp must be the centre of an earthly paradise" (MJP, *Monographs*, 61).

lessons to Ellie. In later years, she moved on to study the lives of master artists, reading Giorgio Vasari's many-volumed *Lives of the Painters* in translation and then writing her own dramatic verses about "Little Titian's Palette," "The Boy Van Dyck," and "Tintoretto's Last Painting."[39]

One day, in a private home, she saw for the first time the well-known marble statue of Prosperine, created by the American sculptor Hiram Powers. Deeply moved by his "grand magnificence of earthly art," Maggie attempted to describe the sculpture's subtlety of curve and expression:

> That half-averted face—how passing fair!
> The smile that lingers round the curving mouth
> With mournful meaning filled; the pensive brow
> So beautifully calm and passionless;
> The rounded cheek that seems as it would yield
> Beneath a finger's weight; the wavy hair
> About the imperial head.[40]

The statue seemed to her almost human, fashioned by the sculptor's "most transcendent skill." It was, she felt, a mortal talent that mirrored the creative genius of God:

> Who fashioned with a word a perfect man,
> And breathed into the clay *a living soul!*[41]

Maggie's years in Germantown also gave her two other important opportunities—to learn to know well her widowed grandmother Miller and to come under the influence of an exceptional teacher at the Manual School, Charles McCay. The location of the Manual School was only a few hours' distance from Oxford, Pennsylvania, where eighty-year-old Margaret Miller spent much of her time with her daughter, Jane Dickey, and her family.

Maggie was her grandmother's namesake, and she resembled the old woman in appearance and in temperament—small, red-haired, and strong-willed. Together the two Margarets took "foraging expedition[s]" into the countryside, gathering "whortleberries— wild raspberries . . . hepatica . . . and dittany, to make the tea she [Grandmother] loved so well."[42] During long evenings round the fireside, Maggie listened to Mrs. Miller's tales from her childhood:

> When day with its bright light is gone,
> And quiet eve comes stealing on,
> When tasks are done—and lessons o'er,
> She often glads us with a store
> Of Scottish tales, which memory's pen
> Has gathered up from many a glen—
> Well do I love to list to her,
> She is so good a *chronicler*![43]

Among the Highland folklore Maggie absorbed was the Scottish explanation for her own small stature. As a toddler she had been "tossed on the horns of a cow," a misfortune, she was told, that always "dwarf[ed] a little child's growth."[44] Years later, Maggie adapted her grandmother's tales into literary ballads about Lady Hildegarde's wedding, a fairies' tablecloth, and the origin of "Christ-Crotch . . . the old Saxon name for Mince Pie."[45]

Maggie's new friend and intellectual mentor at the school, Charles McCay, was a native Pennsylvanian, ten years her senior, who had graduated from Jefferson College in 1829. Though trained as a mathematician and engineer, McCay taught classical subjects at the Manual School, as well as serving as a "tutor to Dr. Junkin's children."[46] Since faculty and students lived together in one large building, it is not surprising that the attractive young instructor and Maggie became fast friends, he interested in stimulating her burgeoning abilities, she enthusiastically responsive to his personal tutelage.

In May of 1831 the Junkins' fifth son was born. "Your kind wishes & your anxious prayers on behalf of my dear Julia are more than realized," Junkin wrote to his brother-in-law, "in the birth of another son, a may flower that began to open its bud with the rising of the beautiful morning & spread his full rosy face to the setting sun. He is a fine, fat good fellow."[47] The child was named William Finney, after an uncle.

Julia Junkin had hardly recovered from the baby's birth when she was asked to entertain a young missionary and his wife about to set sail for the South Pacific Islands. "It requires strong faith to leave country and kindred," Julia wrote to her sister Jane, "to seek a home among savages, cannibals as they are on the island to which they expect to go."[48] Maggie was fascinated by the visitors' exotic vocation, and for the rest of her life remained interested in foreign missions. She founded the first missionary society in Lexington, Virginia, after the Civil War, and among her published poems were two rhymed tales of missionary activity in India.[49]

That same year George Junkin was chosen as moderator of the synod of Philadelphia, a large constituency including Presbyterian churches throughout eastern Pennsylvania and the state of Maryland. The synod's yearly meeting, held in October in Baltimore, was not an easy one over which to preside because of sharp differences between the conservative branch of the denomination (Old School adherents) and the more liberal branch (the New School group). This rift followed George Junkin back to Germantown, where many of the Manual School's supporters were of the New School, while Junkin himself was a staunch and vocal Old Schooler. The resulting theological exchanges, added to the institution's desperate financial situation, forced Junkin to resign his position as principal. At first he had hoped to move the location of the school itself to Oxford. But God had other plans, Julia wrote to her sister. "Tho' a man's heart may devise his way, yet the Lord directeth his steps."[50] Providence had come in the guise of an invitation for Junkin to become president of Lafayette College in Easton, Pennsylvania, a school long chartered but never actually in existence.

"I suppose you know that we are . . . going to move," twelve-year-old Maggie Junkin wrote to her cousin, Helen Dickey, several years her senior. "We have got a house in Easton up the Delaware river. . . . They say it is a beautiful place."[51] She dreaded the move, she wrote Helen, and hated to leave the cultural stimulus of the city which she had come so much to enjoy.

Over the next twenty years, Maggie's opinion of Easton was to change dramatically. Though the family had its share of sorrows and difficulties in their new location, she discovered that "lovely Lafayette "[52] was an ideal locale for her to blossom and mature, as a scholar and as a budding poet.

Chapter 2

The Domes of Academe
1831–1848

The sun has almost set—
Now he is gilding with lingering rays—
And flooding, with his evening's ruddy blaze,
The dome of *Lafayette*.[1]

G eorge Junkin moved his family to Easton because he was
convinced that in that small Pennsylvania town he could
best serve "Zion . . . by devoting my attention to the training of
her sons for the public field of labour."[2] Without realizing it, he
could hardly have chosen a more ideal location for his eldest
daughter to spend her adolescence and young womanhood. In
Easton, over the next sixteen years, Maggie was to find artistic
stimulus from the region's unspoiled scenery and intellectual

invigoration as she flourished in the experimental atmosphere of the new college.

Late in March of 1832, "virtually the entire student body and teachers alike" from the recently closed Manual School traveled "by foot carrying their belongings along the fifty mile journey" from Germantown to Easton.[3] The Junkins, having sold many of their possessions at another "vendue," took the trip in a carriage, accompanied by three black servants. Though the distance was shorter, the move itself was far more difficult than the journey from Milton to Germantown had been. The children were all recuperating from influenza;[4] baby William was not yet weaned; Joseph, never very strong, had recurring ague; and five-year-old George was immobilized in a body cast from his "ribs to the ankle" as treatment for a "disease of the hip joint."[5] After "a good deal of confusion,"[6] the family settled into a tiny rented house in the center of Easton. Nearby was an equally small facility used for class recitation and dormitory rooms. This simple dwelling represented the only real asset of Lafayette, and the students and faculty housed there (almost entirely Manual School personnel) were the embryo school's total academic constituency.

At Lafayette, as at the Manual School, physical labor was an important part of the curriculum. Because the school was in temporary quarters, construction of a college building became the work of highest priority for the students. The indefatigable president, utilizing skills he had learned as a boy, supervised the quarrying and hauling of stone to the undeveloped campus site on nine acres of recently purchased land and worked beside the students to mortar brick walls and fashion joists, doors, windows, and roofs. His enthusiasm was so contagious that the students and his own children eagerly participated in both planning and construction. Only twenty-six months after the Junkins's arrival in Easton, Lafayette College had become a physical reality, with a three-story all-purpose building, sixty students, a curriculum of classics, agriculture, and mechanics, and four faculty members, including the president and his loyal subordinate, Charles McCay. It was an extraordinary achievement.

Meanwhile, the citizenry of Easton had given the Junkins a cordial welcome and applauded the new president's eager self-reliance. Though the community provided fewer cultural advantages than Germantown, it was nonetheless an attractive and energetic town. Located at the confluence of the Delaware and Lehigh rivers, the area not only offered "romantic and magnificent scenery,"[7] but also attracted industry including two blast furnaces, a wire factory, several mills, and a foundry.[8] River traffic and several stagecoaches daily linked the area with Philadelphia, New York City, and western markets. Within the town limits were five churches (three English speaking, two that held services in both German and English), "an academy, a public library, two banks, five weekly newspapers, thirteen lawyers, seven physicians, three drug stores, thirty-three general retail stores . . . five fire engines . . . three tanneries, four distilleries, one brewery" and some six hundred houses, many of brick.[9] Easton even boasted of having a well-respected, if not very able, female poet. Local citizens were proud of their carefully laid out foot walks and street curbs, and an ordinance issued in 1833 required that all residents have "cellars cleaned and white-washed" to prevent cholera.[10]

During her first years in the community, Maggie was too busy with domestic chores to enjoy the advantages the community offered. The small rented dwelling for the president and his family housed Mr. and Mrs. Junkin, Maggie, Ellie, and the five boys, as well as Mrs. Junkin's nephew, Sam Dickey, who was attending Lafayette. Conditions in the crowded home were primitive, the servants were sick, and Julia Junkin reported that she and the girls did all "the work ourselves, except the washing."[11] By winter she was pregnant again, and Maggie became, more than ever before, her mother's principal support. "She . . . had the most watchful care of us all," George Junkin, Jr., remembered years later, "doing what she could to relieve her parents . . . [with] the care and entertainment of the little brood, mothering us with great success."[12] The new baby, a healthy, chubby boy, was born in June, 1833, and named David.

Warmly welcomed into the already crowded household, the child was to live less than a year, and his sudden death would be the first domestic tragedy for the Junkin family, a devastating loss made more intolerable because of his apparent good health, his winsome personality, and the special attention that parents and siblings gave to him. Mrs. Junkin had described him as "the loveliest . . . of our *little* circle,"[13] and Maggie had proudly reported in March of 1834 that "David can stand alone . . .[and] has got eight teeth."[14] Having known that there was smallpox in the area, the family had had the child vaccinated, but despite all their precautions and loving care, he contracted a sudden, fatal disease and died at the age of nine months. "He was full of life, health, & beauty," Julia Junkin mourned, and "now he sleeps beneath the clods of the valley."[15] Bravely, she tried to persuade herself that it was all God's will. "My heart feels sore," she wrote, "yet I think I can say, 'It is well.'. . . The good shepherd has taken him to his own bosom."[16] By contrast, Maggie viewed the baby's death as punishment for the family's having loved him too much:

> He was our idol—and we gave
> Too much to *him*, the love
> That should have gone in thankfulness . . .[17]

to God himself. For many years, she was to be burdened by the belief that God punished those who cared too deeply for their own, a conviction she voiced in 1854 when her mother and Ellie died and again in 1863 when Stonewall Jackson succumbed to his wounds.

The loss of her young brother had a profound effect upon Maggie's poetry, where her already noticeable concentration on death became even more pronounced. Poems that began with cheerful descriptions of flowers, for example, or odes to the new year often changed to sad reflection about life's end:

> The flowers—the gentle flowers—
> We claim a kindred with them—they have birth—
> They live—they die upon the same green Earth,
> Where sleep lost ones of our's [*sic*].[18]

> Time! Time! thou art weeping—ah, well may'st thou weep,
> For cold-hearted Death is just hushing to sleep,
> The youngest and last of thy children—its breath
> Grows fainter and fainter,—the pallor of death
> Around it is strangely and fearfully cast.[19]

A few weeks before David's death the family had moved, along with the student body, into the one completed college building, high on the north bank of Bushkill Creek. On May 1 George Junkin was officially inaugurated as president in a ceremony in which the family participated despite their grief. That evening there was a grand "illumination" of the campus, with candles in every window of the new structure, which held six recitation rooms, a chapel, a refectory, fifty dormitory rooms, and an "apartment for the President and his family."[20] Now living inside the single college building, Maggie found that her days moved in rhythm with the students' rigorous daily schedule: a wake-up bugle call at 4:50 A.M., prayers, labor assignments in early morning and late afternoon, and long sessions for academic instruction.

The last child in the family, a third daughter, was born on June

13, 1835. Named Julia, she quickly became her "Father's pet," a "little plaything" for her siblings, and a balm to Mrs. Junkin, who still felt deeply the loss of young David. The child matured early, in résponse to the stimulation of seven older brothers and sisters. "Julia is as talkative as ever any *woman* was," Maggie commented when her sister was four years old, "and she talks with so much precision and so plainly, that it would astonish you. . . . She can repeat all her letters perfectly." Maggie acknowledged to Helen Dickey, however, that Julia was overindulged: "I would not be speaking truth, did I say that she was not spoiled."[21]

With eight children in the home Mrs. Junkin's domestic chores were greater than ever. When Maggie urged her mother to accompany Mr. Junkin on a business trip to Philadelphia, her mother demurred. "Mother you might know," Maggie confided to her cousin, "has too *many brats* at home to leave. . . . I tried to make her think that I could keep house untill [*sic*] her return, but I suppose she thinks me too young & foolish to trust alone, at any rate, she is unwilling to let me try it."[22] Instead Mrs. Junkin suggested that Maggie assist with the yearly ritual of spring housecleaning. "Housecleaning!" Maggie exclaimed. " 'Tis a *detestable* business."[23]

A portion of the family's responsibility was the increasingly wearing and time-consuming care of Maggie's grandmother, Margaret Miller, who came regularly for long visits. In her happier moments the old woman regaled the family with recollections of "her own Scottish hearth . . . the bright scarlet heath—and the blue heather-bell."[24] But the drafty rooms of the yet unfinished college building exacerbated Mrs. Miller's rheumatism, and she complained bitterly about the cold, damp quarters and her isolation on Lafayette's hill with no road down to the village. "I am sorry on her account," Mrs. Junkin wrote, "it is our wish to make her as comfortable as we can, but she has to submit to many inconveniences which we cannot remedy."[25] Though the old lady

grew more and more unhappy with each visit, the Junkins continued to have her with them for long periods, and every letter
written when she was not in Easton included a message of love to
Grandmother Miller.

With so much to do for siblings, mother, grandmother, and
student boarders, it is not surprising that Maggie found relatively
little time in daylight hours for her lessons. "The only time my
busy father could hear me recite was before our early breakfast,"
she wrote, and she often stayed up well past the college's official
nine-o'clock retirement hour, reading Greek texts by candlelight.
Concerned about her eldest daughter's eyesight, Mrs. Junkin
instructed Eleanor to extinguish Maggie's candle before she herself went to bed. "But when Ellie would offer to discharge her
mission," Maggie recalled, "I would raise my finger in half-
serious threat, and say, 'Touch it if you dare!'"[26] Years later she
acknowledged that her mother had been correct in urging her not
to read by such poor light. At the time she justified her disobedi-
ence by suggesting that her father "encouraged my undertaking
more than I could possibly do in the daytime."[27]

Soon after they reached Easton, both Maggie and Ellie en-
rolled at a small girls' academy within the bounds of Easton
proper. Because she had begun reading Virgil before she left
Germantown, Maggie attended only half a day, spending her
afternoons in private instruction at home with Charles McCay,
her good friend from Manual School days, and later with one of
Lafayette's first graduates, David Moore. Though she was not
fond of mathematics or Roman history, she loved studying the
classics with McCay:

> . . .with you I o'er traced the paths
> The pious Trojan roved;
> And sighed to think how fruitlessly
> The Tyrian Dido loved.[28]

Private tutoring, however, was not enough to satisfy her, and Maggie longed to attend school on a full-time basis, preferably boarding school. "I was anxious for Father to send me to the Lawrenceville Female Seminary," she wrote to Helen Dickey. [29] But it was her brother John, not Maggie, who was to have that opportunity, at "Mr. Phillips school," also in Lawrenceville, New Jersey.[30]

Mr. and Mrs. Junkin had decided in the fall of 1836 that, although they had little spare cash, John needed the discipline of a preparatory school. Mrs. Junkin explained that her eldest son "has never been much of a student, and as he is a good deal of a mechanical genius, he had got into the habit of pottering about the shop and neglecting his books; he also took up a great deal of his time with [his baby sister] Julia: his Father thought if he was taken away entirely, it would perhaps break off these habits."[31] So John was given the opportunity Maggie longed for. Ironically, he hated the experience and could hardly wait to get back to Easton at the end of the academic year, while Maggie remained restlessly at home. There simply wasn't enough money to send two away to school, Maggie sadly reported: "The expense . . . prevents my being sent to school somewhere."[32]

In compensation, her father designed a new curriculum for her, carefully written out in Mr. Junkin's hand: "Rutherfords Ancient History, Gillies' Greece, Fergusons Roman Republic, extracts from Gibbon's Decline & Fall, Hume or Henry's England [and] Irvines Columbus [Washington Irving's two-volume biography of Christopher Columbus]," as well as "Abercrombie on the Moral Feelings" and "Arnot's Physics."[33] The program itself was challenging, but she still longed for close friendship and competition with other young people. For the rest of her life Maggie felt that she had missed a great deal through "loss of the companions and discipline of childish schooling."[34]

As her younger siblings grew older, Maggie finally acquired

more leisure and freedom to enjoy the scenery around Easton. The Lafayette campus was located on Bushkill bluff, high above the Delaware River, with a commanding view of the countryside. Behind the college lay woods filled with wild flowers where Maggie and Ellie often wandered together in the evenings:

> The cooling dew descends—
> The birds have ceased their gentle notes to trill—
> Each flower is folded in its own bright cell—
> And pensive twilight reigns![35]

Little Julia, too, loved to play in the meadows and under the trees. She was fascinated by flowers, bringing home damp bunches of them for Maggie to paint in her sketchbook. "Julia is *exceedingly* fond of 'rambling in the woods,' as she calls it," Maggie wrote to her grandmother. "She has a perfect passion for flowers—and never can find it in her heart to pass by wild ones, however inaccessible they may be, without scrambling after them. . . . She is constantly bringing them to me 'to paint'—and she will say 'Oh! Maggie—they are *so pretty*—do paint them.'"[36] Maggie made watercolor paintings of the flowers Julia brought her, as well as sketches of the Delaware River, Bushkill Creek, and the town of Easton. Ellie also began to paint, under Maggie's supervision, concentrating on birds.[37]

One day, bringing home a rose, young Julia asked her mother where "the scent of the flower lived."[38] Maggie used the incident to pen a whimsical, affectionate poem about her little sister:

> I went to the garden to-night, mamma,
>   To the spot where the rose-tree grows,
> And I bent down a branch of your favorite bush,
>   And gathered a beautiful rose.
>
>   .   .   .   .

So I tore the flower apart, mamma,
  And scattered its leaves around,
But no little fairy with scented wings,
  Was anywhere there to be found.
And now I have gathered another, mamma,
  As fragrant as any that grows,

. . . .

And I've brought it to you to ask you where
  Is hidden the scent of the rose.[39]

The poem is typical of the hundred or more Maggie composed between 1837 and 1841. They include rhymed letters to friends, elegies about students who died young, historical sketches, hymns composed for local congregations, poems based on Old Testament stories, translations of Greek odes, verses about nature, stanzas addressed to her sisters and mother, and accounts of family activities, such as a nostalgic return visit to Milton. After completing her poems and sharing them with family and friends, Maggie carefully copied them into two large, leather-bound notebooks, noting the date of composition and the incident that inspired each poem. After she had made the copies, she continued to revise many of them, scribbling over the pages with almost illegible modifications.

Though most of her poems were serious, even lugubrious, she wrote a few in a humorous vein, such as the one she called "The lament for the lost heart," composed in mock heroic style, in which she regretted that she had not "left *my heart*/Safe on Mount Lafayette!" At the end she gave a sudden light twist to the poem by explaining, "The *heart* was a *sugar one!*"[40] On another occasion she poked fun at an earnest orator who attempted to persuade his audience not to imbibe strong drink. Responding to his intense polemic, Maggie answered that there was ample classical precedent for drinking:

Virgil praised the nectar'd cup—
Horace drunk its contents up—
Revel'd in its honey-dew—
Sang "Evoke Bache"! too!
In our later, happier day
Moore has lent his witching lay
To the "Parting Bumper's" brim,
I will chant its praise with him—
I will tune a simple strain
To the glories of Champaign [*sic*]!

Since the speaker was a very young member of the "New Kirk" (a church in the New School tradition) she suggested that "*Youthful* warnings are in vain,/ They should come from older men." And she ended with a ringing toast:

Here's a brimming bumper then,
To thy glories, Oh! *Champaign*![41]

One cannot help wondering how her father responded to the poem, lighthearted though it was, since for many years he had been in the forefront of the temperance movement in both Milton and Easton.

One of Maggie's most revealing poems, from an autobiographical point of view, is a rhymed description of herself and her siblings, written in 1839 to a cousin, A. B. C. (Andrew Boyd Cross). First, Maggie spoke of herself as being "scarcely five feet, one!" with eyes "the same colour as the sky" and hair "brown/ As leaves which Autumn shaketh down," though a later portrait shows her as having abundant auburn hair. Then, in a single stanza for each, she drew word pictures of her five brothers and two sisters. She described John as quiet and black-eyed, Joe as tall and handsome with red hair, and George as a budding orator. She said little about Eben and Willy, except to give their ages and relative position in the family, and she called three-year-old Julia "younger, lovelier far/ Than aught I have described thee." She told her cousin that:

> I *cannot* paint her—thou must *see*
> Her face, to *feel* its witchery![42]

Maggie's stanza about Eleanor merits a careful look because of her intense feeling about this younger sister. The portrait, appropriately written in lighthearted doggerel, is especially affectionate and appreciative of Ellie's sense of fun:

> Dear Eleanor is just *fourteen*—
> A lively romp as e'er you've seen—
> With hazel eyes—and sunny hair—
> And mirthful face—full, round, and fair—
> Beneath her lids—and round her lips,
> Lurks mischief—when she can, she nips
> The nose, or oftener pulls the hair,
> Or draws away the expected chair—
> Or when our lips just touch the brink
> *Tilts up* the draught we meant to drink![43]

For her part, Eleanor was touchingly proud of Maggie's poetic abilities. "Sister M," Ellie told a cousin in January of 1840, "wrote some beautiful verses (pray excuse a sister's language) to the old Year, on its departure."[44]

Because the family's apartment in the all-purpose college building was very small, Maggie seems to have written much of her verse late at night after her siblings and parents had retired, when she could have some privacy and quiet. She wrote a number of poems on successive New Year's eves, just before or after midnight:

> Depart! Depart!
> The echo trembles thro' my heart—
> I start to hear thy dying knell—
> Old, wearied year! Farewell! Farewell!
> > Written Jan 1, 1840
> > As the clock tolled the last hour of 1839.[45]

During daylight hours Maggie increasingly felt the need to escape from time to time the intrusions of family responsibility and discover a place where she could think, dream, and write without interruption. Her need for privacy was shared by many nineteenth-century women, especially writers. Charlotte Brontë longed for such a retreat where one might be isolated from the "ties" of family "and all their sweet associations, so as to be your *own woman*."[46] Later, Virginia Woolf suggested that every woman needed "a room to herself."[47] This special spot of solitude Maggie found in a clump of hawthorn trees not far from the college, a place where she could "breathe my joy in Nature's ear" and find contentment in the "soothing power/ That speaks in every bird and leaf."[48] Here she reveled in the sounds of bird calls and in the coming of spring:

> The sweet-voiced rivulets—the birds—the many-finger'd
> > breeze
> Harping upon a thousand strings, among the leafy trees,
> Make such heart-thrilling music in Nature's glorious fane
> As never yet from fretted roof has echoed back again!
>
> How beautiful a home—how fair a dwelling place is earth,
> When spring puts on her garniture—and gives her blossoms
> > birth!
> Even when she weeps, as oft she will (tho surely not for
> > grief),

Her tears are turned to diamond-drops on every shining
    leaf![49]

Not surprisingly, Maggie kept the location of the bower secret
from all but a few special friends:

There lies above the Bushkill's bank a nook amid the trees,
As lone as if it heard no sound except the sighing breeze:
It is a lovely spot in which to pass an evening hour,
Screened sweetly by the mantling leaves—we call it "Haw-
thorn Bower."

. . . .

May no intruder enter here. I claim this spot my own,
Where I will often trust to find 'tis sweet to be *alone*.
Where I may come at early morn or at the twilight hour,
And muse and dream my fancy dreams within my "Haw-
thorn Bower."[50]

When she did permit others to visit her leafy retreat, their
number was small and select, only a handful of young women and
students from the college, who gathered to discuss literary topics:

We love it, not because 'tis fair
But we have often wandered there,
When daylight's dazzling beams were gone,
And evening's hush was coming on,
We've sat us down and worn away
The hours in converse sad or gay,
As pleased us best—[51]

Though she relished her periods of quiet reflection in the
bower, Maggie also enjoyed close friendships among both students and faculty at Lafayette. She wrote to her cousin Helen

about the young men she knew, "some half dozen of the *finest looking* fellows ever you saw," but she hastened to add that she had not lost her heart to any of them. "I have it *safe* yet."[52] Rather than having any kind of romantic interest in them, she seems to have enjoyed a companionable, occasionally argumentative, relationship with her father's students. One poem innocently recalls:

> Those pleasant nights of winter weather
> The times we ate *ice-cream* together—
> When gathered round the centre-table,
> We warred as hard as we were able
> About queer things of various kinds,
> From Poets *down* to '*ladies' minds!*'[53]

Among Maggie's undergraduate friends was T. C. Porter, two years her junior. Mentioned in her poems about the hawthorn bower, he was presumably one of the inner circle who shared that hideaway. Many years later Porter recalled an incident in which he and Maggie had been having a heated discussion about poetry. Ellie teased them about their seriousness, suggesting that "it was impossible for us two to be together ten minutes without discoursing about the riders of Pegasus." She made a wager that whoever next mentioned poetry would have to write "fifty lines of verse" about something trivial, such as "a head of cabbage." Porter lost the bet and paid the penalty with fifty rhymed lines about the lowly vegetable.[54]

Though she teased Maggie about her intense interest in poetry, Ellie was in complete agreement with her elder sister about one topic—marriage to a widower. Helen Dickey had sent them a copy of a poem by an unknown poet, entitled "The Widower's Bride." Responding to the verses, Ellie wrote that the sentiment was "so true [,] for both Mag and I believe that 'He who has warmly, truly loved,/ Can never love again!'" Maggie added, at the end of the same letter, that she hoped Helen "could not give [her] hand to one who had ever loved another. 'First love' did I say? There is no second!"[55] It was a theme she would use again, a decade later, in a serialized story entitled "The Step-mother!" Her antipathy to becoming a second wife came back to haunt her, in ironic fashion, when in 1857 Maggie consented to marry a widower with seven children.

Though she insisted to Helen Dickey that she was not in love with any of the Lafayette students, Maggie probably had her share of suitors, even if letters of the period mention no names. Years later she told her stepdaughter that she had fallen in love once while she was in Easton, but her parents disapproved of the match. The only hints of that abortive romance are in an undated poem, written from the "Forks of the Delaware" at Easton:

TO——.
Forget thee! yes—I will forget thee,
    Tho' in the strife my heart should break;
'Twere better I had never met thee,
    So much I've suffered for thy sake.

Henceforth we must be sadly parted,
    And life to me will all be lone;
The very thought a tear has started,—
    There's none to love when thou art gone.

And yet it *must* be—thou hast said it,
    The struggle will be light for *thee*;
The gloomy future—(how I dread it)
    Seems only desolate to *me*.

Forget thee! yes, I will forget thee!
    However vain the boast may seem;

I'll be as tho' I had not met thee,
And all the past shall be a dream![56]

It is possible that the man Maggie cared so much for was not a student at all, but rather her old friend and tutor, Charles McCay, who had stayed at Lafayette only two years before accepting a position at the University of Georgia. He returned to Easton in 1838 and again in 1839, and Ellie assumed that these visits were primarily for the purpose of wooing her sister. With disappointment, she confided to Helen Dickey in March of 1839 that "it is decided I believe that Mr. McCay is not coming back to carry . . . Mag away."[57] Instead, a year later, McCay married a young woman from Georgia. Maggie sent him a polite little poem of congratulations, addressed to the "friend of my childhood's sunny days":

I well remember all your care,
Would I had prized it more!
. . . .
Here's one at least, who will not soon
Her early friend forget,
'Tis she who writes thee, and remains
Thine truly,
Margaret[58]

Although he never again lived in the same community with the Junkins, Charles McCay maintained a close friendship with the family for the rest of his life, and he named one of his daughters Julia Junkin, in honor of Maggie's mother.

McCay's departure had left the college—and Mr. Junkin—with one fewer staunch supporter. Despite increased enrollment and the construction of new buildings, the school was still in deep financial trouble. When his enthusiastic plans for Lafayette exceeded the college's income, George Junkin often put his own money into buildings and salaries. According to one newspaper article, he "spent $10,000 of his private funds" for the upbuilding of Lafayette.[59] He even paid the tuition for a number of students and offered free board to others, including a lad from the "Seminole Tribe, North Fork Canadian River"[60] and two young, newly freed slaves who had belonged to John McDonogh, a Southern philanthropist from New Orleans. In addition to using his own—and his wife's—money to pay the daily expenses of the college, Junkin devoted much of his time to money-raising, petitioning the state legislature for funds, soliciting donations from interested individuals and churches, and attempting to collect monies owed him. Unless an unnamed debtor repaid $2,000, the president asserted in 1840, he would "absolutely sink family, College & all."[61]

For their part, Lafayette's trustees were dismayed by the president's grandiose ideas. The manual labor portion of the curriculum was not self-supporting, in spite of an ingenious invention, a "horse-power machine to facilitate sawing," and the production of well-made "Venetian window blinds."[62] Undeterred by the insolvency of the manual program, Junkin started a normal school, with its own separate building, for the training of elementary teachers. In the agricultural division he urged students to begin cultivating new varieties of trees and animals, Rohan potatoes, Durham cows, and Berkshire pigs.[63] And, finally, he purchased a printing press so that the students could begin publishing a small newspaper. Entitled *The Educator*, the news sheet, printed on "alternate weeks . . . one in English, the other in German," was "to be devoted to education in the modern liberal sense of that term" and "to be a bond of union between teachers all over the country," with articles on a variety of subjects including "every thing that germinates and grows by receiving its nourishment from the soil."[64]

Junkin's latest innovations failed as completely as had the labor enterprise. The agricultural experiments proved to be unproductive. The model school failed because few young men wanted to study pedagogy. And *The Educator* elicited strong protests, including vociferous comments against President Junkin at a public meeting held in the northern part of the state, where speakers denounced "that small 7 by 9 paper, filled with all kinds of uninteresting matter."[65] With such opposition, it is not surprising that *The Educator* survived for only sixteen months. Because Junkin used much of his own money to finance his innovations, the trustees grumbled privately but seldom took public issue with him. Ultimately, it was Junkin's discipline of student behavior that brought them into open conflict with the college president.

From the beginning of his tenure at Lafayette, Junkin had maintained a well-deserved reputation as a stern disciplinarian. Indeed, one of his own nephews characterized him as "Uncle Judgment."[66] Students, feeling his wrath, had made comments among themselves, but there had been little open dissension. Early in 1840, however, an incident occurred that provoked widespread debate. On January 7 the faculty, with Junkin's approval, indefinitely suspended an undergraduate named Andrew Porter because he had "intentionally cut and wounded in the knee" a fellow student.[67] Unfortunately for the administration, the young man in question was the son of the governor of Pennsylvania and the nephew of the chairman of Lafayette's board of trustees, John Madison Porter. The matter quickly became an issue between the faculty's—and Junkin's—right to discipline students and the authority of the trustees. Faculty members and students took sides, townspeople became involved, and several professors resigned in protest.

Maggie was vehement in her father's defense. "You cannot think how heavy" his burdens were, she wrote to Helen Dickey. "*He alone,* humanly speaking, has been the *sole sustainer* of

Lafayette. . . . He has expended his *every* cent, his time, his influence his all in struggling for it . . . and *with all this*, he does not get in return even his family's bare *support—or* the thanks of those for whom he toils." In company with the rest of the family, she was "*indignant* . . . at the injustice which is done him."[68]

The situation remained tense until, late in the fall of 1840, there came an unexpected offer to George Junkin to become president of Miami University in Oxford, Ohio.* It seemed to the long-suffering Mrs. Junkin to be the very "finger of God" pointing her husband to a new opportunity, an "open door" for greater service,[69] and the beleaguered president accepted the offer with gratitude. Though she rejoiced at her husband's new position, Julia Junkin found it difficult to depart from a place "which has been to us in many respects a very—very pleasant home," and especially painful to leave the "dust of our dear little David."[70] Maggie was concerned about the effect the move would have upon her mother, who "will . . . have for the *fourth* time to seek a home among strangers." Still, Maggie noted, she "seems more resigned to our going than I am." She herself hated the thought of leaving close friends and the magnificent scenery around Easton. "It is *hard* to have to leave a place to which we have become so much attached . . . and can I, with a dry eye, think of seeing our beautiful hills . . . no more?" As a dutiful daughter, however, she felt she had no choice but to move with the family. "Wherever my dear Father thinks it his duty to go, surely it is my bounden duty to submit, unmurmuringly—even if it should break my heart."[71]

After selling "a variety of Household and Kitchen furniture, Farming and Gardening Utensils, a Horse, Cow and Hogs," [72] the family prepared to travel by boat down the Delaware River toward Philadelphia. As hundreds of friends stood on the riverbank

---

*The college was so designated, though at the time it had no graduate courses.

waving farewell to Junkin "and his interesting family," the former president prayed for "the town, its inhabitants and his beloved Lafayette." The boat "swung off," the pro-Junkin newspaper report continued, "and the most profound silence reigned . . . a strong evidence of the deep impression which the parting words of this good man made upon their hearts."[73]

The two years the Junkins were to live in Oxford, Ohio, proved to be unhappy ones. Maggie felt she had moved "more than *half a mile* 'this side of sun-down.'"[74] Mrs. Junkin longed for people more "*like ourselves*,"[75] and Ellie hated the flat midwestern terrain, the hundreds of pigs roaming the countryside, and the "*staring red brick*" house the family occupied.[76] The two older boys were almost as discontented as their sisters, John resignedly studying anatomy by himself at home because lack of money prevented his attending medical school, and Joe writing back discouraged letters from his new teaching position miles away.

Though there were few financial problems at Miami, George Junkin soon found himself embroiled in other difficulties. Miami, considered "one of the finest colleges in the West," with 164 students and three substantial buildings,[77] was a state-supported institution that various denominations were eager to influence. Even a college president with unusual tact would have had trouble keeping peace between "Methodists, New School Presbyterians, Universalists, and Campbellites."[78] Junkin, with his blunt, outspoken manner, did nothing to ameliorate the situation.

In addition he infuriated local abolitionists with public statements suggesting that slavery was condoned in the Bible. At a meeting of the synod of Cincinnati in 1843, he delivered an impassioned speech on the subject. The extraordinary eight-hour address received wide publicity and even elicited in 1846 a letter of praise from John C. Calhoun, the South Carolina advocate of states' rights.[79] The abolitionists' opposition, added to the dislike of the college president among local ministerial bodies, made life extremely uncomfortable for Junkin.

The most outspoken resistance, however, came from students. The new president had been called to Miami in part to bring strict discipline to the school, a challenge he confronted head-on in his inaugural sermon, entitled "Obedience to Authority." His audience reacted in anger, "mutter[ing] about a 'reign of terror.'" On one occasion "all the sophomores refused to attend class because of their dislike for a certain textbook [and] seniors talked of cutting the name of President Junkin from their diplomas."[80] One imaginative student even sent a false death notice about George Junkin to the *U. S. Gazette* in Philadelphia, a macabre prank the family learned about only when they began receiving letters of condolence. Hastily, George Junkin wrote to the *Gazette*, assuring readers that he was in "excellent health" and that the alleged death notice had been sent by "a student who had received correction for errors and instead of repentance, resorted to falsehood."[81]

During her two years at Oxford, Maggie was far from idle. She learned to play the piano, nursed her mother through a serious illness, and undertook to serve as teacher for her three youngest siblings. "Maggie's morning is taken up with her duties as *school madam*," Ellie wrote. "There was no good school for Eb and Will so she has undertaken to teach them and Julia, and if she does not get tired it will be the best thing ever happened [to] them."[82] Ellie still stood in awe of Maggie's erudition and her skills at communication.

The young woman was also writing verse, completing at least twenty-five poems between 1841 and 1843, and for the first time she saw a number of them published. Topics for her poetry included homesickness, as in "Sad News from Easton," and historical figures, such as Tasso, Galileo, and the biblical David.

There were the usual poems about death, including "Lines in the evening after the burial of a student of Miami University." In the most notable of these poems, beginning "I, too, shall die," she vividly described her continuing horror of the grave:

> Then the shroud
> My bridal-robe, when I am wed to Death,
> Shall wrap my still, cold form; and they will press
> The coffin-lid upon the frozen lip
> That hath no power to beg a kinder home,
> Than the dark, narrow confines of the grave.[83]

Perhaps because they felt so far away from kinfolk and friends in eastern Pennsylvania, the Junkin siblings grew closer together than they had ever been before. Though they understood that eventually the family would have to separate, they were nonetheless saddened when Joseph left Oxford to take up a teaching position. Maggie consoled herself that although their solidarity had been severed on earth, the family would be reunited forever in Heaven:

> *The chain is broken*—Time which rends so many links apart
> Has spared our circle hitherto, the sorrow of *this* smart—
> Link after link is loosened now, and those that still remain,
> Will fall more easily that some are severed from the chain.
>
> .   .   .   .
>
> *Be this the aim of each*—and then altho' our paths diverge
> Like sun-beams from their centre, still like sunbeams they
>   will merge
> Their points in brighter radiance—when our latest sin
>   forgiven,
> We shall be gathered joyfully—*a family in Heaven!*[84]

In spite of their feeling of isolation, the Junkins kept in touch with friends in Pennsylvania, and they must have found it a source of perverse satisfaction to learn that Lafayette College was not faring well without its energetic first president. Enrollment had dropped, several influential professors had resigned, and the man appointed to fill George Junkin's place had quarreled bitterly with the board of trustees. Junkin had heard of these difficulties through frequent letters from supporters at Easton and had seen the situation firsthand when he and Mrs. Junkin visited Lafayette in the summer of 1842. But, in spite of his realization that the college was experiencing serious difficulties, he was stunned to receive in September of 1844 a totally unexpected and extraordinary letter from Lafayette's board of trustees, informing him that they had unanimously re-elected him president of the college. The letter ended with the words, "We are your friends."[85]

Maggie was appalled. "I need not say that I shed no tears of *joy* last night when I heard the news," she wrote. "I am not considered *obstinate*—yet I did not yield my consent to Father's giving in to the wishes of his enemies in the West, and retracing his steps *back* to his old position. He submitted to too much, lost too much—toiled too much at Lafayette, ever to make me wish to see him there again under *any* circumstances."[86]

But her views had no influence on her father. Without hesitation George Junkin accepted the offer to return to his "lovely Lafayette,"[87] and before winter the family was once again in Easton, where Mrs. Junkin attested that they were "warmly welcomed. . . . Everybody seems glad to have us back." The kindness of friends, she added, took such tangible forms as "pickles, preserves, potatoes, sausages, apples, & &."[88] This time they lived in a separate house away from the college buildings, a stipulation Junkin had insisted upon before he agreed to return. "My reason," he told the trustees, "is to gratify the feelings & promote the happiness of a woman, but for the expenditure of whose patrimony the walls of your lovely edifice would not have been reared." In a private dwelling, he went on, his wife and daughters could avoid being "forever overlooked by boys & young men even in their private yard."[89]

Though Maggie was loath to see her father return to the position that had caused him so much difficulty, she was happy to be back home again. Now in her middle twenties, an age when most of her female friends and relatives were already married, she seems to have been perfectly content to live at home, studying with her brother Joe (now on Lafayette's faculty) and other professors, continuing with her writing, and pursuing her interest in painting and sketching. She had not been back in Easton long before she completed, by herself, all the course work required of young men for graduation from the college and became, according to a twentieth-century historian, the "first coed at Lafayette."[90] She was also gaining a reputation among townspeople as a publishing poet, her verses having appeared not only in Easton newspapers, but also in Neal's *Saturday Gazette* and the *U. S. Gazette* of Philadelphia.

Then suddenly, in March of 1845, her quiet, studious life was shattered by the onset of what Ellie called "rheumatiz" and the doctors termed "billious [*sic*] fever" and "inflammatory rheumatism."[91] Maggie had probably been struck down by a severe, nearly fatal case of acute systemic rheumatoid arthritis,* with symptoms of high fever, periods of delirium, and "severe pain in every part" of her body, "causing her to scream out every few minutes."[92] Though she survived the virulent attack, her recu-

---

*At the time, Maggie's illness was called "rheumatic fever." But today, the more accurate diagnosis is "acute systemic rheumatoid arthritis," an acute reaction of the body's own autoimmune system. The severe shooting pains behind her eyeballs, which she first experienced several months after the attack, came from *rheumatic iritis,* a not uncommon complication of acute systemic rheumatoid arthritis. Along with these recurring pains in her eyes, she complained of other typically rheumatic symptoms at various times throughout the rest of her life.

peration was very slow, and she remained "exceedingly stiff in all her joints." It was not until July that she felt well enough to write a letter to her cousin Helen, admitting that "it quite pains my hand to hold a pen still."[93]

By autumn she had recovered enough to assist with the family sewing and some housework, where her help was much needed, since there were students living in the home and Grandmother Miller was on one of her long visits. Maggie also threw her limited energies into plans for a large fair given by the women of Easton to raise money for the college. "If its results are at all commensurate with the zeal . . . displayed by our ladies, we will realize something handsome," she reported to Charles McCay.[94] Her own contribution, offered for sale, was a "copy in sepia of the pathetic head of Beatrice Cenci,"* an Italian painting widely reproduced in England and America.[95] As secretary of the women's committee, Maggie was pleased to announce that proceeds from the fair totaled $950, to be used to pay off "the debts due against the Model School building."[96]

But her pleasure in reducing this long-standing debt was offset by her discovery that close work on her painting and other activity had brought on blinding headaches and excruciating pains in her eyeballs, probably caused by the *rheumatic iritis.* Alarmed by her condition, the family took her to a doctor in Philadelphia and then sent her to the seashore for a week, hoping the salt air would be restorative. The only palliative the doctors could suggest was a

---

*Beatrice Cenci was a sixteenth-century Italian woman convicted and subsequently beheaded in Rome for plotting to kill her father. Her romantic story was the basis for Shelley's verse play, *The Cenci*, written in 1819. The famous portrait (now recognized as being by a painter other than Guido Reni of someone other than Beatrice Cenci) was, during the nineteenth century, one of the best-known paintings in Italy, hanging in a "place of honor" in Rome's Barbarini Gallery. Dickens "hung it reverently among his Pictures from Italy," Hawthorne called it "the saddest picture ever painted," and Melville described it as "that sweetest, most touching, but most awful of all feminine heads" (Stuart Curran, *Shelley's Cenci: Scorpions Ringed with Fire* [Copyright 1970 by Princeton Press.] Reprinted by permission of Princeton University Press, preface, xi).

drastic restriction of the use of her eyes for a prolonged period. It was a devastating prescription! As long as she could remember, she had built her life around the use of her eyes, studying what her father had plotted out for her. The "father's relentless ambition" had been "matched by the child's, to make her a scholar."[97] Now all scholarship, reading, and writing were forbidden for an indefinite period.

For the next eight years Maggie was forced to abandon painting, and she was able to read very little, for either pleasure or study. No wonder she wrote bitterly, years later, that her "studies were cut short at twenty-one, never to be resumed!"[98] Unfortunately the prohibition seemed to have little benefit. In August of 1847 her mother reported that Maggie still could not "use her eyes . . . without causing them to pain her very much."[99] She was to learn that the headaches, pains in her eyes, and generalized aching and debility recurred at unexpected, random intervals for the rest of her life.

In her restricted routine Maggie came to depend less upon her father and more and more upon Ellie and her mother, who read to her, took her dictation, and helped her in other ways to make the adjustment to a dramatically altered pattern of living. For years Ellie had possessed the ability to keep Maggie's spirits from flagging. With "Sister Ellen" in the house, Maggie asked, "who could complain of feeling lonely?" She "will not let us get the blues."[100] And now Maggie paid tribute to her mother for providing an example of serenity and abiding faith in God, an example Maggie struggled to emulate:

> for thou
> The upward path hast trod
> And with a guiding finger still,
> Hast pointed me to God!

> To *Him*, in gratitude I bow
> *Who gave a Mother such as thou!*[101]

To fill up her days Maggie "took entire charge of the house-keeping . . . and helped on the education of the younger children as far as her 'ball and chain' would permit."[102] But housework was not enough to keep her mind occupied. Within a few months she had begun to compose verses in her head which she later dictated to Ellie or her mother. In one of the most unusual of these poems, entitled "A Ballad in reply to Tupper's Ballad to Columbia," Maggie responded with vigor to an Englishman's antislavery tirade against America. She began with a sarcastic comment upon England's record of oppression against her own forebears, the Highlanders and Scotch-Irish:

> We kindle o'er the record,
>   Of Scotland's martyr soul,
> We sigh o'er Erin's sorrows,
>   And wonder at the wrong,
> That should have bowed her children
>   So sadly and so long.

Acknowledging the blot that slavery displayed on an otherwise noble America, she suggested that people in the United States would free all their slaves if such manumission could be accomplished quickly and easily. "Ah, brother,/ Could we at once obey/ There should not walk a bondsman/ Upon our soil to-day!" She went on to remind the Englishman that it had been his country's ships that had begun the slave trade and had "brought across the waves/ Unwelcome to Virginia/ A human freight of slaves." The poem ended with a plea for emigration to Liberia, where

christianised—enlightened—
Our slaves shall walk abroad
Beneath their native sunshine
The freemen of their God![103]

The dispatching of freed slaves to Liberia was a cause Maggie was deeply committed to until the Civil War made the topic moot.

Perhaps because she was still fragile and overly concerned with her own health, Maggie reacted with unusual distress to her grandmother's nearly fatal illness in the spring of 1846. Grandmother Miller had come to Easton for one of her regular lengthy visits, and since the family home was so small, the ninety-year-old woman had to share a room with her three granddaughters. While Maggie was reading to her one afternoon, her grandmother was suddenly rendered speechless by a debilitating stroke. That night, Maggie and Ellie were given the responsibility of sitting up with the invalid. "About daybreak," Maggie told her cousin, her grandmother "fainted in our arms." Maggie was sure the old woman was dead. Leaving Ellie to cope with the sagging body, she flew downstairs to fetch her parents. Although within twenty-four hours Mrs. Miller was past the crisis, Maggie was still "so nervous . . . as to not be able to guide my pen very well—fright always weakens me so much. We thought her dying."[104] Her abnormal fear of death had not abated.

Grandmother Miller lived for another year and a half, but she never recovered completely from her stroke, and she grew increasingly querulous and paranoid toward those around her. When she died in the spring of 1847 at the age of ninety-one, Mrs. Junkin could only rejoice that the end had been peaceful, though she regretted not having been able to do as much for the old woman as her sisters had done. "The way that we have been situated, moving from place to place, made it impossible for us to have her so much with us," she explained.[105] She must also have felt relief that her mother's death had provided some assistance to the always uncertain Junkin finances, for Grandmother Miller left them one thousand dollars, a sum her husband invested as insurance against future need.

In the first months after her father's return to Lafayette, Maggie reported to Charles McCay that the administration of the school was progressing harmoniously. "Our college is in very successful operation at present," she told her former tutor, "and there is reason to think that hereafter there will be smooth sailing."[106] One of the stipulations George Junkin had demanded before taking up his old position was that the trustees, not he, would be responsible for keeping the college solvent. But within a year he found it necessary to pour his own money into the school and, at the same time, to travel about the state and up to New York City soliciting funds for the college. Mrs. Junkin hated to see him "go a-begging" among rich industrialists, "but he thinks it his duty, so I say nothing."[107]

Not only was the irrepressible Junkin once again heavily committed to fund-raising, but he also seemed unable to stay away from controversy. Somehow, despite his already busy schedule, he found time to organize a new Presbyterian church in Easton, an activity that aroused animosity among members of the original congregation. The most prominent of these disgruntled members was Judge Porter, who had never completely forgiven Junkin for suspending his nephew.

Tensions mounted, as they had before the family moved to Ohio. "College affairs are in a very unsettled state here," Mrs. Junkin wrote to her sister. "*Where we will be, or how situated*, a few *months hence*, is known only to *Him* who guides the falling

sparrow —but I still desire to take *Jehovah jireh* for my motto."[108]*
Distressed as she was over her husband's problems, she was even
more concerned over the health of twenty-five-year-old Joseph,
who was showing early symptoms of tuberculosis, for which the
only known remedy was moving the patient to a warmer climate.

Despite the personal hostility exhibited toward him at both
Lafayette and Miami during his administrations, George Junkin
had become a man of national reputation. Since his early days in
Milton he had served in leadership positions in many church
synods and presbyteries and had held the national post of moderator of the Old School Presbyterians in 1844. His articles had
appeared frequently in church and temperance periodicals, and
his dramatic eight-hour sermon on slavery had been printed and
widely disseminated.

It was not surprising, therefore, that when Washington College
in Lexington, Virginia, was looking for a new president in the
spring of 1848, the trustees should have turned to this Presbyterian divine whose work in education was well known across the
country. The official invitation arrived in Easton in September of
1848. To be asked to become president of yet another college,
this time in the South, seemed to George Junkin heavenly inter-
vention indeed, since he naively anticipated that Virginia's climate
would keep Joseph's pulmonary troubles from worsening. The
beleaguered president took a quick trip to the Shenandoah Valley
school and returned home in ebullient spirits, eager to begin
work in "this new and most inviting field of labour."[109]

The Junkins's departure from Easton the second time elicited

---

*The Hebrew phrase, *Jehovah jireh*, or its English equivalent, "The Lord will
provide," was a motto Mrs. Junkin used frequently to symbolize the "precious,
oft-repeated assurance" of God's providence. The words from Genesis (Genesis
22:14), spoken by Abraham in gratitude for God's gift of a ram as a burnt-
offering substitute for his own son Isaac, became a watchword of Julia Junkin's
own strong faith in God's over-arching care (MJ, *Silverwood*, 263; also JRJ to
JD, December 22, 1840; *Silverwood*, 12, 32, 195, 263, 364, 377, 389).

an even more dramatic response than their exodus to Ohio nine years earlier. Easton women presented Junkin with a silver pitcher. Citizens, remembering him as the "*founder* and firm supporter of Lafayette College," went on record as "lament[ing] the departure of one who has been . . . so deeply cherished,"[110] and twenty-six undergraduates announced their plans to accompany the president south. At graduation exercises students booed Judge Porter and applauded the president when he appeared in the auditorium, prompting one participant to remark that "this is the proudest day in George Junkin's history."[111] As the ceremony proceeded, according to one account, "the young men wept, the President wept, the audience was in tears, whilst no sound was heard except the quiet tread of those noble young men as they advanced to the dais, pressed their President's hand, and retired."[112] It was a moving finale to sixteen years of heroic effort and unremitting turmoil.

Though she was enthusiastic over the move for the sake of her father and Joe, Maggie herself could scarcely bear to contemplate their departure. Earlier in Easton she had overcome much of her childhood shyness and found new self-esteem as a poet. Now, imprisoned in a nonintellectual routine and unable to pursue what meant most to her, she was finding it difficult, even in familiar surroundings, to maintain her sense of purpose. How, as a single woman of twenty-eight, with no outlets for her aspirations, could she hope to make a place for herself in a new section of the country? She wished she could have as much faith as her mother, who stated, "We think we have seen the finger of Providence directing us in times past, & we trust he will not now forsake us."[113] Maggie had no way of knowing that in Lexington she would find a richer, fuller, more rewarding life than anything she could have imagined.

Chapter 3

Maggie and the Major
1848–1857

> Forgive these saddened strains Ellie
> Forgive these eyes so dim!
> I must—*must* love whom *you have* loved
> So I will turn to him,—
> And clasping with a silent–touch,
> Whose tenderness endears
> *Your hand and his between my own*
> I bless them with my tears.[1]

T he journey to Virginia in November of 1848 did nothing to allay Maggie's misgivings. Always short of funds, George Junkin decided that the family should travel part of the way by boat, less expensive than the railroad or stagecoach. The journey took them from Baltimore through the Chesapeake Bay and up the Rappahannock River to Fredericksburg. Unfortunately, the damp winter wind gave Joseph a severe chill that was worsened by a frigid night in an empty, unheated train station after the family missed their connections in Gordonsville. The last lap of the journey, via stagecoach from Staunton to Lexington, began in sleet and ended in driving snow.

Too late, the Junkins realized that their anticipation of warm winters in western Virginia had been a false hope. Fearful that Joe's bronchitis could change to pneumonia if he remained in Lexington, Junkin reluctantly withdrew funds from his wife's invested inheritance and requested twenty-six-year-old John to leave his fledgling medical practice in New Jersey to take his younger brother to Florida. The two young men settled for the remainder of the winter at Marianna, seventy-five miles west of Tallahassee, where they spent much of their time outdoors in the warm sunshine, especially "inviting . . . to the invalid suffering from pulmonary ailments."[2]

Meanwhile, the Junkins made the transition to the new community with relative ease. The president's house stood within a few hundred yards of the buildings of Washington College, a traditional school of classical learning whose history reached back to 1749. Mrs. Junkin found the three-bedroom brick house to be a "comfortable . . . home," and she liked her neighbors, all "Prof's families [who] have been extremely kind to us."[3] Adjoining the college campus to the north stood relatively new Virginia Military Institute, organized in 1839 as a state institution offering both classical education and military training. Lexington was not only the location of two colleges; it was also the county seat and center for trade, with a dozen lawyers' offices, several hat factories, two or three tailoring businesses, several tanning yards, and a variety of other shops including a bookstore where Maggie was happy to find the latest issues of the *Southern Literary Magazine, Knickerbocker,* the *Eclectic,* and the *Southern Planter.*

The majority of the town's nearly one thousand citizens were Scotch-Irish Presbyterians who, according to Washington College professor Daniel H. Hill, were "remarkable for their piety, bigotry, hospitality and intolerance."[4] The Junkins found this strongly Calvinist atmosphere congenial, and they enjoyed being in a community filled with families whose roots were similar to their own. Thirteen-year-old Julia confided to relatives in Pennsylvania that "we soon began to feel at home and to fall into the Lexington ways of living."[5] Within a month after their arrival, Maggie, Ellie, and Mrs. Junkin had transferred their membership to the local Presbyterian church, situated at the intersection of two of the community's six streets. Mr. Junkin began to preach weekly in a small Calvinist church in the country, in addition to serving as president of the college and professor of moral philosophy.

The town's social life centered primarily on the faculty and students of the two colleges. During their first Christmas holidays in Lexington, Maggie and Ellie were "invited to eight parties and two Balls." Their brother George was quick to explain to a cousin that "of course they did not attend the latter—and were not at some of the former."[6] His sisters' strict upbringing did not permit much levity. Besides, the girls' energies were directed primarily toward housekeeping, planning meals, purchasing groceries, and supervising servants, because Mrs. Junkin, now severely deaf, found such chores difficult.

The bitter weather the family had encountered on their arrival did not abate until late spring. George Washington's birthday, chosen as the date for Mr. Junkin's inauguration as president, was especially unpleasant.* "It commenced snowing the night before," Mrs. Junkin wrote to her sister, "& continued to do so

---

*The name of George Washington had long been associated with the college, for in 1796 he had presented the school (then known as Liberty Hall) with one hundred shares of canal stock in the James River Company. In gratitude the trustees of the academy renamed it Washington Academy.

nearly all day, so that the snow was six or eight in. deep." The women in the family drove from the president's house to the Presbyterian church in a friend's carriage, but the new president "had to tramp down in snow, with the procession" of faculty, college students, and VMI cadets.[7] In a moving inaugural address, Junkin emphasized the close relationship between higher education and the church and ended with a stirring appeal: "The watchword of the College must be '*The sword of the Lord, and of Washington.*' "[8]

Though they loyally took part in the inaugural festivities, including a grand illumination of the college, the family continued to feel deep concern about Joseph and John in Florida. Mrs. Junkin sent Joe a bottle of alum water from a nearby spa, hoping that its reputed healing power might bring recovery, and each day the family gathered in the parlor waiting for the daily mail. A letter from John early in February was not hopeful, and Mrs. Junkin admitted to being "exceedingly depressed."[9] Her spirits rose a few days later after receipt of a more cheerful note telling of the invalid's improvement and informing the family that the brothers hoped soon to travel north to Athens, Georgia, where Joseph could spend time with their old friend Professor McCay.

But on the night of April 17, 1849, John Junkin returned to Lexington alone, to tell his parents and sisters that Joe had died two weeks earlier in Marianna. The family realized that he could not have survived the winter with them in Virginia, but they nonetheless agonized over his lonely death so far from kinfolk. "It would have been a great satisfaction to us, had he reached home," his mother wrote, "even if it had been only to die."[10] For Maggie, Joe's passing brought back all too vividly her old horror of death. "Mother . . . has not dwelt as much as I have upon the far-off, lonely grave, and the forsaken clay," she told George, Jr. "I feel as if it would be wrong to go back to life again and find the pleasure in it that we did before this bereavement."[11] In a poetic tribute to Joseph, she described her feelings of desolation:

> Let the breeze unheeded pass me,
> Let the sun unprized shine on;
> What to me is now the freshness—
> What the brightness—*thou* are gone![12]

When he returned to New Jersey John Junkin discovered that during his prolonged absence in Florida his patients had transferred to other doctors. Without income he was forced to ask his parents for a subsidy, and once again Mr. and Mrs. Junkin withdrew money from Mrs. Junkin's inheritance. "We regretted having to break in on the only *capital* we have," Mrs. Junkin wrote,[13] and Ellie confided to a cousin that "having to send so much *pure money . . . makes tight pulling.*"[14]

To augment the family's meager resources, Maggie began writing serialized stories for popular periodicals. Though she discounted both her ability to write fiction and the quality of the publications for which she was writing, she was grateful for the checks that began arriving regularly. When the *Baltimore Weekly Sun* awarded her the handsome prize of sixty dollars for one of her pieces, entitled "The Child of Song," she used the money to purchase earrings for young Julia's newly pierced ears.[15] Another of her stories, "The Step-mother!," was based upon the theme of second marriage, the topic Maggie, Ellie, and their cousin Helen had discussed many years before. Its plot centered upon a young woman married to a widower who had wooed her, not for love, but because he needed a surrogate mother to care for his orphaned children. With grace and tact the young woman not only won over her rich, handsome husband, but also through perseverance garnered the affections of the seven stepchildren who had been reluctant to accept her as a mother.[16]

Cheered by this initial success, Maggie ventured to submit a number of poems and essays to literary magazines. These contributions brought her less financial reward than the stories, but Maggie was pleased that her essay, entitled "Magazine Literature," was published in the *Christian Parlor Magazine* in 1852, while several dozen poems appeared in print between 1850 and 1855. Thirteen of these were printed in the prestigious *Southern Literary Magazine*, including translations of two Anacreonic odes and Sappho's " Ode to Venus." Other poems found their way into issues of *Iris, Fair,* the *Eclectic, Sartain's,* and *Graham's Magazine.*

Maggie's success as a writer won her considerable respect among Lexingtonians, but, more important for her self-esteem, her literary interests helped make her popular with community young people. "Miss Maggie—as we always called her, was the object of my secret enthusiastic worship," wrote one teenager. "She was not exactly pretty, but her slight figure, fair complexion, and beautiful auburn curls furnished a piquant setting for her refined, intelligent countenance, which made up for the lack of mere beauty. I used to thrill with admiration as I watched her riding at a swift gallop, a little black velvet cap showing off her fairness, the long curls blowing about her face." The girl especially admired Maggie's "manner . . . never patronizing nor supercilious," and she went on to recount that Maggie was "constantly lending us books and magazines, repeating poetry to us (other people's poetry), and talking in a way that charmed us about pictures, artists, and authors."[17]

After an appropriate period of mourning for Joseph, Maggie and Ellie once again began to attend lectures, debates, and informal parties, where Ellie continued to be the self-confident participant and Maggie the shy, reticent observer. As she got to know them better, Maggie discovered that most of the people she met socially were more cosmopolitan than she might have anticipated. "Dining the other day at the house of a friend," she wrote,

"I found that not less than four of the company had been abroad, and so we had racy descriptions of men and things in other lands, and spicy anecdotes of celebrities whom we all know upon paper."[18] Among her new friends were a popular Lexington couple, John and Sally Preston, who showed "an extraordinary partiality" toward her. Major Preston taught Latin and English literature at the Virginia Military Institute, and his wife, the niece of Princeton's president Archibald Alexander, was a charming hostess as well as the busy mother of a large family.* Maggie called Sally "one of the loveliest women in the world."[19] Others in her circle of acquaintances included Junius Fishburn, a bachelor Latin instructor at Washington College, and the college's mathematics professor, Daniel Hill, and his wife, Isabella. After each dinner party or lecture, Maggie returned home to give her mother a careful account of the event, since Mrs. Junkin, cut off from ordinary conversation because of her deafness, rarely left the house.

Among those living in the president's household that first year, in addition to Mr. and Mrs. Junkin, Maggie, Ellie, and Julia, were the Junkins' youngest son, William, and Mrs. Junkin's nephew, Ebenezer Finney, both studying at the college. To assist with this large ménage the family at first employed "hired slaves,"[20] bondsmen leased from slaveholders in town. Later in their Lexington sojourn the Junkins acquired a number of slaves of their own. [21] George Junkin, as noted earlier, believed firmly in the biblical justification of slavery. Maggie and Ellie were already accustomed to being around blacks, since they had grown up with Hannah, the cook whom Mrs. Junkin as a bride had taken with her, and had been well acquainted in Easton with two young freed slaves whose tuition at Lafayette had been underwritten by Mr. Junkin and their former owner, the New Orleans philanthropist John McDonogh.

---

*At VMI, faculty members all had military rank according to their academic position, hence Preston's designation as a "major."

For years Maggie had been an admirer of McDonogh and his work for African colonization, and she had written a poem in his honor that ended with the lines:

Let England yield her *Wilberforce* the love he well may claim,
Americans shall venerate and bless *McDonogh's* name! [22]

As soon as she arrived in Lexington she quickly aligned herself with the local effort to send former slaves to Liberia, contributing verses for a rally held in December of 1849 to honor a group of émigrés. At that meeting her new friend, Major J. T. L. Preston, was the principal speaker, and her father delivered the final prayer. Maggie's poem, while suggesting that blacks were fortunate to have experienced "civilization," nonetheless acknowledged slaves' natural yearning for freedom and a return to their ancestral home:

Home, where the hopes now centre,
    That once were vague and vain—
Where bondage cannot enter,
    To bind them down again:—
Home—free from all oppressions
    Home—where the palm tree waves,
Home—to their own possessions—
    Home—to their grandsires' graves! [23]

Her ambivalent attitude toward slavery was similar to that of many of her generation, in the North and even in the South. She supported repatriation, but she would not listen to abolitionist arguments and believed *Uncle Tom's Cabin* to be a "one-sided book." She empathized with slaves' yearnings for freedom yet insisted that most slaves of her acquaintance were happy in their servitude. Describing one Lexington bondsman, she spoke of his "happy, care-free, black face, and sleek, well-conditioned person, set becomingly off in white pants and apron, as he comes to announce dinner."[24] At the end of a letter to friends in Easton, she told of the marriage of two slaves whose wedding and reception had been provided by their owners. If her Northern friends had seen the festivities, she concluded, they would not "have been disposed to waste much superfluous commiseration upon the so-called 'poor, unhappy slaves.' "[25]

While her literary work was appearing frequently, her health improving, and her popularity increasing among Lexington's young folk, one would have expected Maggie to become more content in Virginia. But she continued to regret having left familiar friends and vistas in Easton, and in her despondency she relied heavily upon her mother and Ellie for emotional support. The closeness of Maggie and Ellie remained almost that of twins, as they shared a room, dressed alike, engaged in most of the same activities, and confided to each other their most intimate secrets. Then suddenly—in December of 1852 or January of 1853—Maggie found the old camaraderie threatened by the appearance of an awkward young man named Thomas Jonathan Jackson, who increasingly monopolized Ellie's time and attention.

Tom Jackson had moved to Lexington in the summer of 1851 to begin teaching natural philosophy and military tactics at VMI. Shy and ill at ease among strangers, Jackson had only one acquaintance in the community, Daniel Hill, who had met him during the Mexican War, and it was he who introduced Jackson to the Junkin family. At first the tall, clean-shaven professor spent his time discussing theological matters with Mr. Junkin and inquiring about Presbyterian dogma. But after he had learned a great deal about Calvinism and had become a member of the local Presbyterian church, he continued to frequent the Junkin parlor regularly, drawn there by the presence of Ellie Junkin. When Hill teased him about talking so much about Ellie, Jackson replied, "I don't know what has changed me. I used to think her plain, but her face now seems to me all sweetness." Hill burst out laughing and replied, "You are in love; that's what is the matter!" Jackson "blushed up to the eyes, and said that he had never been in love in his life, but he certainly felt differently toward this lady from what he had ever felt before."[26] It was soon obvious to even the most casual observer that the twenty-seven-year-old Jackson was seeking Ellie's hand in marriage.

Mr. and Mrs. Junkin were surprised by but tolerant of the budding courtship between the solemn professional soldier and their attractive, vivacious, sometimes irreverent Ellie. But Maggie did everything in her power to break up the match. A cousin reported that "Elinor [sic] is in love with a Major Jackson, a professor at the University [sic] and Margaret wont let him come to the house as she is afraid Eleanor will marry him and go away."[27]

From what she knew and had observed about Jackson, Maggie was convinced that he would not be an appropriate husband for her beloved Ellie. His military background was totally different from anything Ellie had ever known. His skimpy elementary education, his training at West Point, his war service, and even the courses he taught at VMI seemed completely alien to Ellie's upbringing in the home of a minister who was also a professor of classics. In addition, Jackson exhibited idiosyncracies that had within months of his arrival in Lexington made him a source of amused conversation on the VMI post and among his fellow residents at the local hotel. Behind his back the cadets called Ellie's suitor "Fool Tom Jackson" and "Old Jack," and they disliked his dull, memorized lectures. Maggie must have known the stories that circulated about his personal peculiarities as well—his diet of "stale bread and buttermilk," his almost fanatical adherence to an exact schedule (including a nine o'clock bed-time), his seeming humorlessness, and his theory that wearing a wet undershirt would help his dyspepsia.[28] She had seen the man in church on Sunday mornings, stiff and ramrod straight in his pew, asleep through most of every Sabbath's sermon. Years later she softened her view, characterizing Jackson more charitably as "*sui generis*," an individual like no other person.[29] But at the time he was courting Ellie, she found his curious manners, theories, and habits unacceptable.

Maggie's opposition to Jackson was stimulated by other, more selfish reasons as well. She was frankly jealous that Ellie should be the first sister to marry, leaving her "an old maid," vulnerable to pity and ridicule. She felt betrayed, believing that Ellie, for years her closest friend and supporter, had now abandoned her for a stranger. And, apprehensive as she always was in facing new situations, she was reluctant to make the adjustment to Ellie's changed status, particularly in Lexington, where Maggie consid-ered herself still to be an outsider.

If her hostility toward Tom Jackson seemed extreme, it was nonetheless consistent with comments she had made years be-fore, when in 1840 she had written a letter of sympathy to Helen Dickey about the "loss" of Helen's sister through marriage. "I remember seeing the tear start to [come] when I spoke of the loneliness you would feel when Margaret would leave you," Maggie wrote. "Do you not sometimes feel disposed to wish that she was Margaret *Dickey* yet?" Maggie then proceeded to offer herself as a substitute sister: "I could talk and laugh, and we could be happy together."[30] In the same vein she expressed in verse her need to keep Ellie to herself:

> Sister! thou knowest not
> How fondly loved thou art
> Unless thou readst the thought

That's swelling in my heart—

. . . .

Together have we read
The poet's thrilling lays—
Together past have sped
Our childhood's sunny days.
Together may we be
For many a year to come.
Together may we be
In an eternal home![31]

A generation earlier Mrs. Junkin had felt a similar need for a mutually supportive relationship with her three married sisters, though she lived far from them throughout most of her adult life. She wrote frequently of her dependence upon their letters and of her wish to be with her "dear friends," as she termed her siblings.*

Despite Maggie's efforts to thwart the romance, Ellie agreed, early in 1853, to marry her suitor. Then she abruptly broke the engagement, perhaps because she did not feel ready to stand up against Maggie's antagonism. Jackson was distraught and asked Daniel and Isabella Hill to intervene for him. Though the Hills did what they could to patch up the lovers' quarrel, the most likely reason for Ellie and Tom's eventual reconciliation was Maggie's change of heart, a lessening of antagonism which she communicated in a poem, "To my Sister." The verses must have meant a great deal to Ellie and later to Tom Jackson, who

---

*In an article entitled "The Female World of Love and Ritual: Relations between Women in Nineteenth-Century America," Carroll Smith-Rosenberg suggests that within many nineteenth-century American families there was a special relationship between "sisters, first cousins, aunts, and nieces," providing unique female support, "an inner core of kin" (*Signs* 1 [Autumn 1975], 11. Copyright 1975 by The University of Chicago).

carefully preserved them.*

Using the stanzas to work through her unhappiness and frustration, Maggie began with an honest recognition of her own deep jealousy of Jackson which she believed grew out of the exceeding closeness the sisters had enjoyed through the years:

> A cloud is on my heart Ellie
> A shade is on my brow
> And the still current of my thought
> Glides often sadly now.
>
> . . . .
>
> From very childhood's years Ellie
> We've known *no separate joy*
> Whatever grieved *your* heart, could bring
> To *mine* a like annoy
> Together o'er one page we bent
> In sunshine and in shade
> *Together* thro' life's summer walks
> Our kindred feet have strayed

Then she acknowledged, with surprising frankness, that her resentment was unfair and that Ellie had every right to seek happiness in marriage:

> But now our paths diverge Ellie
> A thought I may not share

---

*The punctuation of the poem and "missed" rhyme in the third stanza are exactly as they appear in the typed copy. There is no way of knowing whether they were written this way by MJP or altered in transcription. Though it is not possible to date the poem with absolute certainty, it seems very likely that Maggie offered the poem to Ellie as a gesture of reconciliation before Ellie's marriage. In her autobiographical novel *Silverwood* (published in 1858), Edith Irving (the fictional Maggie) gave a slightly altered version of "To my Sister" to her sister Zilpha (the fictional Ellie) before Zilpha's marriage. For plot of *Silverwood* and characterization, see pages 80–84.

Has seized your spirit's sovreignty
And claims to govern these
Yet while as if discrowned of love
I feel an exile's pain
Believe me that I question not
His sacred right to reign

The future seemed bleak to Maggie:

Ah! home must lose its charms Ellie
As fast the years come on
And one by one the cherished hearts
Will go—till all are gone!
'Tis but the common work of Time
To mar our household so
And I must learn to choke the sob
And smile to see them go

But she tried to accept the inevitable—with grim determination, if not with warmth:

Forgive these saddened strains Ellie
    Forgive these eyes so dim!
    I must—*must* love whom *you have* loved
    So I will turn to him,—
    And clasping with a silent—touch
    Whose tenderness endears
    Your hand and his between my own
I bless them with my tears.[32]

The poem was hardly a ringing endorsement either of Jackson or of Ellie's desire to marry the awkward young professor. But it seems to have been enough for Ellie, who again, "after two or three months of estrangement,"[33] promised to become Tom Jackson's wife, provided the betrothal be kept secret from all but close family members. Such secrecy was not uncommon among Lexingtonians in the 1850s, as Ellie's contemporary, Emily Morrison Bondurant, explained. "Engagements of marriage were never announced in old Virginia in those days," she wrote. "We took more pains to keep them secret than family and friends take nowadays to trumpet them abroad."[34]

In spite of her attempt to put a good face on the engagement, Maggie remained privately unreconciled. She "still looks with gloomy fore-bodings to the future," Mrs. Junkin wrote, and "cannot divest herself of the idea that Ellie cannot be to her after marriage, the same companion & confidant she has so long been. When the affair is over, I think & hope she will feel better."[35]

The wedding, held on August 4, 1853, was a simple ceremony at the Junkin home, with Mr. Junkin officiating. The couple left almost at once for a prolonged honeymoon to visit Philadelphia, New York City, and Niagara Falls—accompanied by Maggie. From a twentieth-century perspective, it seems a most unusual arrangement, but in the 1850s "sisters, cousins, and friends frequently accompanied newlyweds on their . . . wedding trip."[36] (Years earlier, Mrs. Junkin's sister Margaret had traveled from Germantown to Milton with George and Julia Junkin only two days after their wedding.) The young couple had a wonderful time on their journey, Jackson writing with enthusiasm of the "magnificent scenery . . . bare and rugged rocks and crags."[37] Not surprisingly, Maggie was less taken with the journey. "That trip was a disappointing affair to me in many respects," she told Helen Dickey. "Ellie and Major Jackson enjoyed it a good deal more than I did."[38]

Upon their return the newlyweds made no attempt to secure separate accommodations. Instead, they settled into a combination bedroom and study that, during their absence, had been added onto one of the first-floor wings of the president's home. Still upstairs were Dr. and Mrs. Junkin, Maggie, now thirty-three years old, and young Julia, aged eighteen.* Maggie remained unable to adjust to Ellie's new status. "I could not tell you how I have felt since Ellie's marriage," she wrote to Helen. "Indeed I shrink from writing that word almost—and as to her changed name—it *jars* my ear to hear it. It took from me my only bosom companion, the only one perhaps I shall ever have—and put between us a stranger."[39]

She recognized that she was being selfish. "I must not rebel—though I'm afraid I have done so too long . . . She will be happy and I—I must be content to . . . be left like 'the last leaf'" on the tree. It would have been easier, she thought, if Ellie had married before they moved to Lexington, because "I am growing old" and no longer "in the home of my childhood, but among comparative strangers."[40] Ellie and the major, by contrast, were too happy to be bothered by her opposition. "Ellie apparently enjoys her married life very much," their brother George wrote. His parents and Julia "like the Major," he said, and he hoped that Maggie would eventually come to tolerate her new brother-in-law, though she "took his *interference* so very much to heart."[41]

During the fall of 1853, Maggie had little time to spend on either resentment or reconciliation, because she was busy coping with her mother's slow physical decline. After Christmas Mrs. Junkin's "protracted and painful illness"[42] grew more severe, but the family was still unprepared for the doctor's announcement, on February 24, that the patient had only hours to live. Stunned, they gathered round her bedside. Maggie implored her mother not to die. "Oh, Mother, what shall we do?" she agonized. "How can we live without you?" Mrs. Junkin quietly replied, "The Lord

---

*George Junkin had been awarded a D.D. degree from Miami University in 1851. He also received LL.D. degrees from Miami in 1854 and from Rutgers in 1855.

will provide." By the use of her old familiar motto, *Jehovah jireh*, she bequeathed to Maggie her personal faith in God's providence.[43]

In the ensuing silence, Junkin began to recite the Twenty-third Psalm, using the metrical rendering the whole family knew by heart, "the old version," as Maggie called it:[44]

> The Lord's my shepherd, I'll not want;
> He makes me down to lie

In a barely audible whisper, Mrs. Junkin quoted the next words:

> In pastures green; He leadeth me
> The quiet waters by.[45]

Reciting antiphonally, the pair went through the familiar verses, until Dr. Junkin came to the words:

> Goodness and mercy all my life
> Shall surely follow me;

His wife struggled to voice a few syllables: "And in God's house. . . ." Here her voice trailed off, and she was dead.[46]

Maggie tried to convince herself that her mother's death demonstrated "how easy a thing it is to die," but her old fear of dying was as strong as ever, and she found she could not even visit Mrs. Junkin's grave in the church cemetery. To lose Ellie to marriage and then to lose her mother to death—the double loss was too much, she felt. "You cannot know the *absolute necessity*" her mother's serene presence had been for them all, she wrote Charles McCay. "*For us* to live without that dearest, sweetest sympathy, that wonderful untiring love that never . . . for one instant failed us . . . it *is* bitter indeed."[47] Wrapping herself in guilt as she had done when her little brother David died, Maggie was convinced she had brought "this anguish upon herself, by loving her mother too much."[48]

Slowly, the girls took up their regular routines again, distributing Mrs. Junkin's clothing among family and friends, answering the many letters of condolence they received, and sewing mourning clothes for themselves. They were touched by the outpouring of affection from the community. Her mother, young Julia wrote, "had lived so short a time" in Lexington and "her deafness had cut her off so much from society" that none of them had realized how popular Mrs. Junkin had been.[49] The calmest member of the family was Dr. Junkin, who wrote to a friend that only after her death had many people learned "the secret he had so long known," that his wife had been a remarkable person. He began preaching a series of sermons using the passages of scripture his wife had repeated in her last hours.[50] As if to mirror the family's distress, the weather turned suddenly cold and forbidding. Early peach blossoms froze on the trees and there was heavy snow.

Maggie's grief, coupled with her lingering unhappiness over Ellie's marriage, brought her to the point of physical collapse. Julia wrote in alarm of Maggie's severe back pains, "and what with that and her eyes and ears she gets very low spirited."[51] Consulted by mail, brother John diagnosed his sister's difficulties as "prolapses,"* and he prescribed total bed rest.[52] Maggie recognized that "grief has a good deal to do with bringing on my disease," and she begged her cousin Helen to pray for her. "I do so need to be taught *submission*."[53]

Five months later, when she was still struggling with poor health and her tumultuous emotions, Tom and Ellie Jackson left

---

*Maggie may have suffered from an uncomfortable hemorrhoidal condition, with "prolapsed" tissue. It is unlikely that she had a prolapsed uterus, since (with no intervening surgery) she became pregnant and delivered a normal baby within four years.

to spend some time with his sister in Randolph County, Virginia (now West Virginia), as well as to visit various healing springs in the area. Ellie was six months pregnant, and she must have dreaded a long journey over bumpy roads. But Jackson, suffering from a variety of ailments, hoped for a cure at one of the many spas whose mineral baths promised instantaneous healing. "The Major's nervous system is out of order," Julia wrote to Helen Dickey, "or he imagines so at least; but to see him you would not think him sick at all."[54] The couple returned late in the summer, Ellie weary but more concerned about Maggie's health than her own. "We are very anxious for Maggie to return to the North . . . & have medical advice," she wrote. She herself was busy making plans for the baby's arrival and asked her sister-in-law, George's wife, to "shop some for us," requesting that the "bundle" be sent to Lexington at once. She ended her letter: "All send love & the Major particularly."[55]

Giving birth was a serious matter in nineteenth-century America, and particularly in the rural South, where "at least one out of twenty-five white women . . . who died in 1850 died in child-birth."[56] A physician often attended a lying-in at the young mother's home, but even the best of practitioners had only primitive knowledge of sterile technique and little ability to prevent hemorrhages, control convulsions, or assist the mother through prolonged labor. Not infrequently, well-meaning doctors, following the advice of the eminent Dr. Benjamin Rush (the Philadelphia physician who had been a friend of Ellie's grandparents), made otherwise normal deliveries complicated by use of so-called "heroic methods" such as excessive bloodletting and use of laudanum or ergot.[57] Though she must have been fully aware of the potential dangers, there is no record that Ellie had any abnormal fear of her approaching labor, perhaps because her mother had successfully survived eight deliveries. Following Mrs. Junkin's example, Ellie probably arranged for a local doctor to assist her during delivery. Without question, both Maggie and Julia were in attendance when she went into labor.

But, in spite of professional care and the loving attention of her sisters, something went terribly wrong, and Ellie died on Sunday, October 22, during delivery of a stillborn child.* There are no family letters to document exact details of the tragedy, only a stark notice placed in a local newspaper four days after Ellie's death and a poem in which Maggie described her sister's last moments. The short obituary in the *Lexington Gazette* stated simply that "Mrs. Eleanor Jackson . . . died, suddenly on Sunday, the 22nd, at the residence of her father, Rev. Dr. Junkin, President of Washington College."[58] In her poem composed in 1856, Maggie wrote that, sitting beside her sister, she had watched Ellie's "eyelids close/ Beneath whose drooping fringes lay/ The charm of all their life's repose," and had observed Ellie's "breath . . . come/ Fainter and fainter till the dumb/ Unanswering lips grew pale in death."[59]

Maggie was devastated by her sister's death. "Ellie's bosom was the repository of all my sorrow and also my joys," she anguished. "Shall I ever cease grieving for its loss!"[60] Later she acknowledged that she could not even follow the coffin to the cemetery, where the family buried mother and child in a single grave beside Mrs. Junkin. Two days later, an early eighteen-inch snow covered the raw, scarred earth.[61]

The president's house held such painful memories that within a few days Maggie traveled north to Philadelphia, to visit doctors and spend the winter with relatives. Because it was the middle of

---

*Family tradition suggests that the stillborn infant was a baby girl, but the assumption is impossible to verify. There is no death notice about the baby and church records do not reveal the child's sex. Neither Ellie's gravestone nor family letters mention the dead baby. Elisabeth C. Robinson, who coauthored *Repassing at my Side* (Blacksburg, Virginia: The Southern Printing Company, 1975), a genealogy of the Junkin family, states: "Everyone just 'knew' that Elinor and Tom Jackson had a girl" (Mrs. Richard Daniel Robinson to Mary P. Coulling, July 24, 1992).

the college term, Major Jackson had no alternative but to remain at his post, teaching his classes without enthusiasm, and visiting Ellie's grave daily. He confided to Daniel Hill that when he was in the graveyard, he "felt an almost irresistible desire to dig up the body and once more to be near the ashes of one he had loved so well,"[62] and he yearned for death himself: "Had I one request on earth to ask in accordance with my own feelings, and apart from duty, it would be that I might join her before the close of another day."[63] When Dr. Junkin and Julia assumed that he would remain indefinitely in the room he and Ellie had shared, the heartsick young man acquiesced.

In his mood of deep despair, Jackson must have been surprised to receive in December a letter from his less than cordial sister-in-law, asking for his sympathy and support. "My dear Brother," Maggie began, "I feel an irresistible desire to write to you today—for my heart has been so exceedingly oppressed in dwelling upon our loss, that perhaps to write to you may be some relief." Acknowledging that she was selfish in asking him to assuage her sorrow when "you have more than enough of your own to bear," she hoped that he would sympathize, "seeing that the source of your own [pain] is the same."[64]

In the middle of the previous night, she continued, she had suddenly been overpowered by the "stunning sense" of Ellie's "being *forever gone*. . . . I seemed for the first time to comprehend that Ellie was *dead*. . . . My heart *ached* to see and speak with my sister once more!" Then Maggie shyly asked the major to write to her, "but I shall know why [if] you don't." If he felt he could not respond, she asked him at least to "remember *me* in your prayers, and believe me, always, your most affectionate and sympathizing sister."[65]

The letter seemed to echo words from the poem to Ellie just before her marriage, when Maggie had promised to "love whom *you have* loved," and the letter's obvious tone of reconciliation appeared to be a hesitant offer to clasp his hand and bless him "with my tears."[66] Touched by her initiative, Jackson replied to his "dear sister," suggesting that her words made him "feel that we are nearer to each other, such as was the case with the now sainted *sister* and *wife*."[67] He was not, he said, a good correspondent, but "if dear Ellie was here, she would answer . . . in her beautiful manner: and how her pure heart would overflow at the thought of your being so affectionately kind to me. You and I were certainly the dearest objects which she left on Earth."[68] He described to Maggie his daily visits to the cemetery, where on more than one occasion he had found Ellie's and Mrs. Junkin's graves "both covered with snow."[69]

He apologized for "say[ing] so much about myself, it looks so selfish . . . Though I have not said much about you here, yet I have thought of you much, and prayed for you much, and your best interests are at my heart. I am very anxious to see you."[70] She had had a miniature of Ellie copied and sent to him, and he was grateful to receive the picture. As soon as she was entirely well, he wrote, she must "come home and warm hearts will welcome you. Your very affectionate brother, Thomas."[71]

Late in the spring of 1855 Maggie did return to Lexington, where she discovered that family problems taxed her still fragile health. The servants were sick, Julia was exhausted from the long, depressing winter, and her father faced unpleasant attacks from Lexington lawyers for taking a stand against the granting of saloon licenses in the community. Her own back pains, she wrote Helen Dickey, were "constant. . . . At times, [I] am greatly discouraged." She still could not bring herself to visit the cemetery. "I have not yet been to the *sad spot*. I *cannot* go. . . . Father, and Julia & the Major unite with me in love."[72]

She and Julia were alone in the house much of the summer, when her father was in Philadelphia and Jackson visited other parts of Virginia. From Neal's Island he wrote to "my dear

Maggie" that, though he still longed for death, her "kindness to me and affection for me has [*sic*] no little influence in lightening up the gloom which for months has so much envelopped [*sic*] me. . . . To sum up all dear Maggie I want to see you again. I desire to mingle in the society of one with whom I have so many endearing associations."[73]

When he returned at the end of the summer, the two began what came to be a daily pattern of visitation. Each evening, after Jackson had finished his class preparation, Maggie would come to his room for "an hour or two of relaxation and chat. . . . In such intercourse," she wrote many years later, "I came to know the man as never before. His early life, his lonely orphanage, his struggle with disease, his West Point life, his campaigning in Mexico . . . all these furnished material for endless reminiscence." During these evening sessions, she said, he would drop his reserve, tell her "amusing stories, and be so carried away with himself, as almost to roll from his chair in laughter."[74] He even taught her Spanish, and when she was in Philadelphia in the summer of 1856, he sent her a letter written entirely in Spanish. "My dearest Sister," the English translation reads:

> I have had no conversation in the Spanish language since I said Good-bye to you. Although I have not had the advantage of your conversation, . . . I had instead the hope of improvement in your health, which to you is of the greatest value. And to me it is more agreeable than being deprived of your precious company, if you can obtain the restoration of your health. . . . I want to see you very much. . . . Write me more frequently if you have the time. Good-bye my dearly loved sister.
> Your very loving brother
> Thomas[75]

In addition to seeing each other in the evenings, Maggie and the major busied themselves with outside activities. Jackson organized and began teaching regularly in a Sabbath school for blacks in Lexington that combined singing, prayer, and oral instruction from Brown's Child's Catechism. The young superintendent kept careful records, and "if any of his regular pupils were absent, he would invariably visit the master or mistress to make inquiries as to the reason of their non-attendance." He learned the names of each of his students, and they, in turn, all knew "Marse Major."[76]

For her part, in addition to keeping house for her father, Maggie started writing again in earnest. In 1855 she saw two newly composed pieces published in the *Southern Literary Magazine* and one in the *Eclectic*, and she wrote a long poem dedicated to her mother's memory. "A Year in Heaven" (which appeared in the *Southern Presbyterian*) contrasted her own despair with what she believed to be her mother's joy in eternity. A year later she completed her only attempt at a novel, which she entitled *Silverwood*. She wrote the book, she said, to "embalm the characters of dear mother, Ellie, and brother Joe," and also to provide comfort to her own aching spirit.[77]

> For I need the wine of solace,
>   Which this cluster sweet supplies,
> Since ye pluck the food of angels
>   'Midst the hills of Paradise.
>
> Or, as Ruth among the reapers,
>   Memory, like a gleaner, strives
> Thus to gather up a handful
>   From the harvest of your lives.[78]

Silverwood was neither a critical nor a financial success, despite the *Southern Literary Messenger*'s praise of the book as a "charming series of sketches . . . pleasant and mournful to the soul."[79] The novel, however, merits more than a casual perusal, since, by Maggie's own admission, several of the fictional personae are patterned after real individuals. "You will recognize the characters," she wrote to a friend, "and many of the scenes are from life."[80]

The novel's plot concerns members of the Irving family,* forced to leave their old home after a disastrous fire to begin life all over again on a rural estate called Silverwood. The tall, attractive, red-haired son Lawrence becomes ill and travels to the West Indies in a vain search to recover his health. Remaining at Silverwood are the widowed Mrs. Irving and her four daughters, Zilpha, Edith, Josepha, and Eunice. Zilpha, a winsome, self-confident young artist, adjusts more easily to their new surroundings than her sister Edith, a shy, bookish writer, "withdrawn, timid and restrained . . . among strangers."[81] Josepha and Eunice are childish figures who do not figure prominently in the story.

Most of *Silverwood*'s 405 pages concentrate upon Zilpha and Edith and a succession of young men with whom they are involved. Dr. Dubois, a physician, falls in love with Edith, but she is enamored of a distant cousin, a minister named Bryant Woodruff, who loves Zilpha. Edith, trying to remember that "there are others to be loved and lived for," resignedly begins to write in order to support her penniless family. Her mother, ever hopeful, quotes a favorite "watchword," *Jehovah jireh*, "the Lord will provide."[82] When Zilpha rejects her cousin Bryant for a Mr. Fleming and tells Edith she plans to marry her new lover, Edith gives way to despair, because to "give her up for another—that will be so hard."[83] Edith writes a poem of reconciliation, "A cloud

---

*In 1852 Maggie had written a series of articles for Easton newspapers, which she called "Letters from a Virginia Cousin." Rather than use her own name, she signed the articles Margaret Irvine. In *Silverwood* she named her family Irving.

is on my heart, darling," which she slips between the pages of Zilpha's Bible. Zilpha marries, Mrs. Irving dies, and an aged Scottish relative leaves a handsome bequest to the Irving family. No longer facing a lonely life as a governess, Edith turns to her old friend Bryant Woodruff for a future of love and happiness.

Though the fictional Irvings are not an exact replica of the Junkin family, several of the characters can be easily identified with members of it. Mrs. Irving is clearly Mrs. Junkin, with her reliance upon God and her use of *Jehovah jireh*. Zilpha and Edith are unmistakably Ellie and Maggie, and Lawrence is a thinly veiled Joseph. Details in the story also come from Maggie's own background. The fire at the beginning of the novel, which sends the family to a new home, appears to represent the "fire storm" of unpleasantness in Easton when Lafayette's trustees turned against George Junkin. The West Indies locale, to which the ailing Lawrence travels for his health, is a substitute for Florida. Silverwood is Lexington, whose scenery includes the crumbling stone walls of "——— Hall" (the ruins, extant even today, of Liberty Hall, the school that became Washington College) and Castlehead (Rockbridge County's landmark, House Mountain).

The men in *Silverwood*—Dubois, Woodruff, and Fleming—are less easily identified. Some readers believe that Maggie used Stonewall Jackson as a pattern for the Reverend Mr. Woodruff, an interpretation that would suggest that Maggie was in love with her brother-in-law. But this analysis falls apart when one remembers Maggie's strong antipathy for Jackson in the years before his marriage. Also, Jackson was a military man, while her fictional bookish minister seems more like Charles McCay or Junius Fishburn, the bachelor professor of Latin at Washington College whom Julia married in August of 1856. Probably Maggie was not patterning the three suitors in *Silverwood* upon any living individuals, as she had intended only "to embalm the characters of dear mother, Ellie, and brother Joe."[84]

By far the most interesting characterization in the book is Maggie's delineation of herself in the person of Edith, rebellious, strong-willed, unwilling to face realities, and lacking in faith. The fictional Edith, still yearning for the burned-out homestead, admits that she "can't think this [Silverwood] is *home*." She acknowledges "how hard it is" to yield gracefully and with "unquestioning submission" to present circumstances, and she tells Zilpha that "I look backward and forward too much, and *upward too little*."[85] By the time Maggie had completed *Silverwood*, she had come to understand herself remarkably well.

Her writing technique in *Silverwood* is similar to the combined verse-and-prose pattern she had employed in her serialized stories, with seven short lyrical poems inserted at key points in the plot. One of these, "A cloud is on my heart, darling," is a slightly adapted, shortened version of "To my Sister."[86] Another, "Left Behind," is a thinly veiled fictional account of her distress at Ellie's death:

> *They* cannot know, by grief untaught,
>   What an unfathomed depth I find,
> Of ebbless anguish in the thought
>   That I am left behind.[87]

Maggie insisted that her novel be published anonymously, though the printer, Derby & Jackson, offered her an additional two hundred dollars if she would place her name on the manuscript. In the past she had been perfectly willing to be identified with her poetry and her serial stories, but with *Silverwood* she seems to have changed her mind and aligned herself with the traditional nineteenth-century practice of women authors not using their own names.* "If [a woman] puts herself in print," Maggie had Edith tell Dr. Dubois, "she belongs no more to herself—she has taken the public into partnership."[88] Within a few years, however, she resumed publishing poetry in her own name.[89] Either she had temporarily yielded to Lexington's conservative views concerning women writers or, more likely, she felt that her novel was so autobiographical that it required anonymity.

With the completion of *Silverwood* Maggie hoped to realize the kind of serenity she had found in the past through writing. But the old memories of Ellie's last moments returned again and again, especially when her close friend Sally Preston died unexpectedly at the age of forty-four in January of 1856 while giving birth to her ninth child. Sally left behind her husband, John, a colleague of Tom Jackson's at VMI, and seven surviving children whose ages ranged from five to twenty-two.

More restorative than her writing, Maggie discovered, were her evening conversations with Jackson. Theirs was a surprising friendship, since in many ways the two were utterly different. In contrast to her unusually broad classical education, his schooling had been largely self-taught until he went to West Point. She had never been outside the mid-Atlantic states and Ohio, while he had traveled widely in Mexico and in Florida. She had been reared in a loving home, surrounded by parents, siblings, and a host of cousins; he was an orphan, for whom the warmth of the Junkin household held special meaning. Her ideal of manhood was formed by the examples of her father, her professional brothers, and her old friend Charles McCay, men with whom she could

---

*Elizabeth Fox-Genovese has explained cogently why so many nineteenth-century women wrote anonymously: "It was one thing to write, quite another to claim the public and unfeminine mantle of authorship. Authorship could not be separated from intended audience, and hence publication could not be separated from unladylike self-display" (Elizabeth Fox-Genovese, *Within the Plantation Household: Black and White Women of the Old South* [Chapel Hill, N.C.: University of North Carolina Press, 1988], 15, 246).

engage in scholarly repartee. Jackson's training was exclusively military, a milieu the Junkins knew little about. "Isn't it odd," Maggie had written to Helen Dickey in 1853, "that E. should have married a *military* man, whose associations and tastes are all with the army and army life?"[90]

In other basic respects, however, Maggie and Tom Jackson were very much alike. Both were painfully shy in public, talkative only with close friends or family members. Both were plagued by ill health, real or imagined. Most important, both were devoutly religious, reading their scriptures daily and attending church regularly, devotional exercises that seemed to bring Tom Jackson greater peace of mind than they did Maggie. One might surmise that this strong sense of religious commitment, coupled with their mutual loss, might have propelled them toward marriage. Perhaps the memory of her early hostility kept them apart, or maybe the fragility of their new friendship, born of a common grief, was not enough to bring about love. Jackson may have felt ill at ease because Maggie's educational background was far superior to his haphazard schooling, and she may have recognized his need for a wife less independent and outspoken than herself.

Whatever their personal feelings toward each other, there was an insurmountable religious barrier that stood against any consideration of marriage. This was a prohibition in the *Constitution of the Presbyterian Church* that forbade a man to marry his deceased wife's sister.* Once Tom Jackson had married Ellie, he and Maggie became forever brother and sister in the eyes of the Presbyterian Church, and any thought of his marrying Maggie after Ellie's death would have been deemed incestuous. Since both Maggie Junkin and Tom Jackson were devout Presbyterians, living in the home of a minister who knew his canonical law as well as anyone in the country, it would have been simply unthinkable for the two of them to defy church, family, and community. They may well have been drawn to each other, but church polity said *no*—and there the matter had to end.

There are hints, however, that their growing mutual affection, in conflict with the absolute nature of the church's proscription, at times brought about an almost unbearable tension, so that each felt the necessity to get far away from the smoldering situation. After several months of seeing each other daily, Maggie fled in the spring of 1855 to Philadelphia, and the major left for a leisurely vacation visiting relatives. Again, in 1856, after another long winter of sharing the same house, Maggie left abruptly to

---

*On page 136 of the 1853 Constitution is the statement that "a man may not marry any of his wife's kindred nearer in blood than he may of his own" (Confession of Faith, Section IV of Chapter XXIV: *Of Marriage and Divorce*, published in Philadelphia by the Presbyterian Board of Publication.) This prohibition was accepted without question by devout believers in the 1850s, much discussed in church periodicals and meetings of the General Assembly of the Southern church (Presbyterian U.S.) in the 1870s and 1880s, and finally repealed in 1884. The prohibition, shared at various times by other denominations, grew out of the belief that once a man and woman married, they became one flesh, a union that was not dissolved by death. Thus, if a man should marry his wife's sister, he would in a sense be marrying his own sister. The same principle applied for many years in civil statutes both in England and in certain states of the U.S. According to one scholar, "No question was discussed with more earnestness in both England and America, with less positive results . . . than whether a man may marry his deceased wife's sister" (J. Schouler, *A Treatise on the Law of Marriage, Divorce, Separation and Domestic Relations* [Albany, New York: M. Bender and Company, 1921], 23). In 1835 the English Parliament had enacted the "Deceased Wife's Sister Act," and though attempts were made repeatedly to repeal it, it remained part of English law until 1907. Virginia's Legal Code of 1819 prohibited such a marriage (Section 17, Chapter 100). The statute was repealed in 1849.

spend time with kinfolk and Jackson suddenly undertook a trip to Europe, the real reason for which may have been his realization that he was beginning to care too much for Ellie's sister.

It seems curious that Maggie, after the deaths of Ellie and her mother, did not turn to Julia for companionship. But the fifteen years' difference in the sisters' ages, coupled with Maggie's sense that Julia was still a child, seems to have precluded any change in their affectionate, but not intimate, relationship. Julia, described by a contemporary as "bright, energetic, amiable, and very pretty,"[91] had been thirteen years old when the Junkins moved to Lexington. When she was eighteen and just beginning to see young men socially, she experienced a frightening episode when the young man who had taken her to church was murdered outside the building, while she waited for him in the pew. Her escort, a VMI cadet named Thomas Blackburn, had shown her to her seat and then had excused himself to meet "at the side of the church" a disgruntled law student named Christian who had been paying unwanted attention to Blackburn's cousin. After accusing Blackburn of alienating his cousin against him, the law student suddenly lunged at the cadet with a knife. Blackburn was discovered just outside the church doors, "dead from a stab in his back . . . and the knife . . . through his throat cutting both jugular veins."[92] The experience was a terribly frightening one for Julia, and two months later she was still fearful. "This makes the third murder in six months," she wrote to her brother Ebenezer. "Christian's trial comes on the 12th of April—no one expects he will be hung."[93] The law student was acquitted because of insufficient evidence.

But, in a community where there were far more young men than eligible young women, Julia did not stay quietly at home for long. Courted by Junius Fishburn, Washington College's attractive professor of Latin, she became secretly engaged to him not long before he left for a year's study in Germany in 1855. When

Maggie returned from Philadelphia in mid-July of 1856, she came home primarily to help Julia prepare for her wedding. Maggie and the bright, articulate Fishburn were good friends, and he had written in his diary during his year abroad that the "pure chaste statues . . . of virtue and benevolence" that he had seen in museums reminded him of his future sister-in-law.[94] In spite of his compliments and their comfortable relationship, Maggie had mixed feelings about the marriage. Perhaps it seemed too painful that Julia, so much her junior, should be getting married, when she herself saw no prospects of matrimony. In a handwritten note, Maggie invited a relative to "witness the catastrophe at 8 o'clock this evening," August 20, 1856, at the Junkin home.[95] Even if she meant the note in jest, the words imply an unpleasant tone of resentment.

After a short trip to visit relatives—"like all Virginians he has a host of *kin*!"—the Fishburns returned to take up residence in the president's house in Lexington. Julia wrote that she was "thankful to be spared the pain of parting from those I love so much. Father's household is so small now that instead of my leaving it Mr. F. will just join our family circle."[96] Like her sisters, she found it hard to separate herself from the family. Now the evening sessions, which Maggie and Jackson had shared alone, came to include Junius, Julia, Dr. Junkin, and sometimes the president's nephew, George, who was also living at the house.

By late fall, however, another regular participant began to take part in the lively discussions in the Junkin parlor—John T. L. Preston, whose wife, Sally, had been such a close friend of Maggie's. It seemed only natural that the lonely widower should drop by frequently to discuss business with Tom Jackson, to talk about pedagogical subjects with Junius Fishburn, and to seek advice on church matters from Dr. Junkin. If the two women of the household, Maggie and Julia, should be present, the evenings became even more appealing to Preston.

In such company, Maggie was completely at ease, winsome, witty, and knowledgeable concerning the classics and art. Not surprisingly, Preston began spending more and more time at the president's home, his chief object now a decorous courtship of Dr. Junkin's elder daughter. At long last, Maggie, "the settled old maid who had dismissed the world of matrimony from my thoughts,"[97] was being wooed by a man whose intellectual pursuits and background matched her own.

After Christmas, winter descended in earnest, reminiscent of the previous January when Sally Preston had died. But February of 1857 brought an unexpected thaw, with aspen "in bloom, and the weeping willow . . . beginning to look green."[98] The early spring suited Maggie's mood perfectly, for suddenly, at the age of thirty-seven, she found herself very much in love.

Chapter 4

The Very Finger of God
1857–1861

> Nothing (I believe) but father's insisting upon it
> that it was the very finger of God pointing me to a
> special work, would have made me consent to it.[1]

J ohn Thomas Lewis Preston was one of the most intellectually
stimulating and attractive men Maggie Junkin had ever known.
A professor of Latin and English literature at VMI since 1839, he
was considered by both colleagues and students to be "an accomplished scholar and gentleman."[2] He was also a skilled orator and
essayist, an influential elder in the Presbyterian church, a long-
term board member of the local girls' school, and a businessman
whose careful property management had made him one of the

wealthiest men in the community.* A handsome man, six feet tall, clean shaven, with piercing blue eyes, prematurely gray hair, and a ruddy complexion, Preston was no effete. Rather he typified the nineteenth-century view of a "man's man," devoted to hunting, dog breeding, and the application of innovative agricultural techniques. It was no surprise that Dr. Junkin looked with approval upon the budding romance between his elder daughter and this fine-looking, mature, influential teacher, churchman, and community leader who promised to bring her financial security as well as happiness.

Nine years Maggie's senior, John Preston had been born in Lexington in 1811. After preparatory schooling at a boys' academy in Richmond where he was a close friend of Edgar Allan Poe, he attended Washington College and then did postgraduate study at the University of Virginia and Yale.[3] Returning to Lexington after his formal education, he became a successful lawyer and active member of the Franklin Society, a local literary and debating organization. During a Saturday debate in 1834, Preston argued forcefully that the state arsenal located in town be transformed into a school for young men to provide military and classical education. A year later, in three widely disseminated newspaper articles, he furthered his new cause, writing so persuasively that, in 1836, Virginia's General Assembly authorized the establishment of an academy in Lexington to be named, at Preston's suggestion, "the Virginia Military Institute." When the fledgling college officially opened in 1839, he became one of its first two faculty members. (His military title of "major" was a

---

*Preston's farm account book, 1834–1887, indicates he owned considerable property in Lexington and Rockbridge County, as well as "prairie lands" in Kentucky, Indiana, and Ohio. He also owned stock in the Lexington Savings Institute and appears to have made large personal loans to individuals in Lexington and the county. In 1860 he purchased a tannery in Lexington, with partners T. J. Jackson, Major William Gilham of VMI, and Jacob Fuller, a classics teacher in a local school (JTLP's farm account book, Stonewall Jackson House, Lexington, Virginia).

purely honorary one, matching his academic position as professor.) He also served from time to time as chief administrator of the Institute whenever the superintendent, Colonel Francis Smith, was away on business.

When he was not teaching, managing his business affairs, or hunting, Preston devoted his time to church activities. At the young age of thirty-two, he had been elected a ruling elder in the Presbyterian church, a position he took so seriously that, according to local tradition, he never missed a session meeting during his fifty-year tenure. Soon after his election he had helped to make plans for the new Greek Revival church building erected in the center of town, to replace a more primitive and much smaller edifice near the cemetery. He was a member of the Sabbath school committee, frequently served as a delegate to presbytery meetings, and for years provided room, board, and tuition costs for a number of preministerial students at Washington College. In 1847 he immersed himself in local ecclesiastical politics by taking a major role in the church's ouster of a controversial and unpopular minister.

When he was twenty-one years old Preston had married his childhood sweetheart, Sally Caruthers. She was a handsome, buoyant young woman who managed her home and her rapidly increasing family with good humor and serenity. The pair made a striking couple, Sally's "tall, ample figure . . . clear blue eyes, beautiful, abundant chestnut hair, and . . . radiant complexion"[4] complementing her husband's erect, courtly physique, and their marriage had been a loving, traditional one. Sally depended upon her husband for advice, support, and the making of all major decisions, while Preston, according to his daughter Elizabeth, fulfilled the role of a Southern patriarch of "the old regime . . . almost feudal in [his] relation to women, children and dependants of all kinds. From such he exacted instant and unquestioning obedience."[5] In one of her few extant letters Sally showed her

longing for her husband's presence. While he was away on business, she had written: "I want to scream when I see other people's
husbands at home, and . . . I am resolved that no earthly power
shall again separate me from you."[6] When he was in Indiana in
1835, she told him of her fears for his safety after she had heard
reports of "cholera, bilious fever, ague & fever & so on . . . from
the west. . . . [D]o my dear love write often, and dont expose me
to such fears."[7] Once he had begun teaching at VMI, Preston's
absences became less frequent, though in 1851 he spent fully half
a year away from home, leaving Sally to manage six children
alone, while he toured England, Italy, France, Switzerland, the
Low Countries, and Prussia.[8]

None of Preston's letters to Sally has survived, but, in a diary he
kept during 1861, he attempted to analyze his ardent love for her
during the first months of their marriage, his "passionate longing,
jealousy lest for a moment our image should be absent from the
mind of the beloved, pride of possession . . . wonder at our own
bliss, a gloating over the past, and romantic anticipation of after
life."[9] In contrast to a young friend who played cards with cronies
and showed little attention to his bride, Preston commented,
with wry understatement, that he had not so ignored Sally during
"the first week of my marriage."[10] Here, and in other journal
entries, Preston portrayed himself as an emotional man with
strong sexual needs who had found contentment and satisfaction
during his years with Sally. Her parents' romantic attachment
never diminished, according to Elizabeth, who one day discovered them rereading old love letters. She remembered that after a
short and embarrassed silence there was "much laughter, and a
look exchanged between the two readers which even a little child
could interpret, in memory."[11]

During the years after the Junkins moved to Lexington, Maggie
became a far closer friend of Sally than of Major Preston. But she
knew him well enough to realize that, though he was charming,

he was also a strong-willed, "masterful" man, with a volatile, not easily controlled temper, and a "biting tongue in the use of ridicule."[12] Seven years after Maggie and Sally became friends, Sally became pregnant for the ninth time.* Already forty-four years old, she grew increasingly apprehensive as the time of delivery approached, and she told her husband "often and often" that, if anything happened to her, he should look to Maggie Junkin as a second wife.† On a snowy day in January 1856, Sally's terrible fears were confirmed when she died in childbirth. No description of her final hours survives, except Preston's poignant comment that his wife's "hand slipped from mine and I was desolate,"[13] and daughter Elizabeth's shadowy memory of "the sounds of distress, the falling snow darkening the sky, the cease-less movements of hushed footsteps . . . the minister's voice [and] the thronged house full of friends, at the final service."[14] Sally—and presumably the dead child—were buried in the Preston plot, not far from where Mrs. Junkin and Ellie lay. Engraved upon Sally's tombstone was a tribute from Major Preston, memorializing her as "the joy of her husband's heart and the light of his household for more than 23 years."[15]

Soon after his wife's death Preston sent the four youngest children and daughter Phebe to stay with his sister, Mrs. Eliza-beth Cocke, who lived on a large plantation in Cumberland County, Virginia. With only Tom and Frank (aged twenty-one and fifteen) still in the house, Preston turned for solace and companionship to old friends and neighbors, including the Junkins and Tom Jackson, recently bereaved himself. In the first months of his widower's state, "dismayed and despairing," Preston was

---

*In addition to the seven surviving children, a daughter, Edmonia, had died in 1842 at the age of four and a half.

†In a letter to Helen Dickey, written in 1857, Maggie quoted Sally's request to "her husband often and often before her death to put *me* in her place after she was gone," MJ to HD, n.d. (after June 15, 1857).

scarcely aware of Maggie, a quiet and unobtrusive presence in the president's parlor. Preston later described how his initial reaction to Maggie had changed. While "my eyes were blinded with tears," he wrote, "I could not see how lovely she was, but my pierced heart cried out in its instinct. . . . I took in mine the hand of comfort [Maggie's] and as the balm of its touch healed my heart my eyes were cleared." Suddenly Maggie was no longer Sally's friend. She was transformed into a woman who might fill Sally's place. "I saw such beauty in her who stood beside me, that I knew she was sister to the blessing of my morning."[16] Slowly, his heart healed, his passionate nature responded to Maggie's own blossoming love, and he dared to hope for a second marriage as emotionally and sexually fulfilling as his first had been.

The lonely widower could hardly have chosen an object of his affection more different from Sally Caruthers Preston. Whereas his first wife had been statuesque and even-tempered, Maggie was scarcely five feet tall, red-haired, and emotional. Sally had built her life entirely around her husband and children. In contrast, Maggie, with a broad classical education, had already begun establishing a literary career for herself. Most important, her natural independence of spirit differed markedly from Preston's notions of a wife's submissive role. Not surprisingly, the court-ship was neither smooth nor easy. Maggie was understandably unsure about yielding her will to this handsome, courtly, imperious Southern gentleman. She was apprehensive about Preston's seven children, whose memories of their mother were strong and affectionate, and she wondered if she had the capacity, so soon after Sally's death, to make him forget his former domestic happiness:

—I doubtingly question my spirit—have I
Strength to summon the sunshine all back to his sky?[17]

Preston also seems to have felt uncomfortable about his apparent haste in seeking a new wife, and he asked himself if he were forgetting Sally too quickly. Describing his first months of loneliness, "when I sighed, nay groaned, to go home [to heaven]," he had discovered in the Junkin home an earthly "angel who . . . waited for me." Was it possible, he wondered, to love both equally? "Which is dearest, the company with whom we begin the pilgrimage, or the one with whom we end it! Very dear are both."[18]

In spite of their personal uncertainties and the sense that perhaps they were approaching marriage too quickly, the couple became engaged sometime in the early spring of 1857—but then quarreled over the setting of a wedding date. Preston insisted on getting married in the summer, five months less than the traditional two years of mourning, because he was lonely, he missed his children, and he was in a hurry to consummate his marriage with Maggie. But he was also a proud and very private man who never would have acknowledged any personal or emotional reasons for wanting to marry quickly. Instead, he stated publicly only his desire to bring his children back home as soon as possible.

Maggie accepted that rationale, but she could not accede to his demand that the wedding date be August 2, which was the anniversary of his first marriage. To the modern reader, Preston's insensitivity to Maggie's feelings is breathtaking. One can only surmise that perhaps he felt dutybound to remember Sally even in the euphoria of his second marriage. Whatever his reasons, Maggie was deeply hurt, "shocked at the choice of his former wedding day," and she absolutely refused. Here was an independence Preston was not prepared for. "After trying to coax and persuade her," Elizabeth Preston recalled, "Father took the bit in his teeth and said she would marry him on that date or not at all!"[19]

Maggie Junkin was not a woman to be cowed by such threats.

Breaking the engagement abruptly, she "dismissed her imperious suitor."[20] There the matter stood, until Dr. Junkin and Tom Jackson intervened. Maggie's father was distressed that a quarrel over a date should jeopardize the bright future he foresaw for his favorite daughter, and Jackson knew only too well how emotionally devastating a broken engagement could be. Between them they persuaded Maggie and Major Preston to compromise upon August 3, still nearly half a year short of the traditional time of mourning, but at least not exactly the first wedding date. Once again Preston devoted himself to being a "fascinating lover," a role in which he boasted "that no man could surpass him."[21] Maggie seems to have found his renewed attentiveness convincing. He was, she wrote, "one of those peculiarly tender, loving, sympathizing men . . . [and] I am *perfectly* persuaded that he loves me." She even turned his constant mention of Sally into a sort of compliment to herself. Admitting to a relative that "I *am* sure you would think it *strange* to know how he comes to me . . . and pours out his sorrow to me," she insisted that "I understand him perfectly and honor him only the more. . . . I don't believe . . . that many women would be content to have it so. *I am.*"[22]

Throughout Preston's courtship of Maggie, Jackson had remained in the Junkin home as an interested bystander who was also contemplating remarriage. The young woman to whom he had turned was a North Carolinian named Mary Anna Morrison, the sister of Daniel Hill's wife, Isabella. Mary Anna had visited in Lexington frequently during the years when Jackson had first become acquainted with Ellie and Maggie. At that time, when he was in love with Ellie, he had looked upon Mary Anna simply as Hill's sister-in-law. After Jackson returned from his European trip in the summer of 1856, however, he wrote Mary Anna a cordial letter and then visited her in Davidson, North Carolina, where her father served as president of a small Presbyterian college.

Additional letters and visits culminated in a formal engagement in late winter or spring.

When Maggie took a trip to Philadelphia in May of 1857, probably to purchase her trousseau, Jackson asked her to pick out a gold watch and other jewelry that were to be his wedding gifts to his bride. "Don't get [the chain] too small," he wrote. "I wish it longer than yours, yet lighter than Ellly's [*sic*] with a massive fastening. I was much pleased with Ellie's . . . but this is a mere suggestion. Your own good taste must make the selection." [23] Doing her best to meet his specifications, Maggie purchased a watch, a gold chain, a coin ring, and a matching set of pearl earrings and pin for the total sum of $123.[24] Her taste must have been satisfactory, because many years later Mary Anna Morrison Jackson recorded that her husband's "bridal gifts to me were a beautiful gold watch and a lovely set of seed pearls."[25]

From Philadelphia, Maggie wrote her fiancé a long rhymed letter in which she poured out her love and her longing for his physical presence:

> Now what shall I call you? What word shall I choose?
> What term of endearment or tenderness use?
>
> . . . .
>
> —Beloved—would anything else I could say
> Be sweeter than *that*?

She imagined herself in his arms:

> Once more do I rest
> Where my cheek feels the steady warm throb of your breast:
> I see your dear fingers in tenderness lay
> All smoothly the curls from my forehead away:
> And the mouth that I praise so—the flexible mouth,
> Full-lipped with the ardor that tells of the South,

Is breathing, "God bless you, my Maggie!" and I
As trustingly echo the prayer in reply—
God bless my Beloved! 'Tis thus I begun,
'Tis thus I would finish—So now I am done![26]

After she had returned home she wrote her cousin Helen
Dickey about her engagement. She was sure Helen would be
surprised that "I, the settled old maid who had dismissed the
world of matrimony from my thoughts, am constrained into an
engagement of marriage. The gentleman is a widower *of course*. (I
had always vowed I never would marry a widower with children
which he *has*!)" It all seemed amazingly like her own serialized
story, "The Step-mother!," written years earlier, "even to the
number of children that are to come into my hands."[27]

She went on to tell Helen of Sally Preston's endorsement of
herself as a second wife. That approval and her father's urging,
Maggie said, had convinced her to accept Preston's proposal. Dr.
Junkin believed "it was the very finger of God pointing me to a
special work," while "the Major [Preston] says it is all heaven
ordained." In an effort to mute any criticism Helen might have of
the August marriage date, Maggie added that "Maj. P. has been
separated from his children . . . ever since their mother's death
and he feels as if he was failing in his duty to them not to have
them under his own eyes."[28] She mentioned neither her original
opposition to the August date, nor the fact that her early reluc-
tance had been erased by Preston's ardent wooing. Perhaps it was
more dignified to suggest that the primary motive for both of
them was concern for the children.

Maggie and John Preston were married in a small, private
ceremony at the president's home on August 3, with her father
officiating. Several of Preston's fellow officers stood up with him,
but thirteen-year-old Willie, the major's third son, was the only

Preston family member present.* "I had no wedding" in the usual sense, Maggie told Helen, "only a dozen people or so—relatives of Maj. P.—and myself."[29] Tom Jackson was absent because three weeks earlier he had departed for North Carolina, carrying the wedding gifts Maggie had purchased for him, to marry Mary Anna Morrison on July 16.

Accompanied by Willie and a servant from the Preston household, Maggie and her husband left Lexington on August 4, traveling in the family coach to Staunton and then by train to Powhatan Court House. From there they took a carriage ride of twenty-five miles to Oakland, the enormous plantation on the James River belonging to Preston's sister, Mrs. William Armstead Cocke. Here Maggie would not only meet her other six stepchildren, but would also experience firsthand "life in the style of the old Dominion."[30]

As the carriage rolled across the twelve-acre Oakland lawn with its fifty massive oak trees, Maggie caught sight of the youngest of her husband's children, nine-year-old Elizabeth and five-year-old John, who ran to meet the approaching vehicle. "My heart sank," Maggie wrote years later, as she stared at the "queer little figures . . . in dark calico dresses, [their] hatless heads . . . covered with short, sunburnt hair . . . [their] faces freckled. . . . Did ever a gentleman's children look so forlorn!" For her part, young Elizabeth remembered vividly her first impression of her stepmother, "so slight and fair and girlish-looking, in her low-cut blue silk gown . . . and wedding pearls." The child was awed by Maggie's "fine trousseau, her gold eye glasses, [and] her pretty curls

---

*William Caruthers Preston (1844–1862) is referred to in manuscript letters as "Willie." His stepmother, Margaret Junkin Preston, calls him "Willie" in her essay memorializing him ("William C. Preston" [BR, Box 284], MSS in possession of Huntington Library, San Marino, California) as does Thomas Jonathan Jackson in his letter of condolence (late 1862) to the Prestons. Only in her books, written years after Willie's death, does Elizabeth Preston Allan use the spelling "Willy." The author has chosen to use the manuscript spelling everywhere, except in quoted passages from Allan's *L&L* and *March Past*.

looped back over her ears," but she was quickly won over by Maggie's "gift for story-telling."[31]

Oakland was an antebellum plantation on the grand scale. More than one hundred slaves lived and worked on the property, and the mansion house itself was large enough to accommodate easily the twenty-five guests who were visiting when the Prestons arrived. Though appreciative of the splendor and antiquity of the place—a "wealth of portraits . . . rare old furniture," and George III's original deed to the property hanging on the parlor wall[32]—Maggie found Oakland's indolent life to be "a trying ordeal."[33] Brought up to utilize her time prudently, she was uncomfortable with "10 o'clock and 11 o'clock breakfasts and 5 o'clock dinners."[34] She found it even harder to adjust to "troops of slaves [who] circled round every function of the day; you were expected . . . to have your hair brushed, your shoes and stockings put on, every hook and eye fastened, every pin put in place, your fan and handkerchief handed to you, by a maid who held herself your special chattel during your stay."[35]

Most troubling of all was the reception she received from her husband's offspring. "The elder Preston children rece[ived] me with decided coldness," she wrote, "wh. made me of course uncomfortable. . . . I don't think the oldest son [Thomas, a twenty-two-year-old ministerial student] ever will give in. . . . Phebe, an elegant, stylish looking girl of 18 and Frank (16) have come to a better mind—and altho' their presence embarrasses me, still I get on better than I feared I should."[36] Happily, the younger children were more open-minded. Willie had already acknowledged the new relationship by attending the wedding, and Randy (aged eleven), Elizabeth, and John treated her, she said, "just as if I were their mother."[37]

Attempting to make friends with her stepchildren and coping with so many servants were difficult enough, but Maggie at the same time found herself under the scrutiny of two dozen friends and relatives of her husband who had known and loved his first wife. According to Elizabeth, her stepmother weathered the trying situation without incident, even winning over Preston's crusty old uncle, Colonel William C. Preston of South Carolina, who had been prepared to dislike "the little red-headed Yankee" whose poetry and name appeared "in print." By the end of the month-long visit, she had gained his wholehearted approval, the old gentleman affirming that his nephew's new wife was "an Encyclopedia in small print."[38]

After four weeks at Oakland Maggie returned to Lexington to face the daunting tasks of being mistress and supervisor of a large household. In addition to herself, her husband, and six Preston children, there were living in the home three of Major Preston's nephews and a college student her husband was helping to educate for the ministry. Before she had had time to adjust to "the regular white family [that] counts 12"[39] and half a dozen slaves, Elizabeth came down with a severe case of typhoid fever that required constant nursing care. The girl was just recovering when Mrs. Cocke arrived for a long visit. No wonder Maggie told Helen that she found "no time to myself in the multiplicity of the calls made on my attention."[40] Though she was grateful that the servants were well trained, she quickly discovered that they spoke with irritating frequency about what "Miss Sally" liked or "Miss Sally never did."[41]

Mrs. Cocke's extended stay was only the first of many long visits from numerous guests. Major Preston was an affable host, ready to show off his new bride to his own and Sally's nieces and nephews. He also liked to entertain local friends at dinner parties and other social gatherings. Among those whom Maggie saw frequently was Mary Anna Jackson, who had returned with Tom from a honeymoon to Niagara Falls to take up residence at the local hotel. Major Jackson's wife, Maggie wrote, "is very sweet and everybody admires her."[42] For her part, Mary Anna was warmed by the cordial reception she had been given by Maggie, who said at their first meeting, "You are taking the place that my sister had, and so you shall be a sister to me."[43]

The Preston home was a large, three-storied structure on the edge of town, set off by "spacious grounds, fine shade trees, extensive orchard and garden and meadow."[44] Slowly, Maggie began to place her own mark upon the house, rearranging furniture and adding sketches, books, and engravings. She also undertook a complete renovation of Elizabeth's and John's clothing, mending what she could and making new dresses for Elizabeth and also for Phebe. Despite the adjustment to a new regime and her many responsibilities, Maggie wrote optimistically of her new situation. "My health is better than it has been for three or four years," she told Helen, "and the Major could not be kinder or tenderer, even tho' he so doats [*sic*] on the memory of the *wife* who is gone."[45] Only at the end of her letter did she sound wistful. Describing one small bedroom that "I have furnished handsomely for myself," she told Helen that it was the only room "in all of the house . . . I feel any right in as yet." She added, "Perhaps I may come to feel more at home after a while."[46]

During these first months of her marriage Maggie found special comfort in frequent visits to the president's house. Here, Julia now served as the housekeeper not only for her father, herself, husband Junius, and their new baby Georgie (George Junkin Fishburn, born June 15, 1857), but also for several young relatives studying at Washington College. Suddenly the fifteen years' difference in the ages of the two sisters seemed less important than their common experiences as young married women. During the winter, when Maggie became pregnant, she leaned heavily upon Julia for reassurance and advice. Ellie's death was still vivid in her memory, and Maggie had been enormously relieved when

Julia's son had been born safely.* Now she was fearful about her own approaching childbirth, and also concerned about bearing a healthy baby after Mary Anna Jackson had given birth in early spring to a tiny, jaundiced girl who died after three months.

In March it was Maggie's turn to offer support to Julia when her husband was vilified by college students. Since the Junkins had come to Lexington, there had been little difficulty with unruly students. But in the spring of 1858 student unrest suddenly erupted, not against the stern college president, but against Julia's husband, Junius Fishburn, who with a fellow professor had discovered two college boys drunk in their quarters. After the pair had been dismissed by order of the faculty, a few of their supporters burned "in effigy Profs. Campbell and Fishburn."[47] The incident was an unpleasant reminder of the various protests that had plagued Dr. Junkin at Miami University.

Then suddenly, at the very time of the student attack, Fishburn fell ill with a deadly combination of "measles and dysentery,"[48] the measles probably contracted from cadets at VMI, where an epidemic was rampant. He died on March 26, 1858, only a few days before his twenty-eighth birthday. Married less than two years, Julia was now a widow at the age of thirty-two. Georgie was eight months old.

On July 2 Maggie gave birth to her first child, a boy also named George Junkin for his grandfather. Major Preston was amazed that his tiny wife could be the mother of such a strapping youngster. "How could such a fairy as she be the mother of such" a boy,[49] he wondered. Elizabeth and Johnny were delighted with

---

*"Our dear Julia has given birth, in safety, to a fine boy," Maggie had written Helen Dickey. "We are all thankful for her safe delivery" (MJP to HD, n.d. [after June 15, 1857]). Maggie's concern for both Julia's safety and her own was understandable. "Women whose mothers or other relatives had died during childbirth carried strong fears for their own possible demise," writes Judith Walzer Leavitt in *Brought to Bed: Childbearing in America 1750–1950* (New York: Oxford University Press, 1986), 22.

their new brother, and Maggie wrote of the baby's birth to Randy, visiting at Oakland. She hoped he would accept "the little stranger . . . for your Father's dear sake."[50]

Dr. Junkin was naturally flattered to have a second namesake, but the old preacher's special pet was Julia's Georgie, who had filled the lonely void in his heart after the deaths of Mrs. Junkin and Ellie and Maggie's departure from the household. It was, therefore, an almost overwhelming blow when in the summer of 1859 the little boy developed a virulent case of scarlet fever, and died in his grandfather's arms on August 19. Dr. Junkin acknowledged that Maggie's "G. is a fine boy; but I cannot love him as I did G. J. F. No! no! nor will I ever love a creature of God *so* again, till I go to the place where love and bliss immortal reign."[51] Though he tried to accept the loss with Christian resignation—"in permitting this trial, God has wise ends"[52]—he found that the best way to assuage his grief came through farming a small piece of land he had purchased near Lexington, which he called "Silverwood."

In a little over a year Julia had lost husband and son. She remained in her father's home, trying to dull the pain through routine chores, but she acknowledged that "life does indeed seem dreary & the way long & weary before me."[53] Desperate to offer some kind of consolation, Maggie wrote a long poem designed to memorialize Julia's winsome child, as well as provide hope and reconciliation. Entitled "The Open Gate," the poem noted the little boy's "loving, broken prattle . . . the patter of his footsteps . . . his bursts of laughter . . . and his golden hair," counseled "heavenly patience," and offered assurance that Georgie was reunited with his father, both eagerly awaiting Julia's own arrival in heaven.[54]

As preoccupied as she was with her own baby and with Julia's loss, Maggie was nonetheless keenly aware of the country's worsening political climate. In Lexington, the Franklin Society wrestled weekly with questions such as, "Would a separation of the states be preferable to a limited Monarchy?" (negative by one vote) and "Is it probable that the Government of the United States will be divided into two or more distinct Governments within the next two hundred years?" (negative seven to five). Both Preston and Jackson argued against a breakup of the union, and "Dr. Junkin," a friend wrote, "roars against [secession] like a lion."[55]

Together with most towns and counties of western Virginia, Lexington was solidly pro-Union and antisecessionist, in part perhaps because few families or businesses depended solely on slave labor. Area slaves, approximately one-third of the local population, were primarily household servants, laborers in shops or mines, or field hands on small plots of farmland.* Maggie's husband, father, and brother-in-law, Tom Jackson, all owned a few slaves,† but despite a rumor of a potential slave uprising in the community in 1857, none of her relatives, before 1859, seems to have had any fear that their servants would turn upon them.

---

*In the Rockbridge County census of 1850, the 11,500 free whites far outnumbered the 4,000 slaves; nearly 400 free blacks lived in the community. By 1860 the white population had grown by 1,300, while the slave and free black populations remained static (1850 U.S. Census, as recorded in the *Lexington Gazette* [February 6, 1851], 2:22). See also Edwin L. Dooley, Jr., "Lexington in the 1860 Census," *Proceedings of the Rockbridge Historical Society* 9 (1975–1979): 189–96.

†At first, Junkin hired slaves belonging to others; by the time of the 1860 census he owned one black servant outright and was listed as a co-owner of two other adults and four children (these latter may have been members of a family who lived and worked on his farm). Mary Anna Jackson had brought three slaves with her from North Carolina. The 1860 census showed Jackson owning four slaves—Mary Anna's slave Hetty, her two teenage sons, and Albert, a forty-year-old black man who was purchasing his freedom through work outside the home. According to his daughter, John Preston had not owned slaves as a young man, but in 1860 he was listed as the owner of three slaves—two women, aged fifty and forty-five, and a young black man, aged twenty-six (Katharine L. Brown, "Stonewall Jackson in Lexington," *Proceedings of the Rockbridge Historical Society* 9 (1975–1979): 209; also U.S. Census Office, 8th census, 1860—slave census, for counties P–R).

Early in April of 1859, not long before Georgie Fishburn's death, that assurance had evaporated when every member of the president's household was poisoned, including Dr. Junkin, Julia, her little boy, and a student in the home at the time. Arsenic was found to have been poured into the supper cream, according to the *Richmond Times Dispatch*, but, fortunately, the offender had used so much of the lethal chemical that "the dose . . . acted as an emetic, thus saving their lives."[56] Arraigned before the local court were Billy, a Junkin slave who had caused trouble before, and Fanny, the cook, who was quoted as saying that "the longer Dr. Junkin lived, the 'meaner' he became." [57] Without conclusive evidence, the case was dismissed.

Six months later the fear of slave uprisings spread throughout the region when the abolitionist fanatic John Brown occupied Harper's Ferry and invited slaves throughout the South to join him. Arrested and convicted, Brown was sentenced to hang early in December of 1859 at Charles Town. The madman's attempt to take over the Federal arsenal had produced such a sense of panic among Virginians that Governor Henry A. Wise ordered 1,500 troops to the site, including VMI's cadet corps. Majors Preston and Jackson were among the school's officers who accompanied the students.

After Brown's hanging, Preston wrote Maggie a long letter, describing the dramatic scene—the "cadets . . . uniformed in red flannel shirts, which gave them a gay, dashing Zouave look, exceedingly becoming . . . the criminal's wagon, drawn by two large white horses, John Brown . . . seated upon his coffin." He then spoke of the gaunt figure standing silent on the platform, "upright as a soldier in attitude & motionless." When the trap door dropped, Preston wrote, "the man of strong and bloody hand, of fierce passions, of iron will . . . the terrible partisan of Kansas . . . the man execrated and lauded, damned and prayed for . . . the man who . . . must ever be a wonder, a puzzle and a mystery—John Brown was hanging between heaven and earth!" It was, Preston commented, a "moment of deep solemnity, and suggestive of thoughts that made the bosom swell. . . . The moral of the scene was the great point. A sovereign State had been assailed."[58]

Brown's subsequent canonization by abolitionists and the election of Abraham Lincoln infuriated moderate Virginians, even those with strong Union leanings. "I have never known the fountains of popular sentiment so thoroughly stirred as they are now in Virginia," a Lexington minister wrote in the fall of 1859. "The election . . . seems to swallow up all other concerns. Books, sports, business, courtships, seem all forgotten, and we hear little of anything but . . . Lincoln's being elected and the revolution to follow."[59] Students and cadets, particularly those from the deep South, began openly espousing the Confederate cause, wearing blue rosettes in their buttonholes and singing "Dixie."

But still the more conservative Lexington citizens were not ready for the state to secede. At a large public meeting Major Preston denounced the "hot haste of South Carolina" in seceding, and he felt sure that "Western Virginia sided with Pennsylvania and Ohio!"[60] Agreeing with his good friend, Tom Jackson wrote to his sister that "I am strong for the Union at present . . . I think that the majority in this county are for the Union."[61] After Mississippi, Alabama, Georgia, and Louisiana had seceded and Lincoln had begun preparing for his inaugural, arguments in the Franklin Society debates became more passionate. Both Unionist and secessionist views were vigorously expressed. "How sincerely and with what boldness was the old Union defended in these Halls!" Preston commented, but also "with what passionate devotion and how ably was States' rights advocated here!" However, most of the speakers, Unionist and secessionist alike, were firm in their loyalty to Virginia. "In one thing we were ever agreed," Preston concluded. "Virginia—Virginia was our mother . . . for her under all circumstances we were willing to die."[62]

In contrast, Maggie's father was single-minded in his belief that the Union should be preserved at all costs, because he considered the U.S. federal system to be a kind of eschatological reality of God's perfect will. Since in his eyes America represented the "millennial model" for the whole world, he was convinced that to break up the Union was to defy the Almighty and thwart the fulfillment of prophecy outlined in the Book of Revelations. "If this nation fails in her vast experiments," he pleaded, "the world's last hope expires."[63] In an open letter to the governor-elect of Pennsylvania, Junkin urged citizens of that state to show moderation toward the South, in order to prevent further secession. Calling himself "A Voice of a Pennsylvanian in the Heart of Virginia," he thundered that if Pennsylvania should become aggressive, "apply the hellish torch, or fan the flames" of hatred, she would "bury beneath the gray ashes of this temple the hopes of freedom for the world."[64]

The old man not only wrote passionately on the subject. He also tried to convince everyone he met of the correctness of his position, including his two sons-in-law, Preston and Jackson. Maggie, "torn between divided loyalties," was miserable during long, angry sessions in which Dr. Junkin assailed her husband's commitment to Virginia. "I remember seeing him, storming up and down Mama's large chamber," young Elizabeth Preston recalled, "fiercely denouncing Father's quiet statement, that his allegiance was due first to Virginia. . . . Dr. Junkin called this belief by all the harsh names that a minister dared to use! Father, recognizing Dr. Junkin's seniority, his profession, and his position as father-in-law, never lost his temper, but he avoided the angry old man as much as possible." The Preston children were "furious at Dr. Junkin's denouncing Father in his own house."[65]

As Christmas approached, Maggie wondered how she could

provide a meaningful holiday for her sharply divided family. Despite her own heartache and her physical condition—she was expecting a second baby early in January—she succeeded so well that twelve-year-old Elizabeth remembered that Christmas as one of the happiest in her memory. The girl was especially excited by Maggie's bringing a Christmas tree for the first time into the Preston home. It was a "green cedar," Elizabeth recalled, "tapering up to the ceiling, aglow with small wax candles, covered with decorations and hung with gifts for old and young in house and kitchen."[66] Throughout the holiday season, Maggie also welcomed large numbers of friends and neighbors to the house for impromptu concerts and carol singing. Among the guests staying at the Prestons' was a young South Carolina cousin who spoke with vigor about the evils of Abraham Lincoln and the merits of secession. Elizabeth was so taken with the handsome, hotheaded cousin that she immediately began wearing the blue cockade of secession in her buttonhole and singing "The Bonnie Blue Flag." Maggie was not amused.

After New Year's the weather turned stormy, "with wet falling snow bordering on sleet."[67] In the midst of this cold snap, on January 24, Maggie's second child was born, another healthy boy named Herbert Rush Preston. Now Maggie had both a toddler and a baby to care for. In the three and a half years since her marriage her life had changed dramatically, as the often conflicting demands of mother, stepmother, daughter, and wife replaced the quiet routine of the author-scholar. But during these years she had made the initial adjustment to her strong-willed husband and had learned to curb to some degree her own emotional excesses. She had also discovered that life as a married woman brought rewards she had only dreamed of before—the deep joy of motherhood, intimate companionship with a man whose literary interests were akin to her own, and a new self-confidence born of knowing she had dealt successfully with troubling situations that would have overwhelmed many women.

There were still problems, to be sure—her occasional unhappiness at what seemed to be Preston's insensitivity to her feelings and the inevitable pressures within a household of children whose ages ranged from a few months to twenty-one years. But for Maggie, the joys of marriage far outweighed the difficulties.

In the past, she had used her writing to relieve tension and cleanse herself of unwanted emotions. But between 1857 and 1861, she put aside any attempt at literary creativity, because her husband, "lukewarm about her [artistic] gift," opposed her writing for publication. Though he was quick to praise her learning and her literary talent, she realized that "in his heart of hearts," he did not "approve of [her] giving any part of herself to the public, even in verse."[68] Her current happiness—and her husband's approval—meant a great deal more to her, in the early years of her marriage, than the creation of her own poetry. She might never have written again if it had not been for the Civil War.

Chapter 5

This Horrid and Senseless War
1861–1865

Disaster follows disaster;
where is it all to end? My very
soul is sick of carnage. I loathe
the word—*War*.[1]

For Maggie the Civil War was a long, torturous, unrelenting
nightmare. She agonized over the deaths and wounding of
many she loved most, continually feared for the safety of her
husband, survived a harrowing week of enemy occupation and
senseless destruction, and in the end experienced the bitter sense
of defeat. Yet from the five years of turmoil she emerged with new
enthusiasm for writing to become a well-known poet, a champion

of regional literature, a book reviewer, and an essayist who accurately foretold the renascence of Southern letters in the twentieth century.

The beginning of 1861 was a tension-ridden period when the whole country held its breath to see whether the Union would be preserved or the Confederacy permitted to function. Yet, despite private and public apprehensions, life in Lexington appeared normal, even placid. For Maggie, the months between January and April were a time to recuperate from childbirth and enjoy her new son. Preston and Jackson continued their teaching at VMI, though they recognized that the 250 cadets were often more interested in political events than in Latin and experimental philosophy. At Washington College Dr. Junkin had a more difficult time. For several years he had been teaching a popular class on the "Constitution of the U.S." One admiring young man had written in 1859 that "old Doc . . . pitch[es] into the politicians. . . . He just dissects them atom by atom and scatters them to the four winds."[2] By late 1860 and early 1861, however, Junkin had alienated many of his students when he insisted that "secession is the essence of all immorality; it neutralizes the highest obligations"[3] of a citizen—to serve Almighty God by preserving the Union. In retaliation, students began calling him a "Pennsylvania abolitionist" and "Lincoln Junkin."[4]

In contrast to the excitable students, the community in general was still opposed to secession. Early in 1861 the county sent Union men to the state convention by the overwhelming margin of ten to one. When a few VMI cadets placed a Confederate flag atop the flagpole near the town courthouse on April 13, Unionists attempted to raise a taller pole at the same location. After the pole broke—or was broken by unruly cadets—Majors Jackson and Preston hastened to the scene to address the corps and restore order.[5]

This strong antisecessionist mood changed dramatically three days later when, after the fall of Fort Sumter, news reached Lexington that President Abraham Lincoln had issued a call for 75,000 troops to put down Southern rebellion. Dr. William White, pastor of the Lexington Presbyterian Church and until that day a strong Union supporter, spoke for many when he interpreted the president's proclamation "as a declaration of war." Having felt, therefore, "forced to fight," Dr. White explained, "I claimed the poor right of choosing whom to fight." In taking his stand against Lincoln, he "became a rebel but never a secessionist."[6]

Earlier that same morning of April 16, a handful of Washington College students placed a Confederate flag atop a wooden statue of George Washington on a cupola of the college's central building. When he saw the flag, Junkin was incensed and ordered it removed. Shouting, "So perish all efforts to dissolve this glorious Union," he set the flag on fire. Students snatched the burning cloth from his hands, smothered the flames, and tore the remaining pieces into shreds which they placed defiantly in their buttonholes.[7]

The next morning a similar flag was again waving over the statue of "Old George." This time the president, with ill-concealed emotion, demanded that his senior class remove the offending banner. When the students failed to respond, Dr. Junkin exclaimed in frustration, "I will never hear a recitation or deliver a lecture under a rebel flag. The class is dismissed."[8] Outside the classroom a crowd gathered to stare up at the Confederate emblem still floating in the spring breeze. Someone began to sing "Dixie." Then suddenly seventeen-year-old Willie Preston stepped forward. He had helped to raise the second flag, and the students all knew of his secessionist sentiments. "Boys, Dr. Junkin is right," he said in words that his sister Elizabeth Preston Allan recorded years later. "Virginia is still in the Union; and he [Lincoln] is still our President. We must wait a few days, and [so]

I am going to take the flag down." Despite the crowd's catcalls and the throwing of bottles and bricks, Willie shinned up the pole, "took down the flag, waved it aloft, and called for three cheers for the Southern Confederacy." Then, with the banner stuffed inside his coat, Maggie's stepson descended to the grudging applause of the students.[9]

Despite Willie's dramatic gesture, George Junkin found the students' insubordination totally unacceptable, and he called a meeting of the board of trustees to demand that the unruly young people be disciplined or he would resign. But Dr. Junkin's action came too late. On the day that the trustees met, the community learned that Virginia's convention had voted for secession. Though its decision still had to be ratified by commonwealth voters, it was now only a matter of time before Virginia would join the Confederacy. Unanimously, the trustees accepted the president's resignation, without comment. Later, however, four members of the faculty wrote him a cordial letter expressing "their profound respect for his integrity" and offering "the hope that the twilight of his life would be his 'brightest and happiest period.' "[10]

In the past Maggie had always championed her father against his critics. Now she could say nothing, because to support him was to criticize her own husband and Tom Jackson, who had also been the object of Junkin's vituperation. During one conversation the old man had even predicted, prophetically, that if Jackson took up arms for the Confederacy, he would die in the conflict.[11]

On April 19, the morning after the trustees' decision, Maggie's father set about selling his property and dissolving his once-cordial relationship with the Presbytery of Lexington.* Not even taking time to pack all his books and papers, Dr. Junkin left hastily in his newly purchased "rockaway," accompanied by an unhappy Julia. Crossing the Mason-Dixon line at Williamsport, Maryland, on May 9, the embittered educator stopped the carriage and, with his pocket handkerchief, wiped from its wheels the dust of the rebellious South.[12] "This wicked rebellion," he explained, "made it necessary either to fly from my home in Lexington, Va., or to abandon my principles & pollute my conscience."[13] In making his dramatic stand, Junkin had been driven by the religious conviction that to dissolve the Union was to thwart God's will. Julia Junkin Fishburn seems to have had no such ideological principles. Having neither husband nor child to claim her allegiance, she evidently believed it her duty to care for her father, whatever her personal feelings. During the war Julia wrote letters to Maggie and visited her afterwards, but she never lived in Lexington or the South again.

All her life until her marriage Maggie had been under the influence of her father. Even after she moved to the Preston home, she had seen him and Julia on a daily basis. Now she had lost them both. Then, before many days had passed, her husband joined General Jackson on the battlefield, leaving Maggie with no one to whom she could turn for assistance during "days and nights of torturing apprehension." She also found herself suddenly thrust into the position of manager of Preston's business

---

*In a deed dated April 28, 1861, George Junkin turned over his farm "Silverwood" to John Thomas Lewis Preston in exchange for property in Indiana, Illinois, and Ohio that had belonged to Sally Caruthers Preston (original deed on file at Stonewall Jackson House, Lexington, Virginia). On April 20 the Presbytery accepted Dr. Junkin's resignation, citing his "long & interesting connection . . . with this Presbytery" and "his pious & earnest attachment to the interests of our beloved Zion." The statement concluded with "warmest expressions of affection" and the assurance that his former associates in the church would "commend him with earnest prayer to the blessing of God" (minutes of Lexington Presbytery, volumes XIII–XV [1848–1880], 227).

affairs—the "many cares incident upon his absence"—as well as supervisor of a household that included five stepchildren (Phebe, Randolph, Willie, Elizabeth, and John), a new stepdaughter-in-law (Tom Preston's bride), her own two little boys, and as many as a dozen slaves. Not surprisingly, she looked back on that unhappy spring as a season of overwhelming "trouble and perplexity."[14]

Within two weeks after Lincoln's call for troops Lexington had shifted to a wartime footing. Most of the VMI cadets left on April 21, ordered to Richmond to train Confederate volunteers in close-order drill and artillery practice. Washington College students signed up for army service in record numbers, and four separate military groups formed in Lexington—the Liberty Hall Volunteers, the Rifles, the Cavalry, and the Rockbridge Artillery, a unit that included Frank Preston, Maggie's second stepson. Maggie, Phebe, and even young Elizabeth joined other women in the community to spend hours knitting for the troops, rolling bandages, and scraping old linen "into piles of soft, snowy lint for wounds."* Soon, civilian supplies of all sorts grew scarce. Precious foodstuffs were carefully hoarded, to be brought out only when young men came home on leave, and everyone seemed ready to sacrifice and "make do." Managing to have fun in the midst of hardships, young people of the community entertained themselves with "starvation parties," quilting bees, bandage-rolling socials, and dances hastily organized when a soldier returned on furlough. Handmade gifts became the order of the day, and when Elizabeth Preston celebrated her thirteenth birthday that first year of the war, she received a "pretty hood" knitted by her sister Phebe and her stepmother's ingenious gift, the "first

---

*At first civilian women made "havelocks," protective neck pieces worn over caps to protect soldiers from the sun. Later, they turned their energies to more productive use—to the knitting of thousands of socks for men whose first supplies of shoes and socks had quickly been expended (Elizabeth Randolph Preston Allan, *A March Past* [Richmond: The Dietz Press, 1938], 129).

grown-up garment I had ever owned . . . a double wrapper . . .
which Mama made out of an old dress of hers."[15]

Though Lexington was far away from early war skirmishes, the
Preston women heard clearly, on July 21, 1861, the sound of
artillery, heralding, they thought, the first major battle at
Manassas.* Maggie knew that her husband had just been transferred from the area of conflict, much to his chagrin. But other
family members were in danger, including two of Major Preston's
sons—Tom, serving as a Confederate chaplain, and Frank, in the
Rockbridge Artillery—as well as "four first cousins . . . [and]
innumerable brothers and kindred of our friends." Elizabeth
remembered that "mama and my sister walked the floor most of
that moonlight night, expecting and reading news."[16] Phebe was
especially concerned for the safety of her first cousin William
Cocke, of Oakland, soon to be her fiancé. The following morning
word came that all the Prestons and Cockes had survived, but
that one Lexington lad, Willie Preston's closest friend, had been
killed.

Lonely and filled with fear, Maggie turned to writing, the
activity that in the past had given her solace. This time, however,
she did not attempt poetry or fiction. Instead she poured out her
emotions in a torrent of letters, to Tom Jackson, to Julia, and
especially to her husband. Major Preston had left Lexington near
the end of April to serve on General Jackson's staff. Four months
later, promoted to lieutenant colonel, he found himself assigned
duty at Craney Island in the harbor at Hampton Roads, a post he
found frustrating and dull. In November of 1861 he returned to
Jackson's command in northern Virginia, to serve as his old
friend's adjutant, share his mess, attend church with him, and
travel for him to Richmond on special assignments.

---

*"The sound or concussion of the firing cannon had been heard on the hills
around Lexington all that July Sunday, and we knew a battle must be in
progress" (Elizabeth Randolph Preston Allan, *A March Past*, 133).

There are no extant letters written by Maggie to her husband during the war and few of his to her, because (many years later) Preston's daughter Elizabeth burned them.* One can, however, get a sense of the passionate nature of Maggie's letters by reading Preston's emotional response, both in the few letters of his that survived and in an extraordinarily revealing diary he kept for three months at Craney Island.

Frustrated and bored with army routine during the latter months of 1861, Preston read and reread his wife's letters. "Got a letter from Maggie," he noted on August 10, 1861. "Read it over twice in the city and once after I came back. She is a genius and she is my darling."[17] Again, he wrote to her: "I had but time to gobble up your letter this morning . . . but to-night I have enjoyed it as an epicure ought to eat. . . . Hardly room left to say—I love you!"[18] "Your dear letter," he told her on another occasion, "came just in the midst of the business mail, and it had to lie unopened for an hour or so. It looked pretty and piteous, like a young maiden asking to be kissed. How often I looked at it and longed for it . . . and how I swallowed its sweetness when I broke it open!"[19]

Her closely written pages, he said, transformed his drab quarters to an abode where "poetry and romance are real" and evoked her image, "sylph like in form, tremulous in susceptibility, poetic in temperament & genius."[20] Such thoughts rapidly evolved into acute physical longing for her presence: "I have loved you all the dreary absence and I love you still. . . . I would so love to press . . . [you] to my arms again."[21]

---

*Elizabeth Preston Allan wrote in 1903 that she had burned all of Maggie's wartime letters to Colonel Preston, because they were too personal: "One feels almost like a vandal in committing to the flames" letters filled with so much "poetry and romance . . . so much sweet philosophy and heartfelt piety; but these things are inextricably interwoven with the lovemaking . . . and must be held sacred. So there they lie, in ashes, on my hearth!" (Elizabeth Preston Allan, *The Life and Letters of Margaret Junkin Preston* [Boston: Houghton, Mifflin, and Company, 1903], 120).

Sometimes this yearning was so intense that it kept him from sleeping. One afternoon, he said, he had gone to his quarters for a much-needed nap, but his physical longing for her prevented sleep. "If I only had my little Maggie in my arms, it would be perfection . . . I thought of her at home with the children . . . and I thought of many other things more foolish. . . . Maggie's image before me, and my lucky drowsiness was gone. . . . I could not even doze."[22] Writing in his diary, he said, was his only antidote.

He was still at Craney Island on August 2 and 3, the anniversaries of his two weddings: "Augt. 2 *(1839)* Augt. 3 *(1857)*. . . . These are the two great days of the calendar of my life." After he had written an anniversary letter to Maggie, he took out the diary to enter there his feelings about the two women he had married. The love he had felt for Sally—his *"first love"*—was now, he wrote, completely "entwined thread for thread in golden tissue with another love. . . . My Maggie, you are to me all that she was, and I so love you that God willing, a long life even down to . . . old age, would still be happiness to me if you will walk with me, and with your loving talk, keep in motion my heart tones to the last."[23]

Preston referred to his diary as a " book. . . . I will not call it a journal,"[24] because he did not write in it every day, and his intermittent notations included far more than comments about Maggie and Sally. There were descriptions of army routine and of Craney Island, reminiscences of his young adult years, short philosophical pieces on the nature of duty and God's providence, and his own hopes for the future. Until mid-August, he wrote in his "book" only to pass the time, with no plans to share his ruminations with anyone else. Then on August 16, when a trusted army courier left for Lexington on official business, he suddenly decided to send the diary to Maggie, so "she may have a peep into the interiour of the heart of her husband."[25] At the end of his last entry, he added a final note to his wife:

I kiss you, my own, I could almost wish
that I were nothing more than an Ordnance
Sergeant, that I might be sent to Lexington
for blunderbusses and other *busses.* Send
back the book to me again by the Sergeant.
We may be here long enough to enable me to
fill it up with my scribbling.[26]

Maggie was surprised when the courier appeared at her door with the diary, and she read it, she said, "with . . . much eager delight."[27] Though his words of endearment probably came as no surprise, she must been especially gratified to read, in his own handwriting, that she was now first in his heart, even though he still referred occasionally to Sally. Further, Maggie must have been pleased to note his heightened awareness of her poetic talents. In an earlier letter he had told her that he wished he "might be able to wield my sword when in battle, as you wield your pen."[28] Now in the journal he wrote that "she dips her pen in magic. . . . Sing to me Maggie—I listen with delight and I believe that what your genius would enable you to say to another without love, your love for me prompts and your poet nature glorifies in utterance."[29]

After savoring the precious "book" in private, Maggie shared portions with the children, omitting the more intimate sections. Then, before sending the diary back to Preston, she wrote on its pages a poem entitled "All's Well," paraphrasing various passages of his about the call of a sentry on night patrol. She ended with a deft compliment to Preston himself. "Insignificant as they [these stanzas] are," she wrote, "may they have a place here. They may profit by companionship. 'Where hast *thou* gathered any sweetness?'—the clay was once asked—and the clay replied—'*I have been with the Rose*'!"[30]

Maggie's other correspondence could hardly offer her the same intense satisfaction as did her husband's letters. But, in spite of her busy schedule, she did manage to write regularly to both Tom Jackson and her sister Julia. The letters to and from General Jackson primarily concerned the welfare of two slaves he had left in her care. After she had told him of the prolonged illness, death, and funeral of Amy, who had been the cook in his home on Washington Street in Lexington, Jackson replied:

> My dear Maggie . . .
> More than once your kind and touching letter
> respecting the sainted Amy brought tears
> to my eyes. . . . I am very grateful to you for
> your Christian kindness to her. I am much
> gratified that you gave her a decent burial,
> and that so many followed her remains to
> the grave.[31]

Maggie also wrote numerous letters to Julia and to her father, but she was never sure how many managed to get through battle lines and on to Philadelphia. In September of 1861, five months after her father's and sister's departure, she received her first letter from Julia, written from their brother's home. Her life, Julia said, was very quiet, so serene one would scarcely know a war was going on. She did not mention that Dr. Junkin had continued to try to dissuade Stonewall Jackson from his ongoing support of the Confederacy. After requesting his youngest brother, David, to carry his personal message of rebuke to the general at Harper's Ferry in May of 1861, Dr. Junkin had also written Jackson a letter urging him to change his allegiance. Jackson had responded cordially but guardedly to his father-in-law, thanking him for his letter and ending with "love to J[ulia], George, John [the two Junkin brothers who had sided with the Union], Uncle D. X. [David Xavier Junkin], and their families. Affectionately yours, T.

J. Jackson."[32]

As December of 1861 neared, Maggie did all she could to make the Christmas holidays a cheerful time for members of the family who had gathered at the Preston home. A year later she remembered the season as surprisingly happy, in spite of the absence of her husband. "*Every one* of Mr. P's children was here, except Frank," she noted, and "the utmost hilarity reigned. We had a beautiful Christmas tree, filled," in spite of various shortages, "with innumerable presents for everybody, servants and all. The Library was a scene of innocent gayety. Dear Willy P. distributed the contents of the tree, as his Father had done the year before."[33]

In February Colonel Preston returned to Lexington, assigned the unenviable task of instructing boys too young for army duty. Though General Robert E. Lee had specified that VMI's military training was essential to the war effort, Preston was painfully aware that cadets, including his own sons Randolph and Willie, were restless and frustrated, longing to be on battlefields instead of in the classroom. Maggie, however, was very grateful he was home, especially when four-year-old George Preston became desperately ill with scarlet fever. Maggie was terrified. She had tried to inure herself to the possible wounding or death of the men in her family, but to have her little son suddenly so sick was totally unexpected. She and Preston took turns nursing the boy in order to keep the rest of the family from undue exposure. Elizabeth and old "Aunt Coralie," the children's mammy, cared for baby Herbert, while Phebe looked after the needs of her own brother John. Once George was out of danger, Elizabeth spent the days with him, reciting poetry to keep him quiet and put him to sleep.

By the time the child was out of danger, Maggie could sense that her husband was eager to get back to active duty. She could have marshalled many reasons for his staying home—the invalid's uncertain health, the cadet corps' need of his instruction, his own farms that required supervision, and his age. At fifty-one, he was surely too old, she felt, for long periods of camp life. "If he goes, he says he will not return until the war closes, if indeed he come back alive." But she hesitated to put too much pressure on him. "May God's providence interpose to prevent his going!" she prayed.[34]

But Preston's request for active duty was approved, and on April 14, 1862, he left in high spirits, bound for Jackson's camp up the valley at Mount Jackson. In a passionate outburst against war's tyranny, Maggie wrote in her diary, "I loathe the word—*War*. It is destroying and paralyzing all before it." Depressed and frightened, she longed for escape: "If we might only be permitted to withdraw ourselves from this turmoil of horrid strife—if it were only to a log cabin on some mountain side."[35]

While her husband was home in the early months of 1862, Maggie had begun keeping a diary of her own, not a day-by-day account, she explained, but rather "brief notes of what was passing under my eye . . . such slight jottings as might serve to recall the incidents of this most eventful year in our country's history."[36] It was a journal she would continue until the end of the war.*

Early entries provide details of the adjustment Maggie made to a wartime economy. She used Randy's and Willie's old trousers to make clothes for John and George, and she "dressed my baby all winter in calico dresses made out of the lining of an old dressing-gown." As food supplies grew scarce, and coffee became impossible to purchase, she learned to make a "poor mixture, half wheat, half coffee" for the family's use. When the supply of

---

*The original diary seems to have disappeared. Relatives know nothing of its whereabouts; libraries have been scoured with no result. Fortunately, large portions of the diary were preserved in Elizabeth Preston Allan's two books, *Life and Letters of Margaret Junkin Preston* and *A March Past*.

candles dwindled, she noted that church services were held only in daylight hours, "to *save* light and fuel." But she found the physical hardships far easier to endure than her personal "undefined fear—the constant dread—which I am never free from."[37] The fear of losing her husband, after only five years of marriage, filled her with dread, and she yearned for the kind of faith her mother had exemplified. "She had such heavenly patience," Maggie acknowledged, "and how exceedingly impatient am I."[38]

A week after he left Lexington for active duty, Colonel Preston was home again, with the explanation that the post offered him, that of inspector general, was one for which he was not well suited. Maggie was delighted, but her relief was short lived. Only a fortnight later, Preston was called out with the VMI corps to support Jackson's army near McDowell, Virginia. "He is gone," she wrote, "to be exposed certainly to the chances of a stern battle. . . . I can't hear from him, and must be content with rumors, which are torturing, because generally so exaggerated."[39] Overcome with fear, she tried to calm herself by reading Preston's small Bible. "I shut myself in his study," she wrote, "and blotted the leaves of his Bible with my tears, while I read on my knees the 91st Psalm." Apprehension gave way to panic when she heard heavy cannonading from the north. "Oh! my husband!" she agonized. "Could I but know he was safe! I wonder at myself that I do not loose [*sic*] my senses. My God! help me to stay my heart on thee!"[40]

Colonel Preston returned safely on May 17, his only battle experience the grim one of helping to bury the dead. But on May 27 there came crushing news. Frank, his second son, had been severely wounded at the battle of Winchester. The distraught father hurried away in a carriage, traveling as fast as possible to Jackson's camp, where he learned that Frank's wound had been so severe that his arm had been amputated. For a few days Preston stayed with the young man, but then battle lines shifted,

Jackson's Confederate troops abandoned Winchester, and Preston had to leave his son and flee to avoid capture. Frank remained behind, too ill to be moved.

Over the next two months the family agonized over Frank's fate. Was he being treated well by Union surgeons? Had he been made a prisoner? If, God forbid, he should die, would they even be notified? Then, as if by a miracle, on July 22 Frank suddenly appeared in the family dining room. He had been placed, he said, in the care of a Confederate woman living just outside Winchester. While she was nursing him back to health, she spirited him away one night in her own carriage, through the lines to safety. The family's rejoicing was muted only by the realization that Frank had missed seeing his brother Willie by two hours.

Willie Preston, now seventeen and a half, had just left to join the Liberty Hall Volunteers. On August 10, 1862, stationed near Manassas, he wrote a long letter to his father, describing a fierce battle in which he had participated near Cedar Mountain. Assuring the family that he was unscathed, Willie spoke of having taken a message to General Jackson during the worst of the conflict. "I was so excited," he told his father, "that I believe I slapped him on the leg, and I know that I slapped his horse so hard that he came near jumping from under the rider." Willie hoped that General Jackson would forgive him as "it was the first time I had ever been under fire."[41]

Two weeks later Willie was dead, killed at the battle of Second Manassas on August 25. The family learned on September 3 that he had been "mortally wounded," and Colonel Preston left immediately for northern Virginia. Maggie's diary entry the following day was poignant. "The worst has happened," she wrote. "Willy, the gentle, tender-hearted, brave boy, lies in a soldier's grave on the Plains of Manassas! . . . I did not know how I loved [him]. My heart is wrung with grief to think that his sweet face, his genial smile, his sympathetic heart are gone."[42]

When Preston reached Manassas village, he found his son's body wrapped in a blanket, his "despoiled face" unrecognizable, and the remains identified only by the boy's shirt on which Maggie had lettered "W. C. Preston." Realizing that it would be impossible to bring Willie home for burial, Preston reached down to try to rescue a single "lock of hair, [but] it crumbled to the touch." Heartsick, he returned to Lexington to pour out to Maggie details "too horrid" to record, "unnumbered dead Federal soldiers covering the battle field; one hundred in one gully, uncovered, and rotting in the sun . . . hospitals crowded to excess, and loathsome beyond expression." After writing it all down, Maggie ended her journal for the day: "How fearful is war!"[43]

Stonewall Jackson had hoped that Willie might serve as one of his aides-de-camp, but the boy had died before assuming the post. "My dear Maggie," Jackson wrote, "I deeply sympathize with you all in the death of dear Willie. He was in my first Sabbath school class, where I became attached to him when he was a little boy. . . . Remember me very kindly to Col. Preston and all the family. Affectionately your brother, T. J. Jackson."[44]

Letters came as well from other friends, for whom Willie Preston had been an especially appealing boy. Maggie remembered him as the one stepchild who had attended her wedding, the sunny, cheerful lad who had been the first to accept her with enthusiasm. Always finding solace in eulogy and poetry, she wrote a lengthy memorial statement about him and probably jotted down at that time verses about his uncoffined grave that she later used in her long war poem, *Beechenbrook*.

Others might have felt special gratitude for Jackson's letter of condolence because he was already a legendary figure. But Maggie appreciated his letter simply because Tom Jackson was her friend. Indeed, she never really adjusted to Jackson's elevated status in the Confederacy. When she learned of the birth of his daughter, Julia, in the fall of 1862, she rejoiced with the couple in the safe arrival of a healthy child, but could not help noting with distaste the adulation given to the infant, "as much talk and ado about it almost, as if it were a little princess!" [45]

Meantime, at home, the universal rhythm of birth and death continued. Early in November Randolph Preston, just seventeen and a cadet at VMI, came home sick. Four days later, when he became delirious, his condition was diagnosed as a severe case of typhoid fever.* After many cycles of false improvement followed by terrible bouts of racking pain and fever, Randy died on December 18, seven weeks after he had contracted the illness. Despite her fear of cemeteries Maggie attended the funeral for her husband's sake. "This evening, just before sunset," she wrote on December 19, "we saw the mortal remains of the dear boy committed to the grave. It is a sore blow to his precious father, to his sisters, and to us all. . . . Three months and a half only, since dear Willy laid down his life on the battlefield, and now another . . . as seemingly fitted for long life as any one I ever saw . . . is cut off. . . . How mysterious the providence [of God] appears."[46]

This time Stonewall Jackson wrote Colonel Preston the letter of condolence. "You have tasted deep of the cup of domestic affliction," Jackson told his old friend. "When I see my friends in deep affliction, I feel my inability to administer consolation. The best I can do is to pray for them." Then, in a postscript, he added, "I send a sword. . . . Please keep it for me." [47] He must have felt that the sword would be safe in Lexington, along with Mary Anna's piano, which had been left with the Prestons when Mary

---

*With no known cure and little knowledge of the cause of the disease, the nursing of typhoid patients was an exhausting experience. "Every thing, sheets, towels [were] all washed or boiled every day," wrote one of Maggie's contemporaries in Lexington, "even a fresh mattress put on; the one used put out in the sun." The prescribed diet for a sufferer consisted of "hot water tea and squirrel broth" (Emily Bondurant, *Reminiscences* [typed manuscript of original, made in 1962, #2430, UNC], 145A).

Anna had returned to North Carolina in 1861 to be with her family.

Within the space of a few months Preston had lost two sons and seen a third permanently maimed. Though he could not bring Willie's body back home, Preston erected a headstone in Manassas where his son's body lay and put an identical marker in the family plot in Lexington beside Randy's. He and Maggie found Frank's amputated arm a daily torture, but the young man quickly adjusted to his disability. A short time after his return to Lexington he began teaching cadets at the institute, one of his duties being to supervise the weekly dress parade. This responsibility required him to wear a sword and scarlet sash, removal of which became a regular task for his younger sister Elizabeth.

In the midst of her distress, Maggie received two reassuring messages about Julia and her father. One was a letter from Julia herself, the first in more than a year, and the other a note from Stonewall Jackson with word from her brother John, a surgeon in the Federal army. When he had met an aide of Jackson's on the battlefield at Fredericksburg (where both men were identifying and removing fallen soldiers) John had asked the Confederate officer to relay the message that he and other family members were well. Maggie was grateful to receive "comfortable tidings of my beloved ones; my dear Father well and in good spirits."[48]

When he left Virginia, George Junkin was seventy-one, an age at which many men would have retired. But the old gentleman spent his last six years in an extraordinarily vigorous way, preaching 700 sermons, serving as a volunteer chaplain to wounded soldiers and prisoners, and writing extensively on the evils of the Confederacy. During the same year in which the Prestons lost one son at Manassas and saw another son's arm shattered by a Union bullet, Junkin continued to urge Stonewall Jackson to desert the Confederacy. He had just published a long polemic against secession, which he called *Political Fallacies*, and he attempted to send an autographed copy of the volume through the lines to Jackson, addressing it, he said, "care of Hooker [Union General John Hooker]."[49] That copy was intercepted and never reached the Confederacy. A few months later he tried again, and this time "the book . . . on Political Heresies" did get through, according to Jedediah Hotchkiss, Jackson's cartographer. In an accompanying letter, Dr. Junkin promised to supply his former son-in-law with "any number" of extra "copies of his book if he wants them."[50]

Maggie was grateful to receive some good news from her family in Pennsylvania, for there was little to be cheerful about within the Preston home. The last week of December was a dreary time for them all, because, she wrote, "the sadness of the house forbids any recognition of Christmas."[51] She used the time she would otherwise have spent preparing the tree to write a long poem she entitled, with bitter irony, "Christmas Carol, for 1862." Contrasting this year's mood with that of happier times, she described the anguish of families waiting "in vain . . . for a footfall" that would never return, yearning for "that dear face . . . hidden cold under the clay." She continued with a description of soldiers in their winter camp, "marching shoeless through the snow."[52] Like her journal entries, the poem was a cry of despair at war's destructiveness, with its "ragged and barefoot soldiery . . . the country laid waste; and the houses burned, and the blackened chimneys standing."[53] Only the final stanza sounded a note of hope, hope that Virginia's struggle might someday achieve recognition by being labeled a latter-day Thermopylae.

Not only was she bitter over the lives that had been lost, she also worried about the effect that the pervasive military atmosphere was having upon her own little boys. Georgie and Herbert had adjusted all too easily to the ways of war, she felt, playing soldiers with paper cutouts and making ambulances and hospitals with chairs and building blocks. While Georgie pretended to outwit the Yankees, little Herbert, nearly two, "also kills 'Lankees,' as he calls them, and can talk war lingo almost as well as George." It was "sad indeed," she wrote, "that very infancy has learned such language!"[54]

By 1863 the naval blockade of Virginia was making itself felt in the scarcity of all kinds of goods. With ingenuity Maggie soaked pulverized peach stones to provide pseudo-almond flavoring, processed peach leaves "rolled and squeezed" as seasoning for custards, set up a small cider mill in the orchard, and adapted old recipes, substituting molasses for sugar. Her husband, she wrote, "has let the Government have every pound of bacon he could spare and put us on a ration of a quarter of a pound of meat a day." [55] The area's limited food supply was made more acute by the influx of refugees from Fredericksburg and Winchester. One Lexingtonian reported subsisting on "rye, sweet potatoes, corn, chestnuts, and all manner of substitutes for coffee."[56]

Maggie also was forced to improvise in order to provide clothing for her family. "Today made two petticoats (for E. and self) out of a window curtain. 'Necessity is the mother of invention.'. . . Cut a pair of drawers for Mr. P. out of a sheet; not because I could well spare the sheet, but because I had nothing else." [57] Though she seriously jeopardized her eyesight by stitching in poor light, she felt she had no alternative. "I *pretend* not to sew any, but am constrained to do so almost every day, though I always suffer in consequence."[58]

Some of her sewing may have been necessitated by Colonel Preston's being chosen as a delegate to the General Assembly of the Presbyterian Church in the Confederacy, meeting in Charleston, South Carolina. Pleased that his friend was so designated, Stonewall Jackson wrote two letters to Preston about the meeting's agenda. He urged the appointment of more army chaplains and expressed hope that the Assembly would bring pressure on the government to repeal Sunday mail service. Unless the Confederate congress adhere to strict Sabbath observance, he wrote, it could not hope to win God's favor: "Divine laws can be violated with impunity neither by governments nor individuals."[59]

Preston returned from the meetings only days before Stonewall Jackson was wounded at the battle of Chancellorsville on May 2, 1863. Once again Lexington townsfolk, hearing distant cannonading that day, knew that a major battle must be taking place. Three days later news reached the community that two of its leading citizens had been killed and General Jackson wounded. "Oh! the sickness of soul with which almost every household in this town awaits the tiding to-morrow may bring," Maggie wrote on May 5.[60] She was not only concerned about Lexington friends and General Jackson, but also fearful for her brother John in battle on the Federal side.

On May 12 she sat down at her small desk to write Jackson a long letter, inviting him to return to Lexington for recuperation in her home. She was just leaving the house the next morning to mail the letter when she learned that he was dead. In tears, she confided to her diary: "My heart overflows with sorrow . . . everybody is in tears. . . . The people made an idol of him, and God has rebuked them."[61] It was the same belief she had voiced after the deaths of her baby brother David, of her mother, and of Ellie—that human love had been idolatrous, so God had snatched away the objects of that love. Maggie was sure, however, that Jackson had been perfectly ready to meet death. "In his last letter to me he spoke of our precious Ellie and of the blessedness of being with her in heaven. And now he has rejoined her."[62]

The last time any of the Preston women had seen Stonewall Jackson was on April 20, 1861, the day before he marched off with the cadet corps. Twelve-year-old Elizabeth had been sitting, cross-legged, on the gatepost of the vacant president's house watching college students practice close-order drill. Jackson, striding by on his way to VMI, had stopped to ask the girl if her parents knew where she was. When Elizabeth replied in the negative, "he lifted me gently down from my desirable perch," she wrote, "kissed me goodbye, and told me to run home at once."[63] Now, two years later, Elizabeth stood on Main Street to watch as Jackson's funeral procession, with its honor guard and its "riderless horse with empty boots swung across the saddle," wound slowly toward the churchyard, "amid the unchecked sobs of men, women and children."[64] At the cemetery Dr. White, pastor of the Presbyterian church, spoke a few words. Maggie's brother, William Junkin, who was a minister serving as a captain in the Confederate army, gave the final prayer. Thomas Jonathan Jackson was buried beside the grave of the baby girl he and Mary Anna had lost in 1858, not far from the graves of Ellie and Mrs. Junkin.

Within a few weeks, Mary Anna Jackson accepted Maggie's invitation to stay at the Preston home for an extended period, probably to attend to various business matters. It must have been a help to the young widow and mother of a six-month-old daughter to stay with friends who also had small children. Maggie was struck by the baby's resemblance to Jackson. "The dear little child is so like her father; she is a sweet thing, and will be a blessing, I trust, to the heart-wrung mother."[65] Years later Elizabeth Preston Allan wrote how grateful they all were to have the privilege of "sheltering the heart-broken wife in the first bewilderment of [her] distress."[66]

Three days after Jackson's funeral, the Reverend David Xavier Junkin, serving as a Union naval chaplain on a frigate in Mobile Bay, learned of the general's death from a Confederate prisoner. Writing to inform Dr. George Junkin of the loss, David Junkin admitted: "I knew not fully how much I loved him. My *heart* cannot but mourn and mine eyes cannot but weep for the loss of one so justly dear (except for the one great error) to us all." He added a final note of sympathy: "God comfort *thee*, my brother."[67]

Within the Preston household, tragedy seemed to mount on tragedy. First there had been Frank's wounding, followed by the deaths of Willie and Randy, and in May the loss of Tom Jackson. Then in July Phebe's fiancé and first cousin, William Cocke, was killed at Gettysburg. "What awful times we live in!" Maggie exclaimed.[68]

Shortly after the battle was over, an aging George Junkin traveled west from Philadelphia to Gettysburg, to bring physical assistance and religious comfort to the wounded and prisoners on both sides. As he walked about the rough terrain, Junkin used a gold-headed cane Jackson had given him to "introduc[e]" himself to Confederate prisoners and to verify his relationship with the hero. On one occasion, he encountered a number of his former students from Washington College. Pulling from his pocket an old class roll, he read off the "history," or academic record, of the surprised young men.[69] Some of them may well have been the students who had defied his order to bring down the Confederate flag two years before. Though he was strident in affirming his belief that secession was evil, Junkin never lost sight of the fact that Confederates were children of God who needed his love and succor.

On almost exactly the same day that he was bringing comfort to the wounded at Gettysburg and invoking the name and memory of Tom Jackson, the *Richmond Whig*, in a shrill editorial, denounced Junkin as "a conceited, irrascible [*sic*] and troublesome old hypocrite," who, the newspaper said, had quarreled so bitterly with Jackson that "the two had ceased even to speak to each other." The paper went on to condemn the "Reverend father in law, whetting his vulturous beak" as he "befoul[s] the memory of the illustrious deceased" by "the rancour of personal enmity . . . at once venomous and putrescent."[70] Either the editor did not know of Junkin's visit to the battlefield on an errand of mercy, or he chose to ignore the information.

During the first two years of the war, Lexingtonians heard only occasionally the ominous booming thunder of artillery, a signal they feared as the prelude to massive battles. But by the fall of 1863, the sounds of cannon and mortar fire had become increasingly familiar, as Union troops raided deep into the Shenandoah Valley. On several occasions they penetrated so close to the town that the VMI corps was mobilized to defend it. "Again the cadets and Home guard are summoned out . . . and Mr. P. went early this morning," Maggie recorded on December 6, 1863. "The reports are that the enemy is advancing . . . from *four* different points." She feared these short, frequent expeditions as much as she had dreaded her husband's longer absences in previous years. One could die as easily in a small skirmish, she felt, as in a large one. Colonel Preston, however, seemed oblivious to her fears. Once, when he failed to return with the corps after a foray, she was in an agony of suspense until he walked in unharmed the next day. Laconically, he explained that since "he [had] failed to find Yankees," he had decided to use the opportunity "to hunt deer on the mountain." Relieved, but understandably irritated, Maggie wrote, "I feel angry when I have been tortured to no purpose, as now."[71] She was also hurt at his seeming lack of empathy.

Temperatures were bitingly cold in December and January, unpleasant conditions made worse by universal shortages of fuel and food. Though the Prestons were better off than many, their dinners often consisted of only a "bowl of hot milk, poured over toast, or, for a change, a bowl of corn meal mush."[72] When the wretched weather continued into March, Maggie came down with a severe cold that quickly escalated into "internal neuralgia" and rheumatism in her hands.[73] Besides being in pain, she was disheartened by her husband's unhappy prediction that "the Valley must be relinquished this summer."[74]

Late in the spring of 1864 Colonel Preston was once again

chosen to be a delegate at the General Assembly, meeting in Charlotte. While he was away, the VMI corps was mustered out, with Frank Preston as their captain, to slow down the Federal advance toward Lexington. On May 15 a dramatic charge under withering fire won for the cadets a short-lived victory at the battle of New Market. But the gallant stand of the young soldiers, whose average age was eighteen, could not deter Federal forces for long. Of the 250 cadets who went into battle, five were killed instantly by enemy gunfire and five others died later from their wounds.

Preston was back in Lexington by the time Frank and the battle-weary cadets returned home. During the next few days Union troops advanced up the valley, past Harrisonburg and Staunton, to the little village of Brownsburg, thirteen miles north of Lexington. By early morning of June 11, it was clear that the enemy would occupy the town before nightfall. In an attempt to hide what she could, Maggie buried the silver and sent the servants to the hills to hide horses and cattle. Meanwhile, Frank Preston and the VMI corps hastily marched southeast toward Lynchburg, while Colonel Preston rushed away to supervise the downstream journey of barges laden with supplies from the Institute. One cadet, too ill to be moved, was left in Maggie's safekeeping. Just before his departure, Preston stored his own uniforms, as well as those of many cadets, in the attic of the house, because woolen goods were too precious to risk their falling into enemy hands.

Shortly after noon, fleeing Confederate troops retreated through Lexington on their way south, burning the North River bridge behind them to impede the advancing Union army. While Federal officers looked for a ford upstream, Union batteries began shelling the town. Most of the cannonballs fell on houses near the river, causing mass evacuation. "Our house," Maggie wrote, "was filled with women and children . . . from the lower part of the town."[75] She tried to calm the hysterical women by offering small cups of blackberry wine. Then suddenly, one shell landed in the Preston orchard itself. At the time, little Herbert was being given a bath, and when the shell burst, his mammy snatched him up and fled into the basement.[76]

This was the most dangerous situation Maggie had ever been in, and she must have wondered if she had courage enough to meet it. In the past, she had shown bravery in facing rheumatoid arthritis, and it had taken courage for her to acknowledge her antagonism toward Jackson and ask for his friendship. She had felt considerable apprehension when she made the decision to marry Preston and accept his large, somewhat hostile brood. "Do you not think I am brave?" she had asked Helen Dickey. "Oh, my dear, I am anything but—as tremulous as possible."[77]

Now, however, there was little time to think of either fear or courage. At four o'clock Yankee soldiers began streaming into town. First came the cavalry, followed by foot soldiers who fanned out across the community and invaded "our yard and kitchen."[78] By sheer willpower, Maggie managed to keep them out of the house, but she could not prevent them from stealing everything in the smokehouse and cellar. She and the children went to bed, but she slept little. The next morning she discovered that Federal troops had broken into the kitchen, devouring the family's breakfast and even stealing the coffeepot. "My children were crying for something to eat," she reported. "I had nothing to give them but crackers."[79]

At nine o'clock that morning, the buildings at VMI were set on fire in retaliation for the cadets' participation in the New Market engagement. "The flames are now enveloping . . . the Institute," Maggie recorded. "The towers have fallen, the arsenal is exploding as I write."[80] Rumors spread that VMI faculty houses in town might be burned as well, and Maggie wondered wildly what she would do if her home were torched. "God protect and have mercy upon us all!"[81]

Fortunately the house was not harmed, and Maggie was assured that the premises would be spared a thorough search if she could promise that no Confederate supplies were inside. Fearful that the trunks filled with uniforms might count as contraband, she and the children rushed to the attic and with pocket knives ripped and tore apart coats and trousers, hundreds of dollars' worth of "nice English cloth."[82] Then Maggie remembered the sword which Jackson had sent them for safekeeping the preceding year. Before the Yankees had come into town, she had hidden it, first in the attic and then inside Mary Anna's piano. Now, "with great trouble," she managed to secrete it under her skirt till she could store it safely in the outhouse.[83] At last, with neither army clothing nor weapons inside, she was able to tell the guard that her home was completely free of Confederate supplies.

But there was still the matter of the sick cadet whom she was nursing. She decided the best course of action was to acknowledge the young man's presence in the house, so she took the Federal guard to see the wounded boy, lying "pale and motionless" in a bedroom.[84] The Union soldier, startled by the sight of the desperately sick seventeen-year-old, spoke kindly to the lad. Tears rolled down the boy's cheeks, Maggie noted, and then Phebe began crying as well.

On Tuesday morning, June 14, the Yankees left Lexington bound for Lynchburg.* Maggie and her children crept cautiously outside to view the destruction and to compare stories with their neighbors. Suddenly, they realized that they had not eaten a full meal during the entire four days of the Federal occupation. Scarcely aware of her own actions, Maggie had managed through the four days of occupation to hold her family together, to keep the Union rabble away from a frightened Phebe, and to save the

---

*Stopped near Lynchburg, Union General David Hunter led his forces back toward West Virginia, bypassing Lexington altogether.

house from search and destruction. She was amazed and pleased that "in the midst of our frightful trouble," she had remained "so calm."[85]

Three days later Colonel Preston returned home, grateful to find his family alive and ready to assess the losses he had incurred during the enemy occupation. Several houses he owned in town had been destroyed, his farm had been stripped bare, and the livestock the family had so carefully sent away had been confiscated or slaughtered.* He estimated that "$30,000 would scarcely cover what he has lost by this invasion."[86] With no habitable quarters or classrooms, the VMI cadet corps received a temporary furlough, then was reassembled in Richmond. From October of 1864 until April of 1865 Preston did his best to teach his classes at the Alms House in Richmond, under extraordinarily adverse circumstances. The city was terribly crowded, there was the constant sound of bombardment from Petersburg, and thoughtful men and women, however devoted to the cause of the Confederacy, realized that the end was not far off.

During the latter years of the war, Maggie had broken her self-imposed ban on writing poetry, in part because of her husband's new appreciation of her talent. In addition to composing the "Christmas Carol, for 1862," she wrote several short poems that appeared in Virginia newspapers: "Virginia," "A Dirge for Ashby," "Hymn to the National Flag," "A Christmas Lay for 1864," and "Under the Shade of the Trees," based upon Stonewall Jackson's last recognizable words—"let us cross over the river, and rest

---

*Preston's need for ready cash may account for his sale of a slave named John on December 12, 1864, for the sum of $5,500.00 (Preston Papers, #1543, UNC).

under the shade of the trees."[87]* Not long after Jackson's funeral, she also wrote poignant stanzas describing his unmarked grave in Lexington's cemetery:

> A simple, sodded mound of earth,
>   Without a line above it;
> With only daily votive flowers
>   To prove that any love it:
> The token flag that silently
>   Each breeze's visit numbers,
> Alone keeps martial ward above
>   The hero's dreamless slumbers.
>   . . . .
> Rare fame! rare name!—If chanted praise,
>   With all the world to listen,—
> If pride that swells a nation's soul,—
>   If foeman's tears that glisten,—
> If pilgrims' shrining love,— if grief
>   Which nought may soothe or sever,—
> If THESE can consecrate—this spot
>   Is sacred ground forever![88]

Preston was unable to return home for this Christmas of 1864. But he did manage to send a belated holiday package, containing a few miscellaneous items that somehow had slipped through the blockade. For Maggie he had a copy of Thackeray's new novel *Philip*, a pair of "rubber shoes" for which he had paid thirty dollars, and a "ream of paper [which] will try your eyes less than

---

*General Turner Ashby was killed in 1862, "the first general of heroic reputation to fall in Virginia," Robert G. Tanner, *Stonewall in the Valley: Thomas J. "Stonewall" Jackson's Shenandoah Valley Campaign, Spring 1862* (Garden City, NY: Doubleday, 1976), 281. The account of Jackson's last words is given by Hunter McGuire, M.D., LL.D., Medical Director of Jackson's Corps, Army of Northern Virginia, in "Account of the Wounding and Death of Stonewall Jackson," *Richmond Medical Journal* (May 1866).

what you have been using." To Phebe he sent some yard goods given him by his sister, Mrs. Elizabeth Cocke. For John there was a "regular Army bridle," and for Elizabeth an orange. "There, now, is my invoice," he wrote, "very small, but it is my little all, and represents more love than many a bride's trousseau, or rich man's legacy!"[89]

Along with another letter he sent Maggie a small book entitled *Wee Davie* which he said was "making a great stir here in Richmond." Then Preston added, "You could do something much better in the same line."[90]* Accepting his suggestion as "a sort of dare," Maggie used her few spare moments to compose a "little ballad story" she called *Beechenbrook*, in which she attempted to give "a true picture of these war-times in which we live." Working at night "without a candle, merely by the light of the fire," she dictated most of the story to Elizabeth "lying on the rug in the fire-glow." It was the only way she could write, Maggie noted, because "my eyes are so weak and give me so much pain."[91]

The poem, written primarily in anapestic tetrameter couplets, is of a young pair named Douglass and Alice Dunbar who live, with their two children, in a country home called Beechenbrook. When the young father enlists, Alice sends her husband to the battlefield to fight:

> For home, and for children,—for freedom,—for bread,—
> For the house of our God,—for the graves of our dead—

---

*Elizabeth Preston Allan remembered the tale as "a pathetic little story . . . in rhyme" (Elizabeth Preston Allan, *The Life and Letters of Margaret Junkin Preston* [Boston: Houghton, Mifflin, and Company, 1903], 199). But there appears to be only one book entitled *Wee Davie* printed in 1864, and it is a prose narrative, written by a Scotsman and published (from the "Twenty-seventh London Edition") by the Presbyterian Committee of Publication, in Richmond. Either Mrs. Allan was mistaken about the book's being in rhyme or there was another booklet by the same title which has since been lost. Norman MacLeod's *Wee Davie* is about a little boy whose death brought both of his parents to membership in the church. Maggie's tale of the war could scarcely be more different.

. . . .

God prosper the right!
To brave men, there's nothing remains, but to fight.[92]

Not long after his departure, Alice and the children hear the dread sound of cannonading. "Again and again the reverberant sound/ Is fearfully felt in the tremulous ground." Alice's little boy reacts to the "thunderous echoes" with envy and the wish that he might participate in battle, while in contrast Alice stands terrified, "as if the low thunder were sounding her fate."[93] The cannonading comes from northern Virginia, where Dunbar is wounded at the battle of First Manassas and brought home in an ambulance to be nursed back to health by Alice.

As soon as he is able, he rejoins his unit in camp, where he is nourished throughout the long, dreary winter by letters from his wife. "What brave, buoyant letters you write, sweet!—they ring/ Thro' my soul like the blast of a trumpet."[94] Here Maggie inserts her earlier poem, "Christmas Carol, for 1862," in which imperative verbs and short, choppy lines of trochaic trimeter underscore the monotony of camp life and the tedium, discomfort, and suffering endured by everyday soldiers:

Halt!—the march is over!
Day is almost done;
Loose the cumbrous knapsack,
Drop the heavy gun:
Chilled and wet and weary,
Wander to and fro,
Seeking wood to kindle
Fires amidst the snow.[95]

One of the young enlisted men serving under Dunbar is a recruit named Macpherson, whose bloody feet attest to his having had no shoes. Dunbar asks Alice to knit socks for the lad, and she sends him a pair for Christmas. Later, Macpherson is severely wounded and sent to Beechenbrook, where he dies far from his own family. The short poem about Macpherson's death is so poignant and personal that it almost certainly grew out of Maggie's own grief at the death of Willie Preston:

> Only a private;—and who will care
>   When I may pass away,—
> Or how, or why I perish, or where
>   I mix with the common clay;
> They will fill my empty place again,
>   With another as stout and brave;
> And they'll blot me out, ere the Autumn rain
>   Has freshened my nameless grave.[96]

Not long after Macpherson's death, the "insolent foe" sweeps through the valley, pillaging and burning. Among the places destroyed is Beechenbrook, whose desolation Alice describes to her husband:

> —Our beautiful home,—as I write it—I weep—
> Our beautiful home is a smouldering heap!
> And blackened, and blasted, and grim, and forlorn,
> Its chimneys stand stark in the mists of the morn! [97]

She could have been describing the ruins of VMI or a host of other houses in the area demolished during Hunter's occupation of Rockbridge County.

Dunbar never receives her letter, having been fatally wounded before it reaches him. Alice hastens to the hospital only to find her dead husband "on the crowded and blood-stained floor."[98] Her first wish is to die herself, as if to atone for his unattended death:

> Break, my heart, and ease this pain—
> Cease to throb, thou tortured brain;
> Let me die,—since he is slain,
> —Slain in battle!
>
> . . . .
>
> Not a pillow for his head—
> Not a hand to smooth his bed—
> Not one tender parting said,
> —Slain in battle![99]

"Slain in battle" is the cry Colonel Preston had repeated over and over again after Willie's death.[100] But the stanzas of the poem also echo the Junkin family's distress after Joe's death and their concern that none of them had been with the dying boy. Years earlier, Maggie had recoiled in horror at shrouds and coffin screws, which to her symbolized death's obliteration of personal identity. By war's end she had learned the terrible anonymity and meaninglessness of death on the battlefield. (Many years later, on July 20, 1891, Maggie offered "Slain in Battle" as her tribute to Stonewall Jackson on the occasion of the dedication of a statue in his memory.)

But Maggie does not leave Alice totally defeated. Pulling herself together because of her children and her country, Alice holds on to the memory of her husband's sacrifice:

> By his death on the battle-field, gallantly brave,
> By the shadow that ever enwraps her—his grave—
> By the faith she reposes, Oh! Father, in Thee,
> She claims that her glorious South MUST BE FREE![101]

The only lines in *Beechenbrook* that glorify war are Alice's final words and her stirring opening phrases when she sends Dunbar into battle. Rather, the poem concentrates upon the loneliness, fatigue, fear, and suffering endured by a civilian population and expresses Maggie's overwhelming revulsion toward war. It may have been this predominant sense of war's horror that kept Maggie from telling anyone about *Beechenbrook* while she was writing it. Only Elizabeth (who took the dictation), Maggie's little boys, and one guest in the home had any knowledge of her literary endeavor. Completing the draft in three weeks, she sent it, with considerable trepidation, to her husband in Richmond.

Her relief was transparent when she received a "letter from my darling husband, expressing extravagant praise of my little poetical story. It delights *him* and that is enough for *me*."[102] He had read the ballad to numerous friends in Richmond, he told her, and all of them had found it moving. To her great surprise he even made plans to have *Beechenbrook* published in Richmond, in spite of the capital's shortages of paper and other supplies. Two thousand copies were "to be gotten up in the *plainest* manner," Maggie reported in her diary, with "dark paper—dim type . . . in stitched brown paper covers."[103]

On March 30, 1865, a notice of the book appeared in the *Christian Observer and Presbyterian*, a Richmond weekly magazine. Calling *Beechenbrook* an "admirable ballad," the notice commented on "its passages of great beauty . . . and its faithful sketches of the war."[104] Unfortunately, only fifty copies had been sent out of the city before Richmond fell to Federal troops early in April. In the ensuing fire that destroyed much of the city, the remaining 1,500 copies were burned. (Reissued in Baltimore in 1866 with a new dedication, "To every Southern woman who was widowed by the war," *Beechenbrook* became a runaway bestseller. Years after its original publication, men and women who had lived through the war testified that they still could not read the book without weeping.)

News of the Confederate surrender at Appomattox reached Lexington on April 10, 1865. Elizabeth was visiting friends, reading aloud from a copy of *Beechenbrook*, when a relative burst in with the electrifying words, "Lee has surrendered!" The girl hurried home to carry word to her family, but as she entered the house she saw Phebe weeping uncontrollably on the sofa and realized that word had reached home already. For the rest of her life Elizabeth associated the scent of the Malmaison rose with that terrible day, because a potted rose bush of that variety stood on the windowsill beside the divan where Phebe lay sobbing.

The following Sunday at the Presbyterian church Dr. White tried to offer consolation to his parishioners when he preached from a long and obscure text in Habakkuk: "Although the fig tree shall not blossom, neither fruit be in the vine; the labor of the olive shall fail, and the fields shall yield no meat; the flock shall be cut off from the fold, and there shall be no herd in the stall: yet will I rejoice in the Lord. I will joy in the God of my salvation." [105] At the end of the sermon the congregation sat silent, many weeping unashamedly. Maggie wanted to be comforted by her pastor's message, but she found it impossible to find solace after five years of pain and loss and senseless killing:

> Why then all these four years of suffering—
> of separations—of horror—of blood—of
> havoc—of awful bereavement! Why these
> ruined homes—these broken family circles—
> these scenes of terror that must scathe the
> brain of those who witnessed them till their
> dying day! Why is our dear Willy in his
> uncoffined grave? Why poor Frank to go
> through life with one arm? Is it wholly and
> forever in vain? *God only knows!* [106]

George Junkin,
Maggie's father
Artist unknown

*Courtesy of
Janet Preston*

Julia Rush Miller Junkin,
Maggie's mother
Artist unknown

Courtesy of Janet Preston

Only surviving photograph of Eleanor (Elinor) Junkin Jackson

*Stonewall Jackson
House Collection,
Lexington, Virginia*

Thomas Jonathan Jackson,
as he looked while he was
at the Virginia Military
Institute

*National Portrait Gallery
Smithsonian Institution*

First building at Lafayette College
built by George Junkin, his faculty, and students.

From David B. Skillman's Biography of a College,
picture facing page 92

President's house, Washington College, in midnineteenth century
After their marriage, the Jacksons lived here with the Junkin family

Michael Miley Collection
The University Library
Washington and Lee University, Lexington, Virginia

VMI barracks, sacked and burned by Federal forces in 1864

Archives, Virginia Military Institute, Lexington, Virginia

J.T.L. Preston
Detail from a sketch by
William Washington of
VMI faculty after the war

*VMI Museum Collection
Virginia Military Institute*

Above:
Interior of Preston house

*Rockbridge Historical
Society Collection
The University Library
Washington and Lee University*

Left:
Herbert Rush Preston,
at the age of eight

*Photograph by Michael Miley
Courtesy of Janet Preston*

Opposite page:
Formal photograph of
Margaret Junkin Preston

Michael Miley Collection
The University Library
Washington and Lee University

Above:
Informal photograph of
Margaret Junkin Preston

Michael Miley Collection
The University Library
Washington and Lee University

Right:
Designed by Maggie for her own
use, this desk was unusually low to
accommodate her short stature

Desk in possesion of Janet Preston

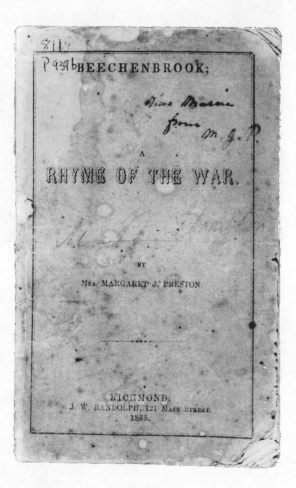

Beechenbrook
One of only fifty copies from the first edition
to survive the catastrophic fire in Richmond,
during the last days of the Civil War

Special Collections
The University Library
Washington and Lee University

The Preston plot in Stonewall Jackson cemetery, Lexington, Virginia
Maggie's tombstone is on the far right

Rockbridge Historical Society Collection
The University Library
Washington and Lee University

Heroic bronze statue of Stonewall Jackson
in the cemetery in Lexington, Virginia

Rockbridge Historical Society Collection
The University Library
Washington and Lee University

Chapter 6

Sonnets and Sauces
1865–1890

> I think I can truly say that I
> never neglected the concocting
> of a *pudding* for the sake of a
> *poem* or a *sauce* for a *sonnet!*[1]

The war years had aged Colonel Preston dramatically. He had lost two sons, seen a daughter's dreams of a happy marriage shattered, and watched the painful adjustment of a third son to the loss of his left arm. Ruined walls and burned-out rubble were all that remained of his beloved VMI, where he had spent a quarter of a century teaching. In the spring of 1865 he looked far older than his fifty-four years, his hair snow-white, his face heavily

wrinkled with "graven lines which were never effaced."² In public, Preston had always seemed a dignified, quiet man. Now,
"long silences . . . broken by grave and serious speech"³ added an
aura of tragedy to his demeanor.

In contrast, Maggie, nine years his junior, was far more cheerful and energetic. To be sure, she grieved for the dead—her
stepsons, Stonewall Jackson, William Cocke, and scores of friends.
But the war had spared her own two boys and her husband. Now
secure in his love and emboldened by his demonstrated willing-
ness to allow her to share her creative talent with others, she
looked forward to a renewed literary career.

Immediately after the war's end, however, no one in Lexington
could afford the luxury of literary pursuits. There were houses to
be rebuilt, businesses and colleges to be reopened, and farms to
be readied for a delayed spring planting. Defeated soldiers who
straggled back to town faced the challenge of beginning their
lives all over again. Preston had suffered huge financial losses
during the Federal occupation of the community, but even so was
more fortunate than many who subsisted that spring on dry beans
and hitched themselves to ploughs because horses and cattle had
been plundered.⁴ Not until gardens produced lavishly and the fall
harvest came in could most Lexingtonians rest easily.

Despite the damage to its buildings and library holdings, VMI
in the fall of 1865 welcomed its first postwar cadets. The eighteen
young men boarded in homes all over town and attended classes
in the only undamaged building, the superintendent's quarters.
In company with a half-dozen other faculty members Preston
began teaching with no salary, "on leave of absence without
pay . . . in order to more nearly balance the [school's] budget."⁵
Regular hours, renewed contacts with young people, and the
opportunity to engage in meaningful work helped to offset his
depression.

Maggie, meanwhile, was making the adjustment to new domestic reality. Several of the Preston slaves had remained with the family after emancipation, but because their wages now constituted considerable expense, Colonel Preston reluctantly let four of them go. "Anakee had lived with him 25 years," Maggie wrote. "He was grieved to give her up, and she wanted to stay. Old Uncle Young manifested no pleasure at the idea of freedom."[6] Both freed slaves and their former master recognized that there was little opportunity at the beginning of reconstruction for blacks to find gainful employment.

Maggie herself probably had mixed feelings about seeing the old, well-trained helpers go. Unlike many of her Lexington friends, she had learned as a girl to perform most household tasks, and she may have felt relief when Sally Preston's servants departed. But working with unskilled assistants was not easy, especially when she had to manage a household with five children still in residence. Frank, teaching Greek at Washington College, and Phebe, unmarried in her late twenties, both still lived at home. John was a teenager studying at a local preparatory school, and the two young boys, George and Herbert, were just beginning their education. Elizabeth, sixteen years old, attended Augusta Female Academy in Staunton in 1865 and 1866, but she was home for the holidays and special occasions.

Though she found housework distasteful, Maggie believed strongly that, for women, domestic responsibility must come before literary pursuits. Only after "a simple woman's household duties" were completed, she said, should she permit herself to "scribble . . . to her heart's relief."[7] Part of her fervor for keeping a spotless home arose from her religious convictions about the work ethic and her adherence to John Wesley's dictum, that cleanliness is next to godliness.[8] But she also knew that her husband expected a well-ordered household, the kind that his first wife had always maintained. So she drove herself to the point of exhaustion, as notations in her postwar diary suggest:

> Covering chairs with new damask . . . have
> fixed five. . . . Varnished a parcel of furniture
> to cover up the wear and tear of the winter. . . .
> Put down matting in the spare chamber . . .
> Busy darning and sewing. . . . Tired with this
> abominable housecleaning. . . . A dozen people
> invited to tea; busy all day making cake,
> ices, etc. and chicken salad *without* any
> celery. . . . Mended and put down the stair
> carpet. . . . Made 22 gallons of blackberry wine
> this morning. . . . Put up 23 bottles of ketchup. . . .
> Boiled jelly, pared peaches for preserves,
> and put up twenty or thirty lbs. of sweet
> pickle. . . . Busy all afternoon with putting up
> the parlor stove, a horrid dirty job; feel like
> a plasterer or bricklayer. . . . Too tired
> in the afternoon to go out; and in a bad humor![9]

Years later Elizabeth Preston Allan commented that her step-mother would "throw herself with passionate abandon into . . . comparatively unimportant drudgery, and then weep bitter tears over what she and her dear ones had missed of peace and home delight."[10]

By now the Preston home was thoroughly Maggie's. She had always had a knack for making a room comfortable. With the use of "silver & pictures & books, etc., she . . . made it [the big old house] a much handsomer interior than it probably had been, in the earlier day."[11] Her husband's penchant for entertaining had continued after the war. There were frequent teas, dinners, and morning socials, all of which were difficult to produce without a cook or with a poorly trained one. When farmhands had to be fed, Maggie often had no recourse but to prepare the meals herself: "Got an old woman for a cook. . . . Eleven black people to cook for here to-night, and I got supper almost entirely myself."[12]

A more pleasant aspect of the return to normalcy was Maggie's opportunity to renew ties with family members who had remained loyal to the Union. As soon as hostilities were over, "even before the rail lines were reconnected," several Dickey cousins traveled to Lexington to "see how the Junkins were." While in Virginia these relatives prevailed upon old "Uncle Young," one of the freed slaves whom Colonel Preston had reluctantly dismissed, to return with them to Pennsylvania, where he remained with the Dickeys for the rest of his life.[13] In the fall of 1865 Maggie traveled to Philadelphia for a happy reunion with Julia and Dr. Junkin. "From that time on," Maggie's stepdaughter wrote, "no shadow ever came between her and those loving hearts whose pleasure it was to lavish affectionate kindness upon her."[14]

During her visit Dr. Junkin and his two daughters must have spoken frequently of their years in the president's house in Lexington, now occupied by Robert E. Lee. Though Washington College had been treated less brutally by Federal troops than had VMI, damage to its laboratories and looting of its library constituted losses of more than $17,000.[15] The college had nearly ceased operation during the war, and after Appomattox the trustees met in a desperate attempt to bring new life to the old school. Their daring move to choose General Lee as president assured the renewal of the college. Within a few months of Lee's arrival in Lexington, the initial student body of 150 had grown to more than 400 young men and veterans, all eager to study under the fallen hero's tutelage.

Maggie had not met General Lee before he moved to Rockbridge County, but she and her husband already enjoyed a family connection with him. Soon after the surrender, Colonel Preston's sister, Mrs. Elizabeth Cocke, had loaned the Lees her cottage in Powhatan County, a small, unpretentious house called Derwent, where the general could rest and recuperate far from the noise and confusion of Richmond. At Derwent Mrs. Cocke and the Lees became good friends, and Lee's two younger daughters learned to know Preston's nephews, Edmund and Preston Cocke. Just before his family joined the general in Lexington in December of 1865, Mrs. Cocke had supplied Mrs. Lee's bedroom with furniture designed by Maggie Preston and made by a one-armed Lexington veteran. Once the family was in the president's house, Maggie paid them frequent calls, and Mildred, Agnes, and their elder sister Mary Lee became fast friends of Maggie's stepdaughter, Elizabeth Preston.*

Fulfilling her social obligations with family and friends, helping her husband adjust to the postwar era, and managing a large household with inexperienced servants required most of Maggie's time and energy in the first months after the surrender. Still, the yearning to write and communicate with others, an urge she had stifled during the early years of her marriage, returned now with rekindled vigor.

She began by reissuing *Beechenbrook*, which was published in 1866 by a Baltimore firm. The company, Kelly and Piet, printed only a few thousand copies at first, but the book sold so well that a second edition appeared later in the same year. Ultimately *Beechenbrook* went through eight printings and became the only one of Maggie's books to make a profit. One unexpected outlet for its sale was the Baltimore Ladies' Relief Fair, held in April of 1866, to raise money for Confederate widows and orphans. With the large sale of *Beechenbrook* and profits realized from hundreds of donated items, Baltimore women raised more than $100,000,

---

*Twenty-five years later, in a long article published in *The Century Magazine*, Maggie painted a warm and humane picture of Robert E. Lee based upon her associations with him, Mrs. Lee, and their daughters (MJP, "General Lee after the War," *The Century Magazine* 38 [1889]: 271–76).

of which nearly a quarter was distributed in Virginia for its refugee work.[16]

Maggie's next literary venture was to contribute poems and book notices to a new Southern magazine, *Land We Love*, edited by Daniel Hill, the Civil War general who prior to 1861 had taught mathematics at Washington College and been a close friend of the Prestons and Jackson. Published for three years (1866–1869) before it merged with the *New Eclectic*, *Land We Love* attracted 12,000 subscribers and served as a forum for Southern writers such as Fanny Downing, Paul Hamilton Hayne, and Francis Orray Ticknor.[17] Maggie contributed seventeen poems to Hill's new venture, as well as reviews of new books, and Colonel Preston wrote an elaborate analysis of Alfred Tennyson's poem, "Tears, Idle Tears."

Though Hill insisted that his magazine's editorial policy was nonregional, its title implied its Confederate bias, and many of the poems and articles within its pages expressed nostalgia for prewar Southern gentility and harsh criticism of Federal reconstruction. Maggie's early contributions reflect this perspective. "Hero's Daughter," for example, is about one of Lee's daughters, and "Regulus" is an angry poem about the mistreatment Southerners believed Jefferson Davis received in a Federal prison.[18] But then in "Acceptation" Maggie rejects both sentimentality and anger to voice instead her gratitude for war's end and her hope for a revitalized Southland:

> our eyes
> Welcome through tears the sweet release
> From war, and woe, and want
>
> . . . .
>
> War has not wholly wrecked us: still
>   Strong hands, brave hearts, high souls are ours;
>   Proud consciousness of quenchless powers—

A Past whose memory makes us thrill—
Futures uncharactered, to fill
With heroisms—if we will.[19]

The reissuing of *Beechenbrook* and the publication of her poems in *Land We Love* made the name "Margaret Junkin Preston" a familiar one throughout the South. Soon she began to receive touching letters of thanks for expressing in her poetry "the sorrow and patriotism" of the region.[20] She was especially flattered in December 1867 to receive an unexpected and most complimentary letter from Paul Hamilton Hayne, one of the South's leading literary spokesmen. "For a long time past," Hayne began, "I have been *one* of the thousands in our section, who read your poetry with a sincere pleasure." Mentioning several of her poems he most admired, Hayne continued: "Your genius, & lofty patriotism have struck me so forceably that I venture thus to address you, & to beg that you will honour me by accepting a copy of the enclosed poem, just published in the Balt. 'So. Society."[21]

Maggie answered a few weeks later, thanking Hayne for his "pleasant words about myself," and acknowledging the receipt of "the glowing, vivid, flashing, sparkling 'Fire-Pictures' you were so kind as to send me." In return, she sent him a copy of *Beechenbrook*. She had never sought to be a true "*litterateur*," she told Hayne, and she knew she could never "enter *your* arena, except for pastime . . . disclaim[ing] all title to the name of Poet, except so far as I share it with Nature's other children—birds and flowers."[22] It was a graceful letter, appropriately humble, but hinting that she was ready to enter into serious correspondence. These two letters were the first in what was to become a nineteen-year correspondence between the two poets, involving more than three hundred letters of mutual support, criticism, and encouragement. Never meeting face to face, the pair continued to refer to each other formally as "Mr. Hayne" and "Mrs. Preston," but from 1867 until Hayne's death in 1886, they shared in an extraordinarily personal way their hopes, their dreams, their disappointments, and their aspirations for a resurgent Southern literature.

Not surprisingly Maggie, exhausted from the double pressures of housekeeping and literary endeavor, began experiencing the old familiar pains in her eyes and back, and she acknowledged that her energy was not what it had been before the war. "Very thoroughly tired tonight," she confided to her diary in April 1868. "Can't work as I used to, without tiring out. . . . More pain in my back than I have had for months."[23] She was not too fatigued, however, to miss the opportunity to write to her father about her rediscovered pleasure in creating poetry.

After the war Dr. Junkin, still vigorous despite his age, had continued his busy schedule. He preached at least once every Sunday, contributed articles for area newspapers, compiled and arranged his voluminous lifetime correspondence, served as chaplain of Magdalene Asylum in Philadelphia (an institution for "females who had deviated from the paths of virtue"), and wrote an exegesis of the Book of Hebrews.[24] He completed the manuscript only days before he was suddenly taken ill in May of 1868. After seventy-two hours of pain and debility he died on May 20, at the age of 78, the day after Maggie's forty-eighth birthday.

Maggie did not try to go to Philadelphia for the funeral, but she was gratified to learn at a later date of the tributes that had been paid to her father.* Charles Elliott, a former Lafayette student, told of his mentor's "power of logic" and his ability to move audiences "to tears by his tender appeals," and John Mason Knox recalled Junkin's "burning words . . . touching pathos . . . [and] brilliant imagery." Even the Lafayette trustees spoke admiringly of the former president's "devoted piety, great learning . . . indomitable perseverance, unsparing self-denials . . . and labors beyond measure."[25] For Maggie the most heartwarming eulogy was printed in the *Lexington Gazette & Banner*. Omitting any reference to her father's unhappy departure when he had wiped the dust of Virginia from his carriage seventeen years earlier, the newspaper spoke instead of Dr. Junkin's years of "labor . . . in which his life was spent for . . . the church he loved," as well as the legacy he left his family, "the precious inheritance of a name without reproach."[26]

By the summer of 1869 the Virginia Military Institute's buildings had been largely repaired, and the number of cadets increased to 270. Encouraged by such achievements, Colonel Preston regained a measure of his prewar cheerfulness, especially after he learned that his son Frank, recently returned from a year's study in Germany, had accepted a prestigious appointment at the College of William and Mary. The family's euphoria, however, was short lived, for Frank's persistent cough worsened into termi-

---

*She would not have been able to reach Philadelphia in time for his burial there in Woodland Cemetery. In 1925 his body and that of his daughter Julia Fishburn were moved to the Stonewall Jackson Cemetery in Lexington, to be reinterred beside Mrs. Junkin, Ellie, Junius Fishburn, and young George Junkin Fishburn, in the family plot—the gravesite Dr. Junkin had purchased years before and called his "cave of Machpelah," referring to Abraham's acquisition of a cave in Israel where he might bury his wife Sarah (*Life of Dr. G. J.*, 518; Genesis 23:19). Interestingly, the Cave of Machpelah was Abraham's "first foothold in the home of his posterity . . . won through his bereavement" (*Abingdon Bible Commentary* [New York: Abingdon Press, 1929], 235. Copyright renewal 1956 Abingdon Press. Used by permission). Similarly, though George Junkin purchased his family plot for the burial of his wife, it, too, became a "foothold" that brought back disparate members of the family to their common resting place.

nal tuberculosis. He died on October 19, 1869, at the age of 28, and was buried a few days later in the Preston plot in the old Lexington cemetery.

In an effort to divert her husband's mind from this newest loss, Maggie persuaded him to assist her in selecting poems to include in her first collected volume of poetry. Such a book, she wrote in her diary, had been "a dream of many years . . . a collection of such verses as I have thought it worth while to keep."[27] Together she and the colonel discussed which poems to choose, which to change, and which to omit altogether. But as she painstakingly copied the poems, she grew increasingly uncertain of the value of assembling "these waifs and estrays of the past years!"[28] She could not help contrasting her work with that of poets like William Morris and Leigh Hunt, whose latest volumes she had just received for review: "When I turn over the leaves of [their] poetry, I am discouraged from all thought of publishing my own. . . . What business have I to be throwing upon the current my poor weak dawdling?"[29]

But still she persevered and by March of 1870 had revised and prepared seventy poems—sixteen sonnets, eleven short religious pieces, thirteen poems on Old Testament and classical themes, more than forty ballads, and a few war lyrics. Once, much of her poetry had been about death. Now, with her postwar self-reliance and her widening interest in people other than herself, she chose poems about Italian artists, Scottish legends, and persons around her whom she cared about. In the last category were three poems that Preston admitted were his favorites—"Nineteen," "Attainment," and "The Dumb Poet." "The first two," he wrote to Paul Hayne, "picture with wonderful insight my two daughters, and the third is a love-blinded portrait of a husband whose only claim to so much as a foot square of Mount Parnassus is that of 'tenant by courtesy,' . . . i.e. by right of his wife."[30] In "The Dumb Poet" Maggie deftly turns upside down her husband's self-diagnosed lack of poetic talent, suggesting that instead of being a voiceless poet, he has unique powers to communicate with her in very special ways:

> O my Dumb Poet, in whose soul
> Love still the mystic psalm rehearses,
> Make thou mine open heart thy scroll,
> And fill it with thy marvellous verses![31]

Though he was enthusiastic about the poetry, Colonel Preston was loath to have the book published by a commercial press, preferring a "private circulation" because he did not like the idea of women "rushing into print."[32] Maggie wrote to Paul Hayne that if private issuance became necessary "that would have satisfied me,"[33] but she wanted at least to try to have the book professionally produced. So she sent the slim volume, entitled *Old Song and New*, to Lippincott's publishing house in Philadelphia. Lest she appear too bold, she modestly characterized herself, in the preface, as a bird with "a slender trill . . . [whose] quiet cooings" she hoped readers would enjoy. She went on to describe her poems as "wayside waifs—sweet-brier and violet" which she hoped would bring "a little tender mist . . . or a sweet sunshine flicker" to the eyes of the reader.[34] Her self-effacement was characteristic of many nineteenth-century women writers who added disclaimers to their works, saying that they wrote only for pleasure, to amuse themselves, and to while away idle time.

In spite of her apprehensions over the worth of her poetry and her avowed humility, Maggie was thrilled when the first copies of *Old Song and New* arrived in Lexington late in August of 1870. "The event of the day," she wrote in her diary, "is the receiving of my book, beautifully printed and bound, just according to my wish." The printed volume provided her with a sense of "real satisfaction that I have been able to accomplish what so long ago

I had desired, yet hardly hoped to see carried out. May God bless the book!"[35] Yet she had no illusions about the financial rewards to be garnered from *Old Song and New*, for she had paid for the galleys herself and agreed to buy up any remainders. It was an arrangement similar to that of most Southern writers of the postwar period who "assumed initial expense of publication," and then shared any profits.[36]

Today's readers may find the poems in *Old Song and New* bland, since they exhibit none of the emotion one senses in *Beechenbrook* or even in the poems Maggie wrote as a girl when she described her horror of death, or anguished over not having the kind of faith she yearned for. Contemporary literary critics, however, were generous in their praise. William Hand Browne, editor of the *Southern Magazine*, wrote that the author was "evidently working her way to a style of her own." The usually acerbic Browne called her ballads the "best specimens of her powers," and he suggested that she "has a true sense of the dignity of the Poet's calling."[37] The *Saturday Review* of London called *Old Song and New* "one of the best volumes of American poetry that have lately appeared," its "domestic pieces . . . marked by a grave and truly feminine tenderness."[38] Not to be outdone by others, Maggie's new friend Paul Hayne wrote a review that Maggie delightedly referred to as "flattering and charming and elaborate criticism."[39]

In spite of the critics' commendations, however, Maggie continued to have doubts about some of the poems in *Old Song and New*. Ten years after its publication she worried that there was within its pages "much that is crude" and unpolished.[40] But Colonel Preston was delighted that his wife's book had been treated with such warmth. "None can be expected to appreciate the poems as I do," Preston wrote to Paul Hayne. "My little wife is as full of faith and reverence as ever was any daughter of Jerusalem; the Greek hardly excelled her in love for the beautiful;

she is as true and trustful as Lady Hildegarde; as simple as a ballad, and as intense as a sonnet."[41]*

Not long after the publication of *Old Song and New*, Julia Fishburn came to Lexington for a visit. It was the first time she had been back to Virginia since her hasty departure in 1861, and the two sisters enjoyed their reunion. Indeed, they had such a pleasurable visit that, when it came time for Julia to leave, Maggie traveled north with her sister for a few weeks' vacation in Philadelphia. While she was there, Maggie learned of the death of General Lee on October 12, 1870. Returning home late in the month, she found the college campus and VMI still draped in black, and "churches & all public places . . . hung with the mournful crepe."[42] During a courtesy call to Mrs. Lee, Maggie was told of the words that the general had murmured "in his unconsciousness . . . 'Let the tent be struck.' "[43] From this brief phrase of General Lee's† came one of Maggie's best-known poems, "Gone Forward," a piece she composed with great intensity in the space of two hours. "Writing it," she confided in her journal, "made the cold perspiration break out over me, which is a token that I was 'i[in] the vein.' "[44]

Yes, "Let the tent be struck:" Victorious morning
        Through every crevice flashes in a day
Magnificent beyond all earth's adorning:
        The night is over; wherefore should he stay?
        And wherefore should our voices choke to say,
        "The General has gone forward"?

---

*Lady Hildegarde, the subject of one of Maggie's poems in *Old Song* (109), exemplified a woman with extraordinary trust in her beloved.

†Because there is some controversy among modern historians as to whether or not Lee really spoke these words—or any words—during his final illness, it is worth quoting Maggie's comment at the end of this letter: "I have verified the expression from the lips of Mrs. Lee herself" (MJP to PHH, November 17, 1870, typed copy of letter, Hayne MSS, Duke).

. . . .] . . . .

We will not weep,—we dare not! Such a story
　　As his large life writes on the century's years,
Should crowd our bosoms with a flush of glory,
　　That manhood's type, supremest that appears
To-day, *he* shows the ages. Nay, no tears
　　Because he has gone forward![45]

————

With the publication of *Old Song and New*, Maggie's life
settled into a pattern that was to continue for the next twenty
years. The major portion of her energy and time she devoted to
her family and to her housekeeping responsibilities. But she
nonetheless managed to squeeze out "spare or unused corners of
filled-up days"[46] in which she wrote hundreds of poems, published four additional volumes of poetry, a travel book, and a
"dialect" story, reviewed countless books for national magazines,
and kept up a voluminous correspondence.

Impelled by her own decision to concentrate upon domestic
details when she longed to be writing, she was continually frustrated. Maggie had been reared to believe with Queen Victoria
that a woman's duty must be to her family first, and only in living
for others could she find fulfillment; yet like many intelligent,

————

*A few women, like Harriet Beecher Stowe, managed to see "the literary role
. . . [as] an extension of her domestic role" (Mary Kelley, *Private Woman, Public
Stage: Literary Domesticity in Nineteenth-Century America* [New York: Oxford
University Press, 1984], 248), but others became bitter, like Cornelia Phillips of
Chapel Hill, North Carolina, who wrote in her postwar diary: "I feel sometimes
such an impatience of my life and its narrow lot as I can scarcely describe. . . . I
want to go, to take wings, and fly" (Cornelia Phillips, quoted in Anne Firor
Scott, *The Southern Lady* [Chicago: University of Chicago Press, 1970], 73.
Copyright 1970 by the University of Chicago. All rights reserved).

articulate, nineteenth–century women, Maggie found it impossible to find satisfaction in domesticity.* One day, she noted in her diary, she spent her waking hours searching in vain for a new cook, mending clothes, and making a cake, rather than in far more meaningful literary activity. Her irritation was the greater because her husband seemed to have plenty of time for activities that gave him pleasure. "Mr. P. out hunting," she wrote angrily in her diary, "and I am in a tempestuous humor—O me!"[47]

Though she insisted that her true role in life was that of "wifehood, motherhood—mistress, hostess, neighbor, and friend,"[48] relatively few comments in Maggie's letters or diary entries speak of her relationship with her husband. It is clear, however, that in the years after the war Preston became increasingly dependent upon her, no longer the domineering partner, but now one who needed her presence to maintain his own emotional equilibrium. In 1870, after Maggie had returned from Philadelphia, she wrote in her diary, "Mr. P. says I shall never go away from him any more." She felt it was almost worth the trouble going away, "to be so welcomed back!"[49]

His reliance upon her, she believed, grew from all the losses he had suffered during the war and, more recently, from Frank's death. In one of her poems she likened Preston to a "ravaged oak" bruised by the elements and badly in want of comfort.[50] Recognizing his need, Maggie carefully adjusted her schedule to fit his, whether he was teaching classes or taking part in a hunt. "My husband started out for a fox-hunt in the morning," she wrote to Paul Hayne in February of 1873, "which left a few hours of partial leisure to me." But she quickly laid aside her own interests when "Mr. P. returned at 4 o'clock [and] I put up my 'Scribbling-book.'"[51] Once, a Lexington friend teased her about never being away from him: "'Mrs. Preston, I believe you think you could not be happy in Heaven without the Colonel!'" Maggie replied "earnestly, 'Indeed I know I could not!'"[52] Years after he retired from active teaching, she wrote in "Winter Love" that though the "summer's solstice days are gone," and the aging couple cannot "turn back" life's seasons, nonetheless the "winter love" they now share is filled with "dreamy bliss":

> I wonder if our summer love
> Was half so sweet as this![53]

The second responsibility Maggie felt most keenly was to her children, both her stepchildren and her own two boys. She had long since won the allegiance of her husband's sons and daughters, who, one by one, left the household after the war. Phebe, the "elegant stylish looking girl of 18"[54] whom Maggie had first met in 1857, had for eight years nursed her grief for her dead fiancé, William Cocke. Finally, in 1871, "after a long and patient courtship," Phebe agreed to marry William's brother Edmund. [55] But her happiness at Oakland, the Cocke plantation, was to be short lived. Only two years after her marriage she died during delivery of her first baby, a little girl named Sally Lyle Cocke. It was a death painfully like the first Sally's death, and the fourth among Colonel Preston's children in a thirteen-year period.

Happily, nine months after Phebe's death Elizabeth Preston married a man whom the family also knew very well. William Allan, eleven years Elizabeth's senior, had served under Jackson during the war and then had come to Washington College to teach engineering. In 1873 he left Lexington to become headmaster of the McDonogh School, a preparatory school in Baltimore endowed by and named for the New Orleans philanthropist Maggie had so long admired. Maggie was closer to Elizabeth than to any other of her stepchildren, and the affection was mutual, as evidenced by Elizabeth's naming her first child Margaret Preston Allan. After Elizabeth sent a telegram in 1875 to announce the new arrival, Maggie replied with enthusiasm:

My darling—thank God first and chiefest of
all, that you are the happy mother of a living
child! And then, thank and bless you that you
have paid me, the sweetest and greatest
compliment of my life—*the very*
sweetest. . . . I dont think I was ever so glad of
a baby's birth—and so relieved, even my
own! except Julia Fishburn's . . . [Your] Father
and I could do nothing but hug each other and
cry for very joy . . . . I wanted the Church
bells rung.[56]

Now that Elizabeth was living in Maryland, none of Maggie's
stepchildren remained at home, for John had finished college a
few months after his sister's wedding and moved on to seminary.
One would have supposed that Maggie, with only her own two
boys in the house, would have savored the relative quiet. Instead,
she took as a boarder a niece, Julia Rush Junkin, daughter of her
brother Ebenezer, who was pastor of a small country church in
nearby Brownsburg. Julia lived with the family for a year while
she attended Lexington's preparatory school for girls, the Ann
Smith Academy. Evidently Maggie was delighted to have a young
girl to fuss over, and she taught Julia to draw and to play the
piano, suggested composition topics for her, and gave her advice
on clothes just as she had once done for her own two sisters. For
her part, young Julia became fast friends with Herbert, just her
age, who enjoyed playing "chess or dominoes" with the girl.
"George," Julia reported, "dont have a thing to do with [us] as
he is *going to college.* We study up in Aunt Maggie's room. Uncle
Preston stays down in the library and reads or smokes."[57]

As for her sons, Maggie's maternal feelings are revealed in a
poem she wrote, entitled "Georgie and Herbert's Letter." Really
a rhymed letter, it was one she sent to the two little boys when she

was vacationing at Rockbridge Baths (a nearby spa) in August of 1867. The children were nine and six, old enough that their mother dared not call them "*my babies* any more." She imagined them playing baseball, climbing trees, riding horseback, and "romp[ing] the live-long day." She wondered whether they were being good, whether they had learned their catechism, and whether they had "gone always cheerfully to bed/ Whenever Mammy bade you!" At the end, Maggie told them how much she missed them:

> I'm longing for you, dears! I pine
> To feel your lips fast kissing mine:
> I often sit and sigh—'If only
> My boys were here to talk and laugh,
> I would not be so still and lonely,
> All thro' the dreamy day—by half!'
> Ah well!—a week or two—and then
> We'll be together all again:
> Good-bye; God bless you! Love each other,
> And don't forget the *little mother*.[58]

As her boys matured, Maggie became concerned that they were not serious students, and she was disappointed that they were not more interested in literary subjects. "They used to rhyme when they were quite little," she wrote to Paul Hayne, "but they have even lost their taste for poetry now—to my chagrin." [59] George, entering Washington and Lee in February of 1874 at age fifteen, when his half-brother John was a senior, made poor grades in both mathematics and French. The following year his grades were not much better, and his professor complained about the "number of unexcused absences" he had incurred. "In most cases," the teacher noted, "*examinations* and *skating* have been offered as excuses."[60] Hoping that a different environment would provide new challenges, George's concerned parents sent him to Hampden-Sydney College, near Farmville, Virginia. After two years away from home, he returned to Washington and Lee, took his degree, and went on to study medicine at the University of Pennsylvania. Herbert seems to have had greater affinity for college work. Washington and Lee awarded him a bachelor of arts degree in 1881 and a law degree three years later.

The departure of her own sons was harder for Maggie to adjust to than the absence of her stepchildren. When both boys finally settled in Baltimore, Maggie wrote to a cousin, "We are lonely beyond everything here since Bert went away. But we would not on any account recall him, for it is such a comfort to us to think that he has gotten actually to work; and I am sure he feels a great deal happier himself."[61]

The Baltimore area was already familiar to the Prestons because, beginning in 1874, they were spending part of every summer with Elizabeth Allan, her husband, and the increasing number of grandchildren at the McDonogh School. Here, in the quiet of the school's rural setting, Maggie found time and leisure to write without interruption:

Hours winnowed of care—
Days hedged from interruption, and withdrawn
Inviolate from household exigence.[62]

And write she did. In the years after the publication of her first book in 1870, she saw more than one hundred of her poems published, not only in regional magazines (such as the *The Southern Churchman* and *Southern Bivouac*) and children's journals (*Wide Awake* and *St. Nicholas*), but also in national periodicals of distinction like *Lippincott's*, the New York *Evening Post*, *Harper's Monthly*, *Literary World*, *The Critic*, *The Century*, and the *Atlantic Monthly.**

In 1873, with a large number of uncollected poems already published, Maggie decided to attempt another book, one she called *Cartoons,* or "little pictures."⁶³ When the head of a Boston publishing company, James R. Osgood, rejected the manuscript, Maggie wrote in great discouragement to Paul Hayne. He replied that she should not be put off by a single rejection: "Perhaps *no one* in this country can enter into, comprehend, or more fully appreciate your present condition of feeling, than myself!" Like her, he had come to "an ever strengthening conviction that the Southern writer—particularly, the *Southern* Poet, must be content with only *partial* recognition from the *Litterateurs* of the North." But she must not give in to discouragement. Earlier in the same letter he had written, "You are a *born Poet* and a *made Artist;*—write! sing! . . . Your literary position is assured; and being in the noonday of your powers, you must not speak, write, or *dream* of *giving up!*" Instead, he advised her to "rest upon your oars . . . wait for brighter times, and a fairer opportunity."⁶⁴

Taking her friend's advice, Maggie sent the manuscript to Roberts Brothers of Boston, which published it in 1875, under a contract that required Maggie to pay all costs. Dedicated to Elizabeth Preston Allan, *Cartoons* is divided into three categories: thirteen poems in the "Life of the Masters," nineteen "cartoons" in the "Life of the Legends," and a final thirty-four in the "Life of To-Day." The first grouping (vaguely imitative of some of Robert Browning's poems) offers imaginary conversations by and

---

*Her poems also came out in journals less well known today, such as *Aldine's Magazine,* 1869–1879; *Baldwin's,* a trade magazine published and given away free by New York City clothiers, 1870–1886 (Paul Hamilton Hayne also published in its issues); *Home Journal,* a family-oriented New York weekly, 1846–1900; *South Atlantic,* published in Wilmington, North Carolina, 1877–1882; the *New York Independent,* a nonsectarian religious newspaper with headquarters in New York and Boston; and *Shakesperiana,* a " critical and contemporary view of Shakesperian literature," published in New York City between 1883 and 1893.

between artists of the Italian Renaissance. The next consists of short poems, with traditional rhyme scheme and meter, that utilize stories of saints and other Anglo-Saxon and European legends. The final grouping includes poems about individuals, most of them contemporaries of Maggie's (Lee, Jackson, Charles Kingsley, Edgar Allan Poe, and Henry Wadsworth Longfellow), and short rhymed essays on religious or devotional subjects.

Though Maggie never again experienced the same thrill from seeing a book of hers in print as she felt when *Old Song and New* appeared, she must have been pleased by the sale of *Cartoons* and by the praise it received from literary critics. The book eventually went into three printings, and most reviewers were favorable. The critic in *Lippincott's Magazine* wrote that "poems of so much vigor as these give fair promise for the future, and deserve more than merely general commendation."[65] A notice in an 1883 issue of *The Critic* (written when the third edition of *Cartoons* appeared) was even more favorable, suggesting that the author combines "virile energy and feminine sympathy and charm."[66] Though the poems in *Cartoons* are more polished than those in her earlier collection, modern readers probably find them intellectually interesting but curiously devoid of personal feeling. One has the sense that Maggie was trying to please the public with narrative and dramatic verse popularized by such well-known poets as Tennyson and Browning but was reluctant to express her true emotions through her poetry.

Driving herself too hard as usual, Maggie became ill in January of 1872, "invalided again," she wrote, as the result of Lexington's "terrible winter climate [which] half-kills me."[67] At the end of March, she wrote to Paul Hayne that she still had debilitating pain in her eyes and general indisposition. "I have been confined to the house most of the time since Xmas," she said, "and have in that time grown a decade older."[68] Congratulating Hayne on the success of his new book of poetry, *Legends and Lyrics*, she herself admitted to being depressed because her book was not selling well and several of her poems had been rejected by magazine editors.

But her spirits and health improved immeasurably in April when she learned of Great Britain's enthusiastic reception of one of her newer poems, "Sandringham," in which she had written about the international concern over the serious illness of the Prince of Wales, news of whose sickness had been reported quickly through means of the new oceanic cable. "Sandringham," she confided to Paul Hayne, had been read aloud by "Mr. Gladstone on the floor of Parliament," where the prime minister called it a "poem of more than ordinary merit."[69] Hayne replied that he was happy over her new accolade. The public recognition of "Sandringham" and its reprinting in the *London Cosmopolitan* would bring credit, he believed, not only upon herself, but also "to Southern letters."[70]

The poem begins with Virginians' concern for the thirty-one-year-old prince:

> Even here, within Sir Walter's Old Dominion,
>   Among Virginian valleys shut away,
> Meeting, we questioned of the last opinion,—
>   "What tidings come from Sandringham to-day?"

The query moves onto far-flung outposts of the British empire where expatriates learn of the prince's dangerous condition:

> From Hoogly's Mouth to Kyber-Pass went flashing
>   The quick inquiry: Where Australia's spray
> Closed o'er dropt anchors, through the breakers dashing,
>   Sailors cried—"What of Sandringham to-day?"

Finally, news of recovery comes to cheer the hearts of all loyal

British subjects:

> In every English home,—by Scottish ingle,—
>   At Ireland's hearths;—on lone Welsh mountains gray,
> All hearts now with the girdling gladness tingle,
>   —"There's life,—hope,—health, at Sandringham
>   to-day!"[71]

That same year Maggie achieved a triumph of a different sort, as eighteen hymns she had written were included in a new Southern Presbyterian hymnbook, called *The Voice of Praise*. When the new hymnal (designed primarily for use by Sunday school children) was presented to the General Assembly in open session, she was singled out for commendation. None of her hymns is in use today, but as the daughter of a minister and a woman who had grown up singing psalms and hymns all her life, Maggie must have found such praise in her own time especially meaningful.

Yet in spite of the public recognition her poetry received, Maggie's satisfaction in writing and in reviewing books was always tinged with a sense of guilt, as demonstrated by her continued insistence that domestic and familial responsibility must have first place in her life:

> I think I can truly say that I never neglected
> the concocting of a *pudding* for the sake of a
> *poem* or a *sauce* for a *sonnet*! Art is
> a jealous mistress—and I have only served
> her with my left hand, because I have given
> my right hand to what has seemed more
> pressing and important.[72]

With candor, she added that she was "quite sure that I have never accomplished what I might have done, if I had concentrated whatever is in me" only upon the art of writing poetry "which after all was my dear delight." [73] If she had taken time to polish and refine her work, she might well have achieved more lasting recognition.

Church work also prevented Maggie from spending as much time as she might have wished on her literary endeavors. In 1873 she and Colonel Preston designed and built an outpost chapel for dock workers on the North River, a chapel she called Beechenbrook because she paid for its construction with proceeds from her first successful book. A few years later she helped form the first Women's Missionary Society in her local church and served as its secretary.

With the publication of two books and the frequent appearance of her poetry in national journals, Maggie was now deluged with requests from book editors to review the newest publications. "Received from Roberts [the publishing firm in Boston] 13 books today," she noted on December 3, 1870. "That makes 15 I have gotten this week."[74] By her own account she served for the next ten years as "literary critic for three Southern papers and . . . conducted the Editorial criticism of *The* (Baltimore) *Southern Review*."[75] Though her book reviews carried no byline and were paid for only by the gift of review copies, she was nonetheless happy to do the work, grateful that "my little critiques amount to something! This is better than making puddings, and so much more agreeable."[76] She was delighted, she said, "to do anything, however little, toward helping forward the recognition of Southern literature."[77] At the end of 1875, she jotted down her literary accomplishments for that year—360 letters, 46 book notices, and 19 new poems.[78] As her personal library overflowed with books, she became a kind of "lending library" to the community. "I supply almost all Lexington with books & mags," she wrote. "Nobody thinks of buying."[79]

Book editors found her to be an ideal reviewer. Not only did she demand neither pay nor personal recognition, but she was also happy to read and comment on a wide variety of subjects, from biographies of famous artists to cookbooks, from theology to current fiction. In the beginning, she tried to entice readers to dip into the books under review and refrained from adverse criticism. Once, when she had nothing nice to say about a particular book's content, she managed to commend "the attractive largeness of the type and the finely leaded lines."[80] But gradually, as her reputation grew, she became more self-confident and more willing to put her views on paper, even when they were uncomplimentary.

Maggie never pretended to be a professional critic. She simply reviewed books as they came to her, judging them from her own perspective, that of a woman educated beyond the average in the classics and in the Bible, who read widely in such diverse fields as art history and contemporary British and American literature. She favored poets who worked in strict meter, disliked those whom she felt to be vulgar (particularly Walt Whitman), and was surprisingly evenhanded in her treatment of Northern writers like Louisa May Alcott.*

Maggie's views were like those of many of her contemporaries. From today's viewpoint, however, some of her critiques seem dated, such as her comments that William Cullen Bryant's "Thanatopsis" was the "most finished" American poem yet written and that Henry Wadsworth Longfellow was the "dearest of all our singers."[81] But she also was perceptive enough to acknowl-

---

*MJP, in her review of *Little Women*, suggests that Alcott "wields . . . a potent influence. . . . What man in these United States has produced direct impressions . . . upon tens of thousands . . . of young minds. . . ? Only here and there, when she runs a tilt with the lance of her New England prejudice in her hand, is there ever anything we would wish altered. Would it were possible to have our Southern life-habits . . . portrayed with the absolute verity with which Miss Alcott has reproduced the young life of New England!" (review in Scrapbook IV:36).

edge the ability of a writer like Oscar Wilde, despite her dislike of his use of sensual language "which the eye of any pure woman would shrink from. . . . He sings," she wrote, "with the pipe of Pan. . . . The poison flower is all the more dangerous because of its bewildering beauty."[82]

Though she reviewed a wide range of books, Maggie gave special treatment to two groups of authors, women and Southerners. Whether or not she cared personally for all the books about or by women that were sent to her, she managed to champion the place of women in literature. She was even more ardent in advocating a high profile for Southern writers, who, she believed, were frequently ignored by regional readers and by critics in both South and North.

When she reviewed Abel Stevens' biography of *Madame de Staël*, for example, Maggie praised the book as "the classic in all that relates to the career of this wonderful woman."[83] She commented that Maria Edgeworth (the subject of a new biography by Helen Zimmern) was "unquestionably a very remarkable woman . . . one of the most literary women of her day." In the same review Maggie mentioned other female writers whose biographies had recently been published by the same company. A new biography of Emily Brontë Maggie considered to be "full of deep interest and painful pathos," and she felt that Margaret Fuller's biography was "a sympathetic, but not overpartial delineation of [a] remarkable woman."[84] She enjoyed reading *The Life of Mary Russell Mitford: Told by Herself, in Letters to Her Friends*, not only because of the number of letters written to Elizabeth Barrett Browning, whom she considered "the greatest of all female poets," but also because the book was filled with "racy anecdote, bits of . . . criticism, literary gossip, personal history—all . . . entertaining."[85] She gave high praise to Harriet Martineau's concern for others—"[her] benevolent helpfulness eager and ungrudging; her bravery not to be questioned; her sympathy for the 'bruised classes,' of the most emphatic sort; her indignation against what she conceived wrong, very pronounced." Still, she found Martineau's *Autobiography* to be a "painful" book, filled with "sharp, acid judgment passed upon her contemporaries," whose "faults [come] out clearer to her vision than virtues."[86] Though she admired the "high religious tone" of certain poems of Christina Rossetti, she disliked the overall "melancholy" of her work, as well as the liberties she took with meter:

> one wail over lost youth, dead hopes,
> defeated life, vanished love, and ineffectual
> endeavor. . . . Miss Rossetti's rhythm, as well
> as rhyme, has always been faulty. . . . She is a
> law unto herself in regard to most of her
> metres, and writes so many pieces in feet of
> such scant measure, that they hobble along
> like baby-jingles. [87]

Maggie was more consistently complimentary when she wrote about contemporary Southern writers. Calling her husband's old friend, Edgar Allan Poe, a "strange rare poet" and an "erratic genius,"[88] she regretted the slurs that had been made on his character and the poverty in which he died. In a poem written for a Poe memorial celebration held at the New York Academy of Music, she rejoiced that:

> *He is avenged to-night!* No blur is shrouding
> The flame his genius feeds
>
> . . . .
>
> —Can we call no man happy till he dies?[89]

She praised Thomas Nelson Page's "incomparable dialect stories"[90] and admired George Washington Cable's story, *The*

Grandissimes, in direct contrast to the view of Paul Hayne, who called Cable "a miserable little *ci-devant* Clerk & Parvenue [and] a *thorough Yankee in blood.*"[91] In her review of *The Poems of Henry Timrod*, edited by Hayne, she paid glowing tribute both to the editor and to the poet: "Timrod's life could not have been as fitly prepared by any other than that of his friend Mr. Hayne. . . . The editing of it has been purely a labor of love." Timrod's poems, she felt, were full of "unstrained pathos . . . vivid, natural emotion . . . clear directness . . . [and] polished but simple rhythms . . . wonderfully free from the problem-haunted spirit and . . . the perplexing mysticism which underlie so much of modern poetry."[92] Maggie's highest praise she saved for Hayne himself, declaring in 1886 that her friend was "what he aspired to be, the Poet of his Southern Land . . . who excels in both prose and poetry."[93] When his book *Legends and Lyrics* appeared in 1872, she called it "the truest book of poems that has ever come from a Southern singer. There is none in the range of my knowledge that can compare with it in fine polished, artistic work—real poet-work."[94]

Not satisfied merely to champion Southern literature in her reviews, Maggie also tried to influence magazine editors and friends to give greater attention to Southern writers. In a letter to Professor W. M. Baskerville of Vanderbilt, she wrote that "if Southern literateurs were more ready . . . to notice the books of their section; there would be much more encouragement given to Southern literature."[95] Addressing G. Watson James of the Richmond *Standard*, she urged him to accept a favorable review of a book by John Esten Cooke, because "we are so apathetic in regard to the claims of our own people."[96] In an attempt to help improve sales of the *New Eclectic Magazine*, she asked Paul Hayne to "speak a good word for [its editors] in one of your Georgia papers. . . . If *it* fails, through the inertia and apathy of the Southern people," she wrote, "then farewell to any attempt to sustain a magazine south of Philadelphia."[97] As to her own poetry, she commented bitterly that "I don't think *three* lines were ever printed in Virginia in notice of *Old Song and New*. I utterly despair of the Southern Editors lending the end of their little fingers to the advance of home-literature."[98]

In 1881 Maggie wrote a long essay entitled "The Literary Profession in the South" in which she spoke of why there had been few professional writers in the antebellum South—lack of patronage and the limited number of Southern readers, as well as what she felt were peculiarly Southern traits, a general "distaste for work of any kind," the popular notion that male writers were "just a trifle effeminate," and an arrogant regionalism that led many to feel "content with ourselves just as we are."[99] Despite this gloomy analysis of the past, Maggie was encouraged by the postwar renewal of centers of learning, the revived importance of the work ethic, and a lively new cross-fertilization of ideas and books between North and South. In her final paragraph, she envisioned a renascence of Southern letters that would use the region's rich heritage as it was refined through the tragedy of war:

> A bright and attractive future, then, we
> believe is about to open before those among
> us who may hereafter give themselves to
> letters. With the possession of genius,
> which nature has not made a matter of
> geography; with the full equipment which a
> thorough culture demands; with the
> priceless inheritance of the richest historic
> associations; with a marvelously
> picturesque past, whose local coloring is
> the fairest which this transatlantic land
> affords; with the material prosperity which
> in time must come . . . what is there to hinder

this wide, vast South from taking its
position as a leader in the world of letters,
as the equal and peer of the North? [100]

Her prophecy was accurate, but it was not to be fulfilled for almost half a century, when William Faulkner, Robert Penn Warren, and Eudora Welty burst upon the American literary scene.

Maggie made her reputation by her books, her reviews, and her essays. But of all her creative activities, she seems to have enjoyed writing letters the best. She corresponded with such prominent figures as Whittier, Longfellow, the critic Edmund Clarence Stedman, and the editor John Reuben Thompson. She enjoyed hearing from "a Scotch friend of my mother's—who writes me from North Castle, Wigtonshire," as well as from Sophia Gilmore, a correspondent in Maine who initiated a fifteen-year correspondence because of her appreciation of Maggie's poetry. And she had other far-flung correspondents, from such English writers as Jean Ingelow and the blind poet Philip Bourke Marston, to missionaries in Hangchow, China, and "the Kyber Pass on the upper Indus."[101]

The person with whom Maggie most enjoyed corresponding was her friend Paul Hamilton Hayne. With him she could speak freely of her hopes and dreams for her literary career, ask for and give critical advice, complain about the unkindness of publishers and critics, and receive welcome encouragement to continue her creative work. The two poets had much in common—poor health, a sense of isolation far from centers of cultural ferment, and the need to fight against personal discouragement and public apathy. His letters always cheered her up. "I hardly know where to begin to express my gratitude," she wrote him in 1873, for "yr delightfully long letter—so full of pleasant talk and sentiment and nice criticism."[102]

In return Hayne found her letters wonderfully meaningful. "I *must answer* your beautiful & affectionate communication at once," he wrote on July 26, 1878. "Its thoughtfulness, its concern for my welfare, bodily & spiritual, its profoundly religious tone . . . all these things combine to make your letter a memorable one, dear to my *heart*, & understanding alike."[103] He wondered whether she could truly comprehend "the real value I place upon your correspondence."[104] He found it amazing that the two of them, living so far apart and never having met in person, could find so much meaning in the letters from the other. "It is a sweet thought to me," he told her, "that you and I—lonely workers in the field of Southern literature—can exchange (as it were) such artistic and poetic confidences."[105] Near the end of his life he tried once more to express how much her letters had meant to him over the years: "What you have been to me, O! dearest of Friends, as a literary Adviser and invaluable Critic in the by gone years, is known only to God, & to my own grateful & affectionate Heart."[106]

Throughout the years of their correspondence, Paul Hayne had suffered from poor health, "oppression on the chest," "a strange difficulty of breathing," and "*nervous* exhaustion coupled with *dyspepsia*."[107] By 1886 his condition had deteriorated to such a degree that Maggie wrote in alarm to Mrs. Hayne, asking for the latest medical news and voicing her sorrow that the two of them had never met: "How bitterly I regret the failure of all my endeavors to have you pay me a visit three years ago; to think that we should be friends so long, and yet never have met!"[108]

Paul Hamilton Hayne died on July 6, 1886. As soon as she heard the sad news, Maggie wrote an emotional letter of condolence to his widow:

> The world to me seems the poorer now that
> this friend has left us. How I shall miss his

letters, his unvarying sympathy, his tender
and kind words! I never had as true a
literary friend, nor one I verily believe, who
was so interested in me.[109]

In the spring of 1882, four years before his death, Hayne had
been awarded (*in absentia*) an honorary LL.D. from Washington
and Lee University, which at the same time conferred an identical
degree upon Colonel Preston on the occasion of his retirement.
Now with her husband home much of the day, Maggie and the
colonel spent more and more time together. They read aloud to
each other, using William Cullen Bryant's translation of the *Iliad*.
He assisted her in various ways to adjust to her increasing deafness, and she nursed him through recurring bouts of the malaria
he had contracted as a young man. When they celebrated their
twenty-fifth wedding anniversary, Preston presented Maggie with
a "silver box holding 25 silver dollars" and a poem. The latter
must have been especially precious to Maggie because of its lines,
its Latin terms, and its symbols of special meaning to them both.
Using the word "lustrum" to describe each five-year period of
their marriage,* Preston played upon the theme of the silver
coins, "circlets," he said, that had been stamped, not with an
emperor's visage, but rather with the "die of Love's delight":

> Five lustrums passed, of which each year
> Hath been a circlet pure and clear,
> Of steady splendor mildly bright,
> Stamped with the die of Love's delight. . .
> So be the future, day by day,

---

*The word "lustrum" was used in ancient Rome to designate the census
taken every five years, hence a five-year period. Preston's choice of the term
seems unusually appropriate, since both he and Maggie were students of Roman
and Greek antiquity.

With thankful hearts, dear wife, we pray,
On this our Silver Wedding Day.—Augt. 3, 1882[110]

Ever since the publication of her first book, *Old Song and New*, Maggie's health had been slowly declining, with hearing loss, aching joints, and severe pain in the eyes. "The old trouble that darkened so many years of my early life return[s] in measure upon me," Maggie had written to Paul Hayne in 1878. "I mean the vexation of my eyes. The persistent pain *behind* and *straight thro'* the ball has been of a two-months duration."[111] In 1882 she undertook an unusually heavy writing schedule, publishing six poems and working on a long introduction for the complete edition of Hayne's poetry.[112] The resulting eye strain and tormenting headaches were so severe that Colonel Preston persuaded her to visit an eye specialist in Baltimore, who assured her that she would not go blind, "at least not now." Unwilling to remain in Baltimore for further treatment, she hurried back to Lexington because "my old Darling [is] at home alone," but she was frightened enough that for the first time she began to use a "blind writer," a kind of slate.[113] Six months later, after more bouts of pain, she had another consultation with the Baltimore physician. This time he discovered that she had serious deterioration of the optic nerve in one eye. The new diagnosis and the doctor's proscription against any use of her eyes "fill me with gloom and apprehension," she wrote in a dictated letter to Paul Hayne. "I feel as if the cords of fate are . . . tightning around me."[114]

In an attempt to relieve her despondency, Colonel Preston in 1884 persuaded Maggie to travel to England and the Continent. It was an adventure he had been planning for years, ever since 1861, when he wrote in his wartime diary: "I think some times I will take Maggie over the sea. How her rich sense would revel there. How her stores replete with historic information and poetic fancy would bring out for her enjoyment and mine everything most noteworthy."[115] Now, twenty-one years after his dream, he insisted that they make the trip together, along with their son George, now a physician; her sister, Julia Fishburn; and two of her brothers, George and William Junkin.

Crisscrossing England and Scotland in a leisurely fashion, the party visited Canterbury, London, Oxford, Stratford, Kenilworth, the Lake Country, and Edinburgh, before crossing the channel to France, Switzerland, Germany, and Belgium. Maggie found "every inch of this English ground" to be marvelously "historic—every foot is instinct with immortal dust." She loved the quiet beauty of Lake Windermere and Lake Grasmere, "redolent all over with the memories of Wordsworth, Southey . . . Hartley Coleridge, Harriet Martineau, Dr. Arnold, and a host of others." At every turn she found echoes of familiar literary figures: "I have dreamed of poor Amy Rosart among the walls of Kenilworth, and sat in Shakespeare's chair in the house where he was born and roved over grand Christ [Church] College and the galleries of the Bodleian Library at Oxford."[116] But the most meaningful place in England for her was Cripplegate Church, where Milton had worshiped before he lost his eyesight:

> I stand with reverence at the altar-rail
> O'er which the soft rose-window sheds its dyes,
> And looking up, behold in pictured guise
> Its choir of singing cherubs—Heaven's *All Hail*
> Upon each lip, and on each brow a trail
> Of golden hair;—for here the Poet's eyes
> Had rested, dreaming dreams of Paradise,
> As on yon seat he sat, ere yet the veil
> Of blindness had descended.
>   Who shall say,
> That when the "during dark" had steeped his sight,

And on the ebon tablet flashed to view
His Eden with its angels, mystic bright,
There swept not his unconscious memory through,
The quiring cherubs that I see to-day! [117]

New scenes in Europe recalled for her verses of Goethe and
Byron, as well as passages in Ruskin, Voltaire, and Madame de
Staël. Switzerland's beauty enchanted her, and she was moved by
"Calvin's haunts" in Geneva, the "gloomy prison-house" of
Chillon, the Flemish art galleries of Antwerp, and "the dear,
strange, old-world city" of Dijon, France.[118] Altogether, she
found the long summer's trip to be "splendid from first to last,
even including the sea-sickness."[119] When she reached home, she
wrote to Paul Hayne that "my Golden Summer is over and gone,
and I'll never have such another." Now, she said, she could face
eventual blindness because "my picture gallery of memory is
hung . . . with glorious frescoes which blindness cannot blot or
cause to fade."[120]

To her surprise and delight she discovered that her vision, if
not improved, had at least not deteriorated. Somehow over the
next two years she found enough energy—and eyesight—to write
a series of sketches about her European journey, publishing them
in a book entitled *A Handful of Monographs* in 1886. The same
year she finished a manuscript copy of a little volume she called
For Love's Sake, published five new poems, and completed her
long essay on Tom Jackson, which was published in *The Century
Magazine*. She had been far more prolific than one might have
expected from a woman with little sight, and there were questions
in various magazines as to whether or not she was really blind.
She was "annoyed beyond expression," she wrote in a dictated
letter to Professor Baskerville, "by having it published far and
wide that I have totally lost my sight. You probably saw this stated
in the July no of Harpers, where it never was denied. All I want

you to know is that I have done all my literary work under great embarrassment, not being able to use my own eyes for reading, writing, proof-correction, or anything. . . . It has affected the quality of my writing, I am sure."[121] Yet despite her insistence that she could still see, her eyes gave her so much trouble that she either dictated her letters or typed them on a primitive typewriter.

For Love's Sake, dedicated to Maggie's sister Julia Fishburn, brought together fifty-seven of her religious and devotional poems, half of which had already appeared in magazines or in one of her earlier collections. Most of the poems concentrated on the sanctity of daily living and homely gifts to be shared with one's fellow man: "Though small/ Your gifts may seem: the Lord hath need of all!"[122] A review in *The Critic* approved of the book's dominant theme, suggesting that she had here "gather[ed] into one vase all the spices and unguents, all the aloes and 'clinging perfumes' of her many devout meditations." The review also praised Maggie for her "mastery of metres of great . . . versatility and [her] facility in the use of complicated verse-forms."[123]

A year later *The Critic* described *Monographs* as a "charming volume of first impressions of Europe . . . a volume made up of isolated 'monographs,' as she calls them." Travel books were much in vogue during the latter part of the nineteenth century, and Maggie had several in her library. In *Monographs* she had made no attempt to offer a guided tour but rather had provided her own enthusiastic response to English and European treasures. This approach was commended in *The Critic*'s review, which endorsed the book's "wealth of contents and power of spirited portrayal."[124]

In the same year, 1887, Maggie compiled her last major book of poetry, *Colonial Ballads*, a collection of 150 sonnets, ballads (many of them based on pre-Revolutionary themes), and short poetic sketches of famous artists gathered into a section entitled "Childhood of the Masters." Reviews were in general favorable,

The Critic calling the author of *Colonial Ballads* a "writer of high gifts. She has ring, rhythm, imagination, force . . . this volume is full of delightful things that ring the changes of her versatility." The reviewer mentioned, however, a single flaw—"a fatal elegance about her work which mars our law of spontaneity."[125]

Such a comment would once have concerned Maggie, but she had now lost much of her enthusiasm for publishing. Her husband was not well, her deafness was cutting her off from ordinary conversation, and her failing eyesight made her dependent upon others for both reading and writing. Julia Fishburn predicted accurately in the fall of 1887 that she would not publish a major book again. "My sister," Julia wrote, "says she is done, she is never going to publish any more!"[126] The two books Maggie had completed in 1887 were indeed her last major publications, though in 1889 she did issue a short volume of children's verse, *Chimes for Church Children*.

She had always been averse to giving out biographical information about herself—"I have been asked a hundred times, more or less, for material to make personal sketches of myself and I have as often refused the data required."[127] However, in the 1880s, she permitted two women journalists to visit her in her Lexington home. From the composite of their descriptions, one can gain an interesting picture of the poet at the height of her literary and personal success. The reporter for *Woman's Magazine* spoke primarily about the Preston home, with its commodious rooms, its tasteful furnishings supplied and arranged by Maggie, and the breathtaking view of the mountains from the rooms' wide windows. The parlor, she wrote, was a "large, square room, hung with curtains of lace falling in graceful folds to the floor, which is carpeted with warm colors of mingled red and oak . . . [with] broad fire-places, and generous windows . . . commanding a view of the Blue Ridge." On tables and walls were memorabilia from relatives' trips abroad and portraits of Stonewall Jackson and such literary figures as "Bryant, Longfellow, Holmes, and Lowell." Crowded onto bookshelves were "several thousand volumes" from her parents' library, Colonel Preston's collections, and the many books she had been asked to review through the years.[128]

In this room, redolent of the arts, a *Washington Post* reporter, Laura Holloway, conducted her interview in 1888. At sixty-eight, Maggie was now "inclined to stoutness," Holloway noticed, with her "rich auburn hair . . . thickly sprinkled with gray." But she had retained a "dignity of carriage" and a clear, gentle voice, "tender and modulated to suit a disposition most quiet and retiring." Behind her spectacles, Maggie's eyes were "as blue and as bright as they were in girlhood."[129] As she approached the age of seventy, Maggie had lost none of her charm.

In 1889 William Allan died, and his widow, Elizabeth, returned to live in Lexington. Though the Prestons were saddened for her sake, they were delighted to have her near them again. Elizabeth's oldest brother, Thomas, was also now living in Lexington, pastor of the local Presbyterian church. In the days of his declining health, with one severe illness after another, Colonel Preston found comfort in having nearby two of his three surviving children from his first marriage.

In March of 1890, Maggie wrote to Mrs. Paul Hayne that her husband was in very poor health, with "a long and wearisome illness. . . . Of course I have been distracted with anxiety. . . . You can well understand that I have had little time to give to anything else."[130] Exhausted with nursing, she was brusque and understandably cross, a month later, when she answered a query from Professor Baskerville, who had written her for literary information. "I have been watching for ten weeks over my sick husband," she wrote, "and when I tell you that only this morning, has he been having the Scripture passages which he wants read at his death-bed, prepared and copied, you will understand, perhaps, of how little moment all other interests are to me."[131] Preston was to live on until mid-summer, dying during the night of Tuesday, July 15. Maggie and all the children were with him.

He was buried the next day in the Preston plot, after a simple service at the Presbyterian church. (One of the officiating ministers at the funeral was the husband of Julia Rush Junkin, who had spent the winter of 1874–75 with the Prestons.) For many in Lexington, his death marked the end of an era, the departure of one of the community's most familiar citizens. He had been the oldest living member of his church and the oldest native-born Lexingtonian. Townspeople remembered him as the founder of VMI, "a gaunt old man with piercing blue eyes, white of hair, almost stern of mien who could quote at any length from the Bible."[132] Without question he had been the most influential man in the area, as his friend Professor James Harrison noted: "A power in the town, a power in the church, a power in the lecture-room, and a power in his home."[133]

Months later, these accolades would bring some comfort to Maggie. But at the moment of his death, she only knew that she had lost her life's companion, the father of her children, the man who had inspired her fiercest devotion and her gentlest care. To be sure, there had been times when he had irritated her, but the quarrels were forgotten in the sweet memories of passionate young love and quieter old age. Her husband's death also ended the joy she once had taken in literary activity. "I have given up writing entirely," she wrote, "and have cut off most of my literary correspondents, for which I have no heart now."[134] She had willingly given up writing for the sake of her husband. Then, during the war, he had asked her to "sing to me, Maggie." For thirty years she had responded. Without him, her pleasure in singing was over.

Chapter 7

Singing Her Own Song
1890–1897

> So let me sing because I must,
>   To nature's order clinging,
> Nor seek, with conscious aim, to thrust
>   Myself into my singing.[1]

M aggie was seventy years old when her husband died. She had lived in the Preston home for nearly half of her life, and understandably she felt threatened and disoriented when the house was put up for sale.* "I was obliged to give up my lovely home of thirty years," she told a friend in Maine, "and break up a thousand holy associations connected with it . . . even now its grounds are being divided into building lots."[2] Equally distressing was the distribution of the treasures inside the house, items that had been there when she married or that she had accumulated over a third of a century.† Four years earlier, sympathizing with Mrs. Paul Hayne on the loss of her husband, Maggie had commented on the importance of inanimate objects when one loses a loved one. "I see you looking round on his books, his papers, his writing desk, his chair, his piles of letters," she wrote, "with an anguish of feeling that can find no expression."[3] Now with the dispersal of possessions intimately associated with her husband, Maggie experienced the kind of loss she had once imagined to be the lot of Hayne's widow.

The original plan had been that, once arrangements were complete, Maggie would move to Baltimore to live in a small house near George and his family. Before she could make the change, however, she suffered a serious stroke that left her paralyzed on one side. Nearly blind, almost totally deaf, and unable to walk without assistance, she had no hope now of living by herself. Indeed, her condition was so fragile that she could not even endure the journey to Maryland. So she made a temporary move to Elizabeth Allan's house on Main Street, a few blocks from the

---

*J. T. L. Preston's will stipulated that his estate, "real and personal," was to be divided among his heirs "as it would have been had I died intestate." In order to comply with this provision, his executors, Thomas and Herbert Preston, evidently had to dispose of much of the real estate, including the house (Will of J. T. L. Preston, Will Book #2, 1874–1904, Rockbridge "Old" Circuit Court, pages 246–49, County Courthouse, Lexington, Virginia).

†The will also specified that "silver, library, and pictures" were to be divided "share and share alike." Janet Allan Bryan, J. T. L. Preston's granddaughter, remembered vividly the day that her mother, Elizabeth Preston Allan, and other relatives divided up the various items in the household (Janet Allan Bryan to Herbert Preston, Jr., September 7, 1957; letter given to the author by Mrs. Herbert Preston, Jr.).

beloved old homestead. Though she had always felt close to her stepdaughter—"I am very comfortable with Elizabeth Allan and her dear young children," she said—the boisterous youngsters made her nervous, and she longed for familiar and quiet surroundings. "I dare not speak of the anguish of my desolate home," she told Mrs. Hayne, "now being altered so as to destroy all its hallowed associations for me. I never want to look upon it again."[4]

In the past she had often tried to imagine how it would feel to be isolated from others. As her deafness increased, she wrote to a friend in 1886 of her worry that she might someday "become shut out from my fellow creatures,"[5] and she wondered how she would react when "left . . . a prisoner still in . . . [her] room."[6] In a rhymed letter to an invalid, Maggie identified with the "patient sufferer" in her "quiet invalid chair" who feared that old friends would forget her:

> Outside of my lonely chamber,
>   Do they think of me often yet?
>
> As they meet in the daily places,
>   Smiling and talking about
> A thousand things—is always
>   The invalid's name left out?[7]

Now Maggie herself sat in the invalid's chair, and she worried that she would be forgotten, not only by neighbors, but also by literary friends and correspondents. She was to experience no such isolation, however. Though she complained that "time drags heavily with me often,"[8] she kept surprisingly busy, with the help of a "sweet girl amanuensis,"[9] answering letters of condolence and concern. The Allan children, sitting close and shouting into her hearing trumpet, read books to her and rolled her out on the porch each day so that she might feel the fresh air, even if she was unable to hear the sounds or see the sights of the neighborhood.

A few months after her move Maggie received requests to write two commemorative poems. Twice before during the decade she had written odes for special occasions. Calling upon her intimate knowledge of the college and her friendship with Robert E. Lee, she had composed in 1885 a twenty-five-stanza poem entitled *Centennial Poem: 1775–1885* for Washington and Lee,* which ended with a call to future greatness:

> Ye will not walk ignoble ways:
> Ye dare not seek unworthy aims:
> Ye cannot do a deed that shames
> These heroes of our holiest days!
> Your oath a Roman oath must be,
> Sworn with a faith that will not yield—
> Sworn on the doubly sacred shield
> Of WASHINGTON and LEE![10]

And in 1889 she had written a special piece for VMI's semicentennial celebration. On this occasion she dwelt at length on Jackson's association with the Institute, his leadership during the Civil War, and his death, and she brought the poem to a climax by describing the monumental task that her husband and other faculty members had to face in rebuilding the gutted school after the war:

> O'ermastered, beaten, ruined, lost,—

*The title of the poem suggests that late in the nineteenth century, college officials considered 1775 to be the real beginning of the college, when "the academy in Augusta [County]" was brought under the patronage of the Presbytery of Hanover and a collegiate curriculum established (Crenshaw, 3). Today Washington and Lee traces its origins back to 1749, to the establishment of the fledgling academy in the Valley of Virginia.

The past a wreck, the future tossed
On seething billows, black as death,

. . . .

So, back again, they came,
To rear new walls above the ashes,

. . . .

Prepared to pluck, with one strong aim,
Triumph from fell defeat.[11]

Both odes, well received, were promptly published as small booklets.

Now, in 1891, the trustees of McDonogh School in Baltimore wanted her to write a poem for the dedication of a bust of the school's first headmaster, William Allan. Maggie wondered if she had the strength to compose anything, especially since she would have to dictate it. Still, she was eager to make the attempt as a tribute to Elizabeth's husband. "You may feel assured that it is my desire to add even a little if I can to the interest of the occasion," she told the requesting committee, "for in no one's estimation did Col. Allan stand higher than in mine." She promised that "if I find within the next week or two . . . my condition of health will admit of this much mental exercise and if it turns out that what I may write is worth sending on to you, I will let you know."[12] The poem was dictated, sent off by mail, and read at McDonogh School on November 21, 1891, just prior to the unveiling of Allan's bust. Friends and students were touched by her tribute to William Allan's dedication to teaching and by her recollection of his early death:

Boys of McDonogh! each who owns
The pathos of this life's pure story,
Remember,—ye are living stones
Set in the temple of his glory—

.   .   .   .
—His monument is all around us![13]

A member of the audience reported that the recitation of the poem was received "with breathless silence till the last syllable fell."[14]

The second invitation was to write an ode in honor of her old friend, Tom Jackson. His admirers had long hoped to place an appropriate marker over his grave, and twenty years after his death a committee had been formed in Lexington to raise money for a large statue of him for the local cemetery. Maggie had been a member of the ladies' fund-raising organization. As a columnist for state newspapers she had written at length about the Stonewall Jackson Memorial Fair, and she had loaned her precious copy of the painting of Beatrice Cenci for exhibition at the 1886 event. It was fitting, therefore, that she should be asked by the Memorial Association to prepare a poem to be read on July 21, 1891, on the occasion of the official unveiling of the oversized bronze statue by the sculptor Edward V. Valentine.

Perhaps the Jackson committee's invitation—in February of 1891—came too soon after her widowhood for Maggie to undertake composition. Whatever her reasons, she seems to have found it impossible to write a new poem. At the last moment the planning committee decided to use the poem "Slain in Battle" from *Beechenbrook,* which she had written in 1865.

When July 21, the day for the statue's dedication, arrived, Maggie was not well enough to take any part in the elaborate ceremonies. The morning began with speeches and the recitation of poems—Maggie's and others'—on the campus of Washington and Lee. Afterwards, the huge crowd of nearly 25,000 persons surged up Main Street toward the cemetery. Because the weather was exceedingly warm and sunny, Maggie was probably sitting on the porch of Elizabeth's house, across the street and to the south of where the statue stood, but with her poor vision she could only have sensed the excitement in the air and the size of the crowd. Resting quietly in her wheelchair, Maggie would have had her memories to keep her company, recollections of the events and emotions of thirty years earlier when she had opposed Jackson's courtship of her beloved Ellie and then had promised to befriend him. Suddenly, the air was shattered by a fifteen-gun salute by the old Stonewall Battery, indicating that Jackson's grandchildren, Julia and Tom Christian, had pulled the cord to unveil the statue.

After the orators, the veterans, and the local townspeople had departed, one likes to think that perhaps Elizabeth's children wheeled the invalid across the street to stare up with blurred vision at the shining replica of Stonewall Jackson, standing at ease, his gaze directed southwest toward the distant hills, one hand holding his field glasses, the other resting on the scabbard of his sword. What she could not know, that hot July day in 1891, was that Julia Christian, the five-year-old granddaughter who had pulled the cord to unveil Jackson's likeness, would, sixteen years later, marry Maggie's step-grandson, Edmund Randolph Preston, thus bringing together in perpetuity the families of Preston and Jackson.* Maggie had abided by the prohibition against marrying Tom Jackson, but she would have been pleased by this union of a later generation.

Maggie and Mary Anna Jackson had stayed in touch after the war, though their letters and visits were infrequent, in part because of the financial straits in which Mary Anna had found herself

---

*Julia Christian was the daughter of Julia Jackson [Christian], who had been born in 1862 only a few months before Tom Jackson died of his wounds during the Civil War. Jackson's daughter had died two years before her father's statue was unveiled in Lexington. In 1907, when she was twenty years old, Julia Christian married Edmund Randolph Preston, son of John Preston, the lad whom Maggie had first met at Oakland in 1857 soon after her marriage to his father. (Julia Christian Preston was still living but unable to celebrate the centennial of the Jackson statue's unveiling on July 21, 1991. She died two months later, at the age of 104.)

on the death of her husband in May 1863. At his request, much of Jackson's property had been sold at the beginning of the war and the proceeds converted into Confederate bonds, which became worthless after Appomattox. He had also died without a will, and by the time the courts had settled the estate, there was little left to support Mary Anna and her fatherless child. Later she seems to have believed that she was owed a financial settlement on the portion of the tannery and other assets that her husband, at the time of his death, had owned in partnership with Preston, Major Gilham, and Jacob Fuller. But her legal attempts to gain what she believed to be her share failed. (Years later the North Carolina legislature voted her an annual pension of one hundred dollars a month, money she felt obliged to decline because by now she had more than five hundred dollars' worth of personal property.)[15] She must have been keenly aware of the contrast between Maggie's life of financial ease and literary success and her own role as the impoverished, self-effacing widow of one of the South's principal war heroes.

Not long after the dedication of the statue, Mary Anna began writing a "memoir" of her husband, hoping to garner some much-needed additional income. Collecting material and putting it into readable prose proved to be beyond her ability, so she turned to the Reverend Henry M. Field of New York City, with "the urgent request" that he assist her to "revise and edit" what she had assembled. Field, a man of integrity and some editorial skill, found the manuscript chaotic. "The matter was so mixed together," he remarked, "that it was difficult to say where a quotation should begin, or where it should end."[16] Not surprisingly, the manuscript when it was finally prepared for the printers included numerous quotations inserted into the text as though they had been written by Mary Anna herself.

When Harper and Brothers of New York City published *Memoirs of Stonewall Jackson by His Widow* in 1892, Maggie discovered that large portions of her "Personal Reminiscences of Stonewall Jackson" appeared in the narrative with neither quotation marks nor acknowledgment. Concerned on her own behalf and also for the editors of *The Century Magazine*,* she wrote asking for advice from her friend James Harrison, professor of English at the University of Virginia and later an eminent Poe biographer. He replied angrily that he could not "conceive what possesses Mrs. Jackson . . . to act in this childish way. . . . Your copyright—& that of your publishers—should be protected." Mary Anna, he went on, should be forced to "acknowledge her cribbings & refer them to their proper place."[17] A few weeks later, however, after he had thought the matter over more carefully, he advised Maggie "to pass it over in silence. Any other course might rouse a hornet's nest & involve you in personalities."[18]

Meanwhile, Field had learned of Maggie's concern and written a hurried letter to the publishers. Absolving himself from any blame, he urged the editors to write immediately to Maggie with a promise to "make such corrections as shall give the proper place to one whose contributions to Southern history all will recognize."[19] The publishers promptly wrote Maggie a letter filled with profuse apologies. If she would mark the passages that had been quoted from her article without authorization, they assured her that "proper acknowledgment may be made in future editions."[20] Subsequent printings of the book carried an explanatory "note" at the end of the preface: "The appropriate credit for the use of . . . frequent and extended extracts from an interesting article by Mrs. Margaret J. Preston . . . was inadvertently omitted from the first edition of this work, and the Publishers are glad of the opportunity to make this acknowledgment to the author of the article referred to."[21] There is no record to indicate that Mary

---

*Maggie's article, "Personal Reminiscences of Stonewall Jackson," had appeared in *The Century Magazine* six years earlier (*Century* 32 [October 1886]: 927–36).

Anna knew anything about what could easily have erupted into an unpleasant and public incident.*

But neither her concern over plagiarized material nor her effort to write poetry for the McDonogh celebration relieved Maggie's continuing depression. The loss of her husband, she wrote to a friend in Los Angeles, "wrecked me of almost everything—home, spirits, health."[22] Her sense of gloom was intensified by the sudden deaths of several persons close to her—one of Elizabeth Allan's children and a number of Lexington friends who had begun visiting her in her seclusion. Perhaps, she thought, life would be more endurable after she moved to Baltimore. "You will understand," she told a friend, "how naturally a Mother's heart must long after her own sons" and her grandchildren, a little girl and a "splendid little grandson, a year old, whom I have never seen."[23] It was not until December 1892, however, that Maggie was finally well enough to travel north to Maryland.

Dr. George Junkin Preston's home, on one of Baltimore's most fashionable streets, was a large, brick, three-story row house with white marble steps. The young physician, who specialized in women's diseases, had remodeled several rooms on the first floor as his office, and Maggie was grateful, as she put it, to "have my doctor beside me all the time." But, despite her warm reception, Maggie did not find the tranquillity she had hoped for. The strange house and unfamiliar surroundings made her "feel very much as if I were transplanted to another sphere," she wrote. "Here my large airy room faces brick walls and housetops, and when I sit at the library windows, I only see throngs of passers-

---

*Though Maggie said nothing publicly, other family members were unhappy that in her book Mary Anna had scarcely mentioned Jackson's marriage to Ellie. Many years later Mary Anna's granddaughter, Julia Christian Preston, recalled that in 1907 Maggie's son George had told her with some vigor that "your grandmother ignored Ellie" in the *Memoirs*. (postscript of letter from Julia Christian Preston to Margaret Preston [George's daughter], n.d. [1955?], Stonewall Jackson House, Lexington, Virginia).

by" instead of the woods and hills of Virginia. Her one real joy came from the grandchildren, George, Jr., and Margaret, who, she said, "are merry little things. . . . It is not easy to be low-spirited or morose or despairing in their presence." With obvious delight, she went on to describe the children: "George is a beautiful child, very gentle and docile; Margaret is fuller of life, with a very bright face and invariably the mistress in their plays and quarrels."[24] The little girl's red hair and lively personality must have been a great deal like her grandmother's.

One happy surprise about Maggie's new location was that nearby lived a daughter of her old friend and mentor, Charles McCay. After years of serving as a professor and college president in Georgia and South Carolina, McCay had left academic life in 1858 to enter business. In 1872 he had moved his family to Baltimore, where he died three years before Maggie left Lexington.[25] His youngest child, Julia, named for Maggie's mother, now lived with her husband and children almost directly across the street from Dr. George Preston's home. Julia Junkin McCay Buchanan became one of Maggie's scribes, taking the invalid's dictation of four to five letters a day, and listened as well to Maggie's reminiscences of long-ago days at the Manual Labor Academy and Lafayette.

Though she had had no enthusiasm for writing poetry since Colonel Preston's illness and death, Maggie's name continued to appear occasionally in national periodicals. A short poem, "One of God's Little Heroes," was printed in 1890 in the children's magazine *Youth's Companion*. *The Critic* published four of her poems in 1890 and 1891, and another poem, "Poet's Rose," came out in *The Century Magazine* in 1893. During this same period her essay on "Giving Children Right Impressions of Death"* appeared in the *Sunday School Times*.[26] In all likelihood,

---

*In this article in the *Sunday School Times* 33 (November 1891): 708–9, Maggie tells of her early experience when she and her father visited the family of a dead boy in Milton, Pennsylvania (see Chapter 1, pages 16–17).

Maggie had written the essay and the poems—and submitted them for publication—well before Colonel Preston's death.

In addition, she received new attention in response to the appearance in book form of her dialect story, *Aunt Dorothy*, after it had appeared serially in *Harper's Magazine*. *The Critic* gave the tale a short and not especially favorable review, suggesting that "the dialect is ordinary [and] the story only one of the many that have been written of late about life on the Southern plantations."[27] But others were more appreciative. James Harrison, for example, wrote years later that he considered *Aunt Dorothy* to be "a delightfully humorous story of Old Virginia plantation life . . . a story reproducing faces and atmosphere of the Old Dominion long years ago, 'befo' de wah.' The book shows Mrs. Preston's understanding of the negro nature both on its humorous and on its pathetic sides."[28]

But comments about *Aunt Dorothy* and the publication of her poetry had little meaning now for Maggie, confined and helpless as she was. Her family and friends read books to her, and she dictated answers to the letters that came in, but she was too nervous, she said, to meet new people, and she continued to find "city life . . . intensely dreary."[29] In response to one letter from a relative she referred to herself as "your tired and invalid cousin."[30] And, fully aware "that the bottom of the hill is . . . near," she continued to dread the physical experience of dying, the old "fear . . . that has 'held me in bondage' all my life."[31] One day she spoke of her anxiety to Elizabeth Allan when the younger woman came to Baltimore for a visit. Elizabeth told her stepmother about a mutual friend who had died in her sleep, and Maggie exclaimed, "Oh, my dear, pray that my going, which cannot be far off, may be like that!"[32] The Lexington friend's quiet release stayed in her mind, and that evening, in a mood of unusual creativity, she took up her blind slate and wrote out a short lyric she called "Euthanasia." The poem expressed not only her longing to be freed from the fear that had so long gripped her, but also her weariness and a yearning for the unwavering faith Mrs. Junkin had demonstrated years earlier:

> To kneel, all my service complete,
>   All duties accomplished—and then
> To finish my orisons sweet
>   With a trustful and joyous "Amen."
>   .   .   .   .
>
> Without a farewell or a tear,
>   A sob or a flutter of breath,
> Unharmed by the phantom of Fear,
>   To glide through the darkness of death!
>
> Just so would I choose to depart,
>   Just so let the summons be given;
> A quiver—a pause of the heart—
>   A vision of angels—then Heaven![33]

This last poem, scribbled almost illegibly in her own handwriting, was published in *The Critic* in April 1894.

Though her prayers would eventually be answered, she lingered on for three more years of blindness and incapacity, suffering from what she termed "spiritual . . . paralysis" and "nervous exhaustion."[34] Fortunately, she was not too sick to enjoy one last literary encounter, a "delightful interview" with Rose Kingsley, when the daughter of the English author, Charles Kingsley, made a visit to Baltimore in 1896. The meeting meant a great deal to Maggie. "I would have been willing to have had an additional attack of nervous prostration rather than not have seen Miss Kingsley," she reported.[35] Some ten months later, Maggie lapsed into a coma from which she never regained consciousness. She died, in just the peaceful manner she had hoped for, on March 29, 1897, a little less than two months before her seventy-seventh birthday.

The children brought her body home to Lexington for a short funeral service at the Presbyterian church, attended by old friends, family members, and the entire cadet corps of VMI, which marched in formation "as a mark of respect to the memory of her husband, whose whole life was spent as an honored professor at that institution."[36] Afterwards, Maggie was buried in the Preston plot, where her husband, his first wife, and her stepsons Frank and Randolph already rested. Nearby was the headstone of Willie, whose body lay far away on the fields at Manassas. Across the pathway were the graves of her mother, Ellie, Julia's husband, and little Georgie Fishburn, and beyond them stood the imposing statue of Stonewall Jackson. Surrounded by those she loved the best, Maggie had come home.

On her tombstone her sons inscribed an epitaph. Though worn by wind and rain, the words are still legible:

> Her song cheered the hearts
> of the Southern people in the
> hour of their deepest distress.
>
> "And they sing a new song
> before the throne."*

---

*Revelation 14:3. Interestingly, the date of birth given on Maggie's tombstone is incorrect. On the grave marker the date is given as May 24, 1820. The correct date is May 19, 1820, as indicated in George Junkin's letter of May 20, 1820, telling of her birth the previous day (GJ to JD, May 20, 1820). Elizabeth Preston Allan also records her date of birth as May 19, 1820 (*The Life and Letters of Margaret Junkin Preston* [Boston: Houghton, Mifflin, and Company, 1903], 6).}

On March 31, 1897, the *Lexington Gazette* in a lengthy obituary praised Margaret Junkin Preston as "the sweet poetess of our Sunny South" and lauded her "clear, bright [intellect] . . . warm heart, and . . . abiding faith in God."[37] A week after her death, her friend and longtime correspondent, Sophia Gilman, wrote an appreciative eulogy for *The Outlook*. Maggie's talent, Gilman noted, "was a many-sided one . . . [that] showed itself in song . . . in sonnet, in graphic pictures . . . and in bright, sparkling letters of travel. . . . There is a finish about her work like polished or carved marble, but it has also in it much of the fire of the opal, and now and then the flash of the diamond."[38]

Such praise would have pleased, but not surprised, Maggie. Though she often complained about having scant notice from Southern critics, in the final years of her life she had received considerable appreciation from literary figures in both the North and the South. Edmund C. Stedman, "the foremost American critic" of the period,[39] had written her that "much of the South's repute . . . rests upon your shoulders,"[40] and Maurice Thompson, an Indiana author and journalist who had fought for the Confederacy, had called her "the strongest and best of our living Southern poets [and] the best living woman poet in America."[41] The *Washington Post* had declared that she was "one of the really famous American authors of the day." The *Boston Evening Traveller* noted that she was "a poet who has assimilated classic feeling with classic knowledge," and the *Quebec Chronicle* praised her as "a true poet" whose writing "is characterized by grace, beauty, and simplicity."[42] Finally, her good friend Paul Hamilton Hayne had enthusiastically, if mistakenly,* acknowledged her as "the sole female poet of Southern birth."[43]

Her poetry had also been included in various anthologies

---

*Even if Hayne had remembered that Maggie was born in Pennsylvania, he, along with most other writers and critics, would still have considered her a "Southern poet."

immediately after the war. William Gilmore Simms used two of her poems in his collection, *War Poetry of the South*, and five of her poems were included in another publication, entitled *Southland Writers*.[44] In the 1880s Longfellow had asked to use three of her pieces in his multivolumed collection, *Poems of Places*, and she had been one of only eighteen women* whose sonnets found their way into *The Canterbury Poets: An Anthology of American Sonnets*.[45]

In the first two decades after her death her work was regularly included in anthologies designed for Southern high schools and colleges, and her poetry continued to receive praise. The *Nation*, in 1904, suggested that "in the comparatively short list of men and women of the South who have deserved literary distinction, she holds an honorable place for poetic talent."[46] W. P. Trent, in his book *Southern Writers: Selections in Prose and Verse*, published in 1905, wrote that "she was plainly the representative woman singer of the Confederacy."[47] Charles W. Hubner, editor of *Representative Southern Poets*, asserted that "the people of the South, especially, should be very proud of her and cherish her memory. She has been largely instrumental in establishing the high esteem in which Southern literature is now held among all discriminating students in this country and in Europe."[48] In the same vein Mildred Lewis Rutherford, "chair of Literature" at Lucy Cobb Institute in Athens, Georgia, declared in 1906 that "the best woman poet in the South is undoubtedly Margaret J. Preston."[49] In 1923 Armistead C. Gordon, Jr., suggested that Maggie was one of a small number of Southern poets "whose work compares more than favorably with that of their predecessors."[50]

But, despite the fame she achieved during her own lifetime,

---

*Other contributors to this volume included Poe, Hayne, Longfellow, Lowell, Whittier, and Oliver Wendell Holmes. It had been Hayne who suggested to both Simms and Longfellow that they use certain poems of Margaret Junkin Preston in their anthologies.

Margaret Junkin Preston is virtually unknown today, and her poems have completely disappeared from anthologies of Southern literature. In part her dramatic eclipse may be explained by the fact that she was a woman writing didactic and sometimes sentimental poems for a particular region at a unique time. Her readers and her critics expected her poetry to reflect faith in God, submission to divine will, women's subservience in a male world, the sanctity of the family, and carefully defined boundaries of subject matter and use of language. Today, many of Maggie's poems no longer seem relevant.

But changes in literary taste cannot entirely explain her sudden disappearance from anthologies. There is also the uneven quality of Maggie's poetry. Unfortunately, she was not adept at culling her material or willing to revise her work again and again. Only a few of her poems, such as the short lyrics in *Beechenbrook* and some of her sonnets, show the ability one wishes she might have exhibited more often. Despite being "fully aware what a valuable thing artistic finish is," she herself admitted that "I haven't the patience, the time, or the seclusion from interruption wh. all this necessitates."[51] Though he calls her "the best of the Southern poets of her sex," one recent critic, Jay Hubbell, finds her excuse of busyness a poor justification. Had she "been a great poet, like Emily Dickinson," he suggests, she somehow would have freed herself from the "handicaps [of housework and family distractions] or have written great poetry in spite of them."[52]

Still, one must concede that, in spite of her shortcomings, she influenced a generation of Southerners. Colonel Preston once told Maggie that she had dipped her pen in magic, and unquestionably she had the ability to move others by the power of her writing. Living through the Civil War, she wrote about its horror and despair with few illusions and little sentimentality, and her story *Beechenbrook* served as a catharsis for others who had shared her pain. Later she championed the cause of Southern letters, arguing with fervor for a recognition of their importance that was to come after her death. Ultimately, her literary influence became more than regional, for her memorable essays on Lee and Jackson made an entire nation aware of the character of these Confederate heroes.

In her letters, her essays, her poems, and her reviews, Maggie showed herself to be a woman who grew in depth and complexity of character throughout her seventy-seven years. As a child she had been tormented by the fear of death, yet she showed extraordinary courage when Yankees shelled her home and vandalized her possessions. As a young girl she was driven by an ambitious father to jeopardize her health in pursuit of a rigorous classical curriculum; then, utilizing what she had learned from the past, she wrote poetry and essays designed to meet the needs of her contemporaries and to challenge them for the future. Plagued from childhood by poor eyesight, she survived bouts of debilitating illness to live a long, full, and vigorous life. Heavily dependent in her early years upon her mother and Ellie for reassurance, she later found the inner strength to offer solace and companionship to Tom Jackson.

Before her marriage she had enjoyed few friendships with men; then at the mature age of thirty-eight Maggie had the courage to embark upon a successful and satisfying marriage with a strong-willed man ten years her senior, a man who still loved his first wife and was devoted to his seven children. Determined to be a model Victorian wife, mother, and housekeeper, Maggie nonetheless found the time and the self-confidence to promote her own poetry, to offer independent opinions about poets and books, and to enjoy a close literary friendship with a man other than her husband. Tormented by the horror and destruction of the Civil War, she transformed the pain of those years into her most realistic poetry, poetry about war and its aftermath that touched the hearts of her readers.

Amazingly, Maggie managed to be a remarkable woman in her own right, even though she lived her entire life in the presence of three imperious men. Her childhood was dominated by a restless, energetic father whom she felt she could never satisfy. In her early adult years she challenged the strong will of Thomas Jonathan Jackson when he wooed Ellie away from her smothering closeness. When she married John Thomas Lewis Preston, Maggie temporarily surrendered her independence for the sake of passionate love and the security of marriage. But then, through her wartime letters, she not only made her husband aware of his dependence upon her, she also garnered his endorsement of her literary ambitions.

All her life Maggie believed that her "rhyming pen" was a talent given her by God, "a gift of song . . . entrusted to her by her Creator."[53] She once likened herself to a bird that sang only because God had given it the ability to sing:

> If bird and bee, if earth and sky,
>   The lesser and the greater,
> Fulfill their law of being, why
>   Should such as I prove traitor?
> So let me sing because I must,
>   To nature's order clinging,
> Nor seek, with conscious aim, to thrust
>   Myself into my singing.[54]

Like a caged bird, Maggie was silent during the early years of her marriage until she was freed by her husband's wartime request that she sing for him. Her productive years ended with Colonel Preston's death, but the melodies she had created echoed in the hearts of her adopted Southland. From her childhood in college towns in Pennsylvania and Ohio, through the agony of the Civil War, and almost to the twentieth century, Margaret Junkin Preston listened to the insistent voice within herself, and she sang her own song.

Family Connections

Allan, Elizabeth Preston (1848–1933), youngest daughter of J. T. L. and Sally Preston, wife of William Allan, and early biographer of Maggie.

Allan, William (1837–1890), husband of Elizabeth, Confederate officer during Civil War, first headmaster of McDonogh School in Baltimore.

Christian, Julia Jackson (1862–1889), daughter of T. J. "Stonewall" Jackson and Mary Anna Jackson.

Cocke, Edmund Randolph (1841–? [after 1893]), son of Elizabeth Cocke, husband of Phebe Preston Cocke.

Cocke, Elizabeth Preston (1808–1889), sister of J. T. L. Preston, owner of Oakland in Cumberland County, Virginia.

Cocke, Phebe Preston (1839–1873), daughter of J. T. L. Preston and Sally Preston, who married her first cousin, Edmund Cocke.

Dickey, Ebenezer (1771–1831), Maggie's uncle, Presbyterian minister, husband of Jane, father of Helen Dickey.

Dickey, Helen (1816–1882), Maggie's first cousin and longtime confidante.

Dickey, Jane Miller (1785–1850), Maggie's aunt, mother of Helen, who lived at Oxford, Pennsylvania and kept the family papers intact.

Finney, Margaret Miller (1790–1865), Maggie's aunt, who was married to a Presbyterian minister in Maryland.

Fishburn, George Junkin (1857–1859), son of Julia and Junius Fishburn, Maggie's nephew, who died at the age of two.

Fishburn, Julia Rush Junkin (1835–1915), Maggie's youngest sister, who (as a young widow) left Lexington with her father in 1861.

Fishburn, Junius (1830–1858), Maggie's brother-in-law, husband of Julia, teacher at Washington College.

Jackson, Eleanor "Ellie" Junkin (1825–1854), Maggie's favorite sister, wife of Stonewall Jackson, who died in childbirth.

Jackson, Mary Anna (1831–1915), second wife of Stonewall Jackson, longtime widow and preserver of Jackson's memory.

Jackson, Thomas Jonathan "Stonewall" (1824–1863), Maggie's

eccentric brother-in-law, famous Confederate general.

Junkin, David (1833–1834), Maggie's little brother who died in Easton, Pennsylvania, at the age of fourteen months.

Junkin, David Xavier (1808–1880), brother and biographer of George Junkin, chaplain in Union army.

Junkin, Ebenezer (1829–1891), Maggie's brother, Presbyterian minister, Southern sympathizer.

Junkin, George (1790–1868), Maggie's father, Presbyterian minister, president of Lafayette, Miami (Ohio), and Washington colleges.

Junkin, George (1827–1902), Maggie's brother, Philadelphia lawyer, Northern sympathizer.

Junkin, John (1822–1889), Maggie's physician brother, who served as a surgeon in the Union army.

Junkin, Joseph (1823–1849), Maggie's brother, who died of tuberculosis.

Junkin, Julia Rush (1795–1854), Maggie's capable, pious, long-suffering mother.

Junkin, William (1831–1900), Maggie's brother, Presbyterian minister, who served in the Confederate army.

McLean, Helen Miller (1787–1822), Maggie's aunt, daughter of John and Margaret Miller, who died when Maggie was two years old.

Miller, John (1759–1814), Maggie's grandfather, émigré from Scotland, Philadelphia marble worker.

Miller, Margaret (1756–1847), wife of John Miller, Maggie's feisty, red-haired grandmother, who taught Maggie Scottish folklore.

Preston, Edmonia (1837–1842), eldest daughter of J. T. L. and Sally Preston, who died at the age of five.

Preston, Edmund Randolph "Randy" (1845–1862), son of J. T. L. and Sally Preston, victim of typhoid fever during Civil War.

Preston, Edmund Randolph (1880–1957), son of John Preston, husband of Julia Christian Preston.

Preston, Frank (1841–1869), son of J. T. L. and Sally Preston, who lost an arm at battle of Winchester, later taught at VMI, Washington and Lee, and William and Mary.

Preston, George Junkin (1858–1908), Maggie's elder son, physician in Baltimore.

Preston, Herbert Rush (1861–1937), Maggie's younger son, lawyer in Baltimore.

Preston, John (1853–1901), son of J. T. L. and Sally Preston, Presbyterian minister.

Preston, John Thomas Lewis (1811–1890), Maggie's husband, founder of VMI, officer under Stonewall Jackson during Civil War.

Preston, Julia Christian (1887–1991), granddaughter of Stonewall Jackson, wife of Edmund Preston.

Preston, Margaret "Maggie" Junkin (1820–1897), daughter of George Junkin, wife of J. T. L. Preston, author, "poetess of the South."

Preston, Sally Caruthers (1811–1856), first wife of J. T. L. Preston and close friend of Maggie.

Preston, Thomas (1835–1895), son of J. T. L. and Sally Preston, minister of Lexington Presbyterian Church for many years.

Preston, William (1844–1862), son of J. T. L. and Sally Preston, who died at battle of Second Manassas.

Notes

All personal letters not otherwise identified are unpublished and belong to Janet Preston, Baltimore, Maryland. Punctuation and spelling appear as written. Dates of letters have been standardized.

Abbreviations

Persons

DXJ	Rev. David Xavier Junkin
ED	Rev. Ebenezer Dickey
EJ[J]	Eleanor [sometimes Elinor] Junkin [Jackson]
EP[A]	Elizabeth Preston Allan
GJ	Rev. George Junkin
HD	Helen Dickey
JD	Jane Dickey
JRJ	Julia Rush Junkin
JTLP	John Thomas Lewis Preston

Julia J	Julia Junkin [Fishburn]
MJ, MJP	Margaret Junkin [Preston]
PHH	Paul Hamilton Hayne
TJJ	Thomas Jonathan Jackson

Manuscript Collections

Duke - Manuscript Department, Duke University Library, Durham, North Carolina.

Lafayette - Skillman Archives and Special Collections and College Archives, Lafayette College, Easton, Pennsylvania.

UNC - Southern Historical Collection, Library of the University of North Carolina, Chapel Hill, North Carolina.

VMI - Virginia Military Institute Archives, Lexington, Virginia.

W&L - Special Collections, the University Library, Washington and Lee University, Lexington, Virginia.

Books, Notebooks, and Scrapbooks
of Margaret Junkin Preston

Beechenbrook - Margaret J. Preston, *Beechenbrook: A Rhyme of the War*. Richmond: J. W. Randolph, 1865. Later editions: Baltimore: Kelly & Piet, 1866; 1867; 1868; 1872.

Cartoons - Margaret J. Preston, *Cartoons*. Boston: Roberts Brothers, 1881.

Colonial - Margaret J. Preston, *Colonial Ballads*. Boston: Houghton, Mifflin, and Company, 1887.

FLS - Margaret J. Preston, *For Love's Sake*. New York: Anson D.

F. Randolph and Company, 1886.

Monographs - Margaret J. Preston, *A Handful of Monographs.* New York: Anson D. F. Randolph & Company, 1886.

Notebook I - Notebook of poems, handwritten by MJ. 1837–1840. W&L.

Notebook II - Notebook of poems, handwritten by MJ. Primarily 1840–1850. W&L. Pagination added.

Old Song - Margaret J. Preston, *Old Song and New.* Philadelphia: J. B. Lippincott & Co., 1870.

Scrapbook I - Scrapbook of printed poems, stories, etc., all written by MJ. 1850–1857. W&L. Pagination added.

Scrapbook II - Scrapbook of both handwritten and printed poems, stories, notes, hymns, all written by MJ/MJP. 1839–1865(?). In possession of Janet Preston, Baltimore, Maryland. Pagination added.

Scrapbook III - Scrapbook of primarily handwritten poems, a few diary entries, and printed poems, written by MJ/MJP. 1865–1870. UNC.

Scrapbook IV - Scrapbook of printed poems, book reviews, stories, essays, obituaries, all written by MJP. 1870–1880. W&L. Pagination added.

Silverwood - [Margaret Junkin], *Silverwood: A Book of Memories.* New York: Irby & Jackson, 1856.

Other

Biography of College - David Bishop Skillman, *The Biography of a College*. Easton, Pennsylvania: Lafayette College, 1932.

Couper - William Couper, *One Hundred Years at V.M.I.* Richmond: Garrett and Massie, Incorporated, 1939. Four volumes.

Crenshaw - Ollinger Crenshaw, *General Lee's College*. New York: Random House, 1969.

Hill - Daniel H. Hill, "The Real Stonewall Jackson," *The Century Magazine* 47 (February 1894): 623–28.

JTLP Diary - Handwritten diary by JTLP, 1861. Microfilm, Manuscript Division, Library of Congress.

L&L - Elizabeth Preston Allan, *The Life and Letters of Margaret Junkin Preston*. Boston: Houghton, Mifflin, and Company, 1903.

Life of Dr. G. J. - David Xavier Junkin, *The Reverend George Junkin: A Historical Biography*. Philadelphia: J. B. Lippincott, 1871.

Man of Letters - Rayburn S. Moore, ed. *A Man of Letters in the Nineteenth–Century South: Selected Letters of Paul Hamilton Hayne*. Baton Rouge: Louisiana State University Press, 1982.

March Past - Elizabeth Randolph Preston Allan, *A March Past*. Edited by her daughter, Janet Allan Bryan. Richmond: The Dietz Press, 1938.

Pope - Earl A. Pope, "George Junkin and his Eschatological Vision." Jones Faculty Lecture, Lafayette College, February 10,

1970. Special Collections and College Archives, Lafayette.

Weaver - Ethan Allen Weaver, *Local Historical and Biographical Notes.* Germantown, Pennsylvania, 1906.

Introduction

1. *Rockbridge County News,* July 23, 1891.

Chapter 1. Scenes of Childhood, 1820–1831

1. MJ, "Scenes of Childhood," ca. 1840, Notebook I:19.
2. GJ to JD, May 20, 1820.
3. Ibid.
4. Ibid, quoting from Exodus 2:9.
5. Ethan Allen Weaver, "Margaret Junkin Preston," address at meeting of the Northampton County, Pennsylvania, Historical and Genealogical Society, September 20, 1921. Special Collections and College Archives, Lafayette.
6. DXJ, quoted in Pope, 1.
7. MJ, "Scenes of Childhood," Notebook I:19.
8. Pope, 4.
9. JRJ to JD, July 28, 1819.
10. MJ, "A Letter to a Cousin," [1838], Notebook I:66.
11. GJ to JD, May 20, 1820.
12. JRJ to ED, February 22, 1821.
13. *L&L,* 15.
14. MJ's Testament, W&L.
15. MJ, "Scenes of Childhood," Notebook I:20.
16. Notebook I:84, 41, 31, 157.
17. Ibid, 148.
18. Ibid, 135.
19. JRJ to ED, January 5, 1830.

20. GJ to ED, April 5, 1830.

21. JRJ to JD, October 12, 1825.

22. GJ to ED, February 16, 1824.

23. MJ to HD, n.d. [1846] and July 27, 1840.

24. MJ, "Wishes for my Sister Ellen," Notebook I:14.

25. MJ, "The Two Stars," March 12, 1839, Notebook I:15.

26. JRJ to JD, October 12, 1825, and JRJ to ED, July 1, 1829.

27. MJP, "Giving Children Right Impressions of Death," *Sunday School Times* 33 (November 7, 1891): 707.

28. Ibid, 707–8.

29. MJ, "Our Burial-place," Notebook I:153.

30. *L&L*, 20.

31. Ibid, 19.

32. MJ to HD, December 8, 1836, and July 27, 1840.

33. MJ to HD, November 23, 1840.

34. MJP, "Comforted," *Cartoons*, 218.

35. *L&L*, 20.

36. JRJ to ED, July 27, 1830.

37. Ibid.

38. *L&L*, 9.

39. *Colonial*, 243, 256; *Cartoons*, 66.

40. MJ, "Thoughts: Suggested by Power's Prosperine, a beautiful work of art in the possession of H. D. Maxwell, Esq., of Pennsylvania," *Southern Literary Messenger* 15 (February 1849): 100.

41. Ibid.

42. MJ to HD, March 29, 1840, and June 27, 1840.

43. MJ, "A letter to my dear Mother," Notebook I:125.

44. *L&L*, 14–15.

45. *Old Song*, 109; *Colonial*, 133, 171.

46. Mrs. Mark Sullivan to David Bishop Skillman, August 4, n.d., Skillman Archives 1848, #4, Lafayette.

47. GJ to ED, May 3, 1831.

48. JRJ to JD, October 3, 1831.

49. MJP, "A Bird's Ministry" and "The Brahmin's Test," *Cartoons*, 221, 224.

50. JRJ to JD, February 23, 1832.

51. MJ to HD, March 20, 1832. This two-page letter, written in a firm, neat hand, is the earliest extant letter of Maggie's, one of many letters she was to write to Helen Dickey over the next thirty years.

52. GJ, quoted in *L&L*, 27.

Chapter 2. The Domes of Academe, 1831–1848

1. MJ, "Evening," Notebook I:4.

2. GJ to Rev. Nicholas Murray, July 17, 1832, Gratz Manuscripts, "University & College Presidents," Case 7, Box 14, Historical Society of Pennsylvania.

3. Pope, 9.

4. JRJ to HD, January 5, 1832.

5. JRJ to JD, February 23, 1832.

6. JRJ to JD, April 17, 1832.

7. Local newspaper, July 20, 1836, quoted in Weaver, 103.

8. *North American* (Philadelphia), September 25, 1839, quoted in Weaver, 124.

9. *History of Northampton County*, under supervision of William J. Heller (Boston: American Historical Society, 1920), 1:399.

10. Weaver, 84.

11. JRJ to JD, October 3, 1832.

12. George Junkin, Jr., quoted in *L&L*, 10–11.

13. JRJ to HD, January 1, 1835.

14. MJ to HD, March 8, 1834.

15. JRJ to JD, January 1, 1835.

16. JRJ to JD, May 2, 1834.

17. MJ, "To my Sister Julia on her 5th birth-day," June 13, 1840, Notebook II:20.

18. MJ, "A thought or two on flowers," Notebook II:31.

19. MJ, "Lines on the Year's last hour," January 1, 1842, Notebook II:160.

20. *Biography of a College*, 94.

21. MJ to HD, March 8, n.d. [1839 or 1840].

22. MJ to HD, August 29, 1836.

23. MJ to HD, May 1839.

24. MJ, "A Letter to my Cousin Susan Finney," Notebook I:42.

25. JRJ to JD, May 26, 1834.

26. *L&L*, 16.

27. Ibid.

28. *L&L*, 21; also MJ, "A letter to Prof. C. F. McC—— of the University of Georgia," November 13, 1840, Notebook II:63.

29. MJ to HD, June 30, n.d. [1837].

30. JRJ to JD, June 14, 1837.

31. Ibid.

32. MJ to HD, June 5, n.d. [1837].

33. Dr. Junkin's "Course of reading in History & Philosophy for M.J.—1839—," handwritten by GJ, inside back cover of Notebook II.

34. *L&L*, 7.

35. MJ, "Evening," June 23, 1837, Notebook I:5.

36. MJ to Mrs. Margaret Miller, June 27, 1840.

37. Maggie's and Ellie's sketchbook, filled with ink and pencil drawings by Maggie and watercolor sketches by both Maggie and Ellie, is in the possession of Janet Preston, Baltimore, Maryland.

38. MJ, "The Scent of the Rose," 1840, Notebook II:27.

39. Ibid, 27–28.

40. MJ, "The lament for the lost heart," Notebook I:82.

41. MJ, "Written after hearing a Temperance Address delivered in a *New church* by a very young man," January 1, 1839, Notebook I:45.

42. MJ, "A Letter to a Cousin," [1838], Notebook I:68.

43. Ibid, 66–67.

44. EJ to Samuel Dickey, January 1840.

45. MJ, "A Requiem," Notebook II:230.

46. Charlotte Brontë, in Elizabeth Gaskell, *Life of Charlotte Brontë* (New York: D. Appleton and Company, 1857), 2:243.

47. Virginia Woolf, "Women and Fiction," March 1929, in *Collected Essays* (London: The Hogarth Press, 1966), 2:142.

48. MJ, "Hawthorn Bower," n.d., Notebook II:34.

49. MJ, "The birth of the Flowers," 1840, Notebook I:158.

50. MJ, "Hawthorn Bower," n.d., Notebook II:34.

51. MJ, "To Miss R—," Notebook II:83–84.

52. MJ to HD, July 5, n.d. [1837].

53. MJ, "A letter to Harry Green," Notebook II:113.

54. Rev. T. C. Porter, quoted in *L&L*, 25; poem reprinted in *The Lafayette*, November 22, 1910, Lafayette.

55. EJ and MJ to HD, March 29, 1839.

56. MJ, "TO——," composed at the "Forks of the Delaware," printed, Scrapbook I:28.

57. EJ to HD, March 29, 1839.

58. MJ, "A letter to Prof. C. F. McC—— of the University of Georgia," Notebook II:63, 68.

59. Frederic A. Godcharles, "Dr. George Junkin," Special Collections and College Archives, Lafayette.

60. 1844–45 Lafayette College catalogue, 13, Special Collections and College Archives, Lafayette.

61. GJ to Rev. Alvin H. Parker, January 11, 1840, Gratz Collection, Historical Society of Pennsylvania.

62. *The First Annual Report of the Board of Trustees*, 1833, 7. Special Collections and College Archives, Lafayette; also local Easton newspaper, September 9, 1835, quoted in Weaver, 97.

63. Attributed to J. M. Porter, Special Collections and College Archives, Lafayette.

64. *The Educator*, 1:1, 1838. Special Collections and College Archives, Lafayette.

65. Account of public meeting, Upper Mount Bethel, Pennsylvania, March 13, 1839, Special Collections and College Archives, Lafayette.

66. Ebenezer Dickey, Jr. to John Dickey, February 4, 1839, item #2, 1839, Skillman Archives, Lafayette.

67. *Biography of a College*, 1:130.

68. MJ to HD, November 23, 1840.

69. JRJ to JD, December 22, 1840.

70. Ibid.

71. MJ to HD, November 23, 1840.

72. Easton newspaper, March 1, 1841, quoted by Weaver, 138.

73. *The Whig*, March 31, 1841, Item #1, 1841, Skillman Archives, Lafayette.

74. MJ to HD, November 23, 1840.

75. EJ to HD, July 10, 1841.

76. EJ to HD, April 17, 1841.

77. Pope, 12; *The Sixteenth Annual Catalog of Miami University*, July 1841, The Walter Havighurst Special Collections, Miami University, Oxford, Ohio.

78. Pope, 13.

79. John C. Calhoun to GJ, September 17, 1846, Preston Papers, #1543, SHC.

80. Walter Havighurst, *The Miami Years, 1808–1969* (New York: G. P. Putnam's Sons, 1969), 84.

81. False death notice dated April 5, 1842, Oxford, Ohio,

Pope, 14; George Junkin's reply dated April 20, 1842, Weaver, 159.

82. EJ to HD, July 10, 1841.

83. MJ, "I, too, shall die," July 7, 1840, Notebook II:122.

84. MJ, "Lines suggested by the first Family Separation," November 7, 1842, Notebook II:233–34.

85. *Biography of a College*, 1:153.

86. MJ to HD, October 3, 1844.

87. GJ, quoted in *Life of Dr. G. J.*, 164.

88. JRJ to JD, December 18, 1844.

89. GJ to trustees of Lafayette College, September 24, 1844, Special Collections and College Archives, Lafayette.

90. Pope, 19.

91. EJ to HD, March 26,1845; also JRJ to JD, May 8, 1845.

92. EJ to HD, March 26, 1845.

93. JRJ to JD, May 8, 1845, and MJ to HD, July 24, 1845.

94. MJ to Charles McCay, November 24, 1845, quoted in *L&L*, 22.

95. *L&L*, 23.

96. Letter from managers of the fair, January 1846, Item #23, 1846, Skillman Archives, Lafayette.

97. *L&L*, 8.

98. Ibid, 16.

99. JRJ to JD, July 8, 1847.

100. MJ to HD, June 5, n.d. [1837].

101. MJ, "To My Mother," January 20, 11 P.M., Notebook II:163.

102. *L&L*, 17.

103. MJ, "A Ballad in reply to Tupper's Ballad to Columbia," Oxford, November 5, 1848, Notebook II, insert between pages 50 and 51.

104. MJ to HD, April 25, n.d. [1846].

105. JRJ to JD, March 22, 1847.

106. MJ to Charles McCay, quoted in *L&L*, 30.

107. JRJ to JD, October 4, 1847.

108. JRJ to JD, August 10, 1848.

109. Trustees papers (028–126, July–December 1848), Washington and Lee University, W&L.

110. *Life of Dr. G. J.*, 488–89.

111. Pope, 17.

112. *Life of Dr. G. J.*, 486.

113. JRJ to JD, August 10, 1848.

Chapter 3. Maggie and the Major, 1848–1857

1. MJ, "To my Sister," n.d. [1853?], typed copy, T. J. Jackson Papers, #370z, UNC.

2. Sidney Walter Martin, *Florida During the Territorial Days* (Athens: University of Georgia Press, 1944), 98.

3. JRJ to JD, March 1, 1849.

4. Daniel H. Hill to Phelps Collins, January 31, 1841, Daniel Harvey Hill Papers, W&L.

5. Julia J, quoted in *L&L*, 39.

6. George Junkin, Jr. to HD, January 25, 1849.

7. JRJ to HD, March 1, 1849.

8. Crenshaw, 115.

9. JRJ to JD, March 1, 1849.

10. JRJ to JD, June 1849.

11. MJ to George Junkin, Jr., May 4, 1849, quoted in *L&L*, 47.

12. MJ, "The Solaced Grief," Easton newspapers, October 10, 1849; *Lexington Gazette*, December 19, 1849; Scrapbook I:28.

13. JRJ to JD, March 1, 1849.

14. EJ to HD, July 6, 1849.

15. *L&L*, 59–60.

16. MJ, "The Step–mother!," Scrapbook II:86–107.

17. *L&L*, 37–38.

18. Margaret Irvine [pseudonym for MJ], "Letter from a Virginia Cousin," September 9, 1852, published in an Easton newspaper; printed copy in Scrapbook II:43.

19. MJ to HD, n.d. [after June 15, 1857].

20. George Junkin, Jr. to HD, January 25, 1849.

21. Crenshaw, 115.

22. MJ, "To Mr. McDonogh after reading his Letter on African Colonization," Notebook II:249.

23. MJ, "Stanzas Sung on the occasion of the departure of a party of Emigrants to Liberia," Scrapbook I:31.

24. Margaret Irvine [MJ], "Letter from a Virginia Cousin," September 9, 1852, Scrapbook II:42.

25. Margaret Irvine [MJ], "Letter from a Virginia Cousin," November 25, n.d., Scrapbook II:49.

26. Hill, 625.

27. Quotation from unnamed Dickey cousin, mentioned in letter of Eleanor Hosie to Herbert Preston, Sr. (letter in possession of Janet Preston, Baltimore, Maryland). As may be noted in this single letter, the spelling of Ellie's name varied. Mrs. Junkin always called the girl "Eleanor," and so she signed her own name when she made sketches in Easton. On her marriage certificate, in August of 1853, her name is listed first as "Eleanor," and that is scratched out and "Elinor" written over it. The name "Elinor" appears on her tombstone.

28. Reprinted with permission of Charles Scribner's Sons, an imprint of Macmillan Publishing Company, from *Lee's Lieutenants*, by Douglas Southall Freeman. Copyright 1942. C h a r l e s Scribner's Sons; copyright renewed (c) 1970, Inez Goddin Freeman, excerpt from page 350. Lenoir Chambers, *Stonewall Jackson* (Wilmington, North Carolina: Broadfoot Publishing Company, 1988. [Copyright New York: William Morrow and

Company 1959]), 1:237–38; Hill, 625, 627.

29. MJP, "Personal Reminiscences of Stonewall Jackson," *Century* 32 (May 1886–October 1886): 927, 930, 933, 936.

30. MJ to HD, March 8, n.d. [1839 or 1840].

31. MJ, "Lines Addressed to Sister Eleanor," Notebook I:134–35.

32. MJ, "To my Sister," undated [probably 1853], typed copy in Thomas Jonathan Jackson papers, #370z, UNC.

33. Hill, 625.

34. Emily Morrison Bondurant, *Reminiscences* (typed manuscript of original, made in 1962, #2430, UNC), 76.

35. JRJ to HD, July 22, 1853.

36. Carroll Smith-Rosenberg, "The Female World of Love and Ritual: Relations between Women in Nineteenth-Century America," *Signs* 1 (Autumn 1975): 22. Copyright 1975 by the University of Chicago.

37. TJJ to "my dear sister" [Laura Arnold], October 19 and November 30, 1853, Thomas J. Jackson Collection, VMI.

38. MJ to HD, September 9, n.d. [1853].

39. Ibid.

40. Ibid.

41. George Junkin, Jr. to HD, January 6, 1854.

42. *The Presbyterian*, Philadelphia, March 11, 1854, quoted in *Life of Dr. G. J.*, 499.

43. Julia J to Lizzie Webster, March 14, 1854, W&L. See also Chapter 2, page 55.

44. MJ to Charles McCay, June 1854, quoted in *L&L*, 67.

45. *Scottish Psalter*, 1650.

46. MJ to Charles McCay, June 1854, quoted in *L&L*, 67.

47. Ibid, 66, 67.

48. Ibid, 65.

49. Julia J to Lizzie Webster, March 14, 1854, W&L.

50. Julia J to Ebenezer Junkin, March 30, 1854 (original

letter in possession of Agnes Junkin Peery).

51. Julia J to HD, July 24, 1854.

52. Ibid.

53. MJ to HD, postscript to letter of Julia J to HD, July 24, 1854.

54. Julia J to HD, July 24, 1854.

55. EJJ to HD, 30 [no month] 1854.

56. Sally G. McMillen, *Motherhood in the Old South: Pregnancy, Childbirth, and Infant Rearing* (Baton Rouge: Louisiana State University Press, 1990), 81.

57. Ibid, 9–10.

58. *The Gazette*, Lexington, Virginia, Thursday, Oct. 26, 1854, (no. 9), 3.

59. *Silverwood*, 384.

60. MJ to HD, September 14, 1855.

61. Couper I:291.

62. Hill, 625.

63. TJJ to "my dear sister" [Laura Arnold], June 1, 1855, Thomas J. Jackson Collection, VMI.

64. MJ to TJ, December 19, 1854, Thomas J. Jackson Collection, VMI.

65. Ibid.

66. MJ, "To my Sister," n.d. [1853?], typed copy, T. J. Jackson Papers, #370z, UNC.

67. TJ to MJ, March 1, 1855, Preston Papers, #1543, UNC.

68. TJ to MJ, February 14, 1855, Preston Papers, #1543, UNC.

69. Ibid.

70. Ibid.

71. TJ to MJ, March 10, 1855, Preston Papers, #1543, UNC.

72. MJ to HD, September 14, 1855.

73. TJ to MJ, August 16, 1855, Preston Papers, #1543,

UNC.

74. MJP, "Personal Reminiscences of Stonewall Jackson," *Century* 32 (May 1886–October 1886): 932, 933.

75. TJ to MJ, May 31, 1856, Preston Papers, #1543, UNC; translation by Dr. Wilfred Readsly.

76. MJP, "The General's Colored Sunday School," *The Sunday School Times*, December 3, 1887; printed copy in Scrapbook III:142.

77. MJ to Miss Rebecca Glasgow, n.d. [1856], quoted in part in *L&L*, 85.

78. MJ, introductory poem to *Silverwood*.

79. *Southern Literary Messenger* XXIV (January 1857): 80.

80. MJ to Miss Rebecca Glasgow, n.d. [1856], quoted in part in *L&L*, 85.

81. *Silverwood*, 187.

82. Ibid, 252, 261.

83. Ibid, 354.

84. *L&L*, 85.

85. *Silverwood*, 120, 109, 313.

86. See Chapter 3, footnote, page 69.

87. *Silverwood*, 384.

88. Ibid, 176–77.

89. MJP, "The Open Gate," Scrapbook II:55; "Lalisillia of Argos," *Eclectic Magazine* (May 1859); review of Elizabeth Barrett Browning's poems, *Southern Literary Messenger* 30 (February 1860): 146–53.

90. MJ to HD, September 9, n.d. [1853].

91. Clement Fishburn, quoted in W. W. Pusey III, "Junius M. Fishburn (1830–1858): Professor of Latin," *Proceedings of the Rockbridge Historical Society* 9 (1975–1979): 149.

92. Mrs. John Moore [Sally Alexander Moore], *Memoirs of a Long Life in Virginia* (Staunton, Virginia: The McClure Company, 1920), 37–40.

93. Julia J to Ebenezer Junkin, March 30, 1854 (original letter in possession of Agnes Junkin Peery, granddaughter of Ebenezer Junkin).

94. Junius Fishburn's diary, quoted in W. W. Pusey III, "Junius M. Fishburn (1830–1858): Professor of Latin," *Proceedings of the Rockbridge Historical Society* 9 (1975–1979): 150.

95. MJ to Betty Alexander, Wednesday, August 20, n.d. [1856], W&L.

96. Julia J to Lizzie Webster, August 4, 1856, W&L.

97. MJ to HD, n.d. [after June 15, 1857].

98. TJJ to "my dear sister" [Laura Arnold], February 26, 1857, Thomas J. Jackson Collection, VMI.

Chapter 4. The Very Finger of God, 1856–1861

1. MJ to HD, Lexington, n.d. [after June 15, 1857].

2. V. C. Saunders to his parents, November 23, 1839, in Couper I:66.

3. BA, Washington College, 1828; MA, University of Virginia, 1829; additional study at Yale College, 1829–1830 (Washington and Lee Alumni Catalog, W&L; *National Cyclopedia of American Biography*, 245; *Catalog of the Officers and Students of Yale College*, 1829–1830, 7, Yale University Library).

4. *March Past*, 40.

5. Ibid, 87–88.

6. Ibid, 25–26.

7. Sally Lyle (Caruthers) Preston to JTLP, November 4, 1835, Preston Papers, #1543, UNC.

8. Visa attached to JTLP passport, issued May 11, 1851, J.T.L.Preston Collection, VMI.

9. JTLP Diary, August 15, 1861.

10. Ibid.

11. *March Past*, 44.

12. *L&L*, 93; *March Past*, 20.
13. JTLP Diary, August 2, 3, 1861.
14. *March Past*, 44.
15. Gravestone of Sally Lyle Caruthers Preston, Preston family plot, Stonewall Jackson cemetery, Lexington, Virginia.
16. JTLP Diary, August 2, 3, 1861.
17. MJ to JTLP, n.d. [1857], quoted in *L&L*, 97.
18. JTLP Diary, August 2, 3, 1861; also September 13, 1861.
19. *March Past*, 89.
20. Ibid.
21. Ibid, 87.
22. MJ to HD, n.d. [after June 15, 1857].
23. TJJ to MJ, May 25, 1857, Preston Papers, #1543, UNC.
24. Bill of sale from a Philadelphia jewelry store, made out to "Miss Junkins," original at Stonewall Jackson House, Lexington.
25. Mary Anna Jackson, *Memoir of Stonewall Jackson by His Widow* (Louisville, Kentucky: The Prentice Press, 1895), 104.
26. MJ to JTLP, n.d. [1857], quoted in *L&L*, 96, 98.
27. MJ to HD, n.d. [after June 15, 1857].
28. Ibid.
29. MJP to HD, October 10, n.d. [1857]; also Thomas H. Williamson to Colonel F. H. Smith, August 6, 1857, Colonel F. H. Smith's Official Correspondence, 1857, VMI Archives.
30. MJP to HD, October 10, n.d. [1857].
31. *L&L*, 100; *March Past*, 93.
32. *L&L*, 102.
33. Ibid, 99.
34. MJP to HD, October 10, n.d. [1857].
35. *March Past*, 93.
36. MJP to HD, October 10, n.d. [1857].
37. Ibid.
38. *March Past*, 95.

39. MJP to HD, October 10, n.d. [1857].

40. Ibid.

41. *L&L*, 104.

42. MJP to HD, October 10, n.d. [1857].

43. Mary Anna Jackson, "With Stonewall Jackson in Camp," *Hearst's Magazine* 24 (1913): 386.

44. *L&L*, 105.

45. MJP to HD, October 10, n.d. [1857].

46. Ibid.

47. Trustees Papers, 1858, W&L, quoted in W. W. Pusey, III, "Junius M.Fishburn (1830–1858): Professor of Latin," *Proceedings of the Rockbridge Historical Society* 9 (1975–1979): 153.

48. Ibid, 154.

49. JTLP Diary, September 13, 1861.

50. *March Past*, 113.

51. *Life of Dr. G. J.*, 506.

52. Ibid, 505.

53. Julia J. to Lizzie Webster, May 18, 1858, W&L.

54. MJP, "The Open Gate," Scrapbook II:55–56. Years later a much revised version of "The Open Gate" appeared in *Old Song*, 229–30. The poem was shortened and the rhythm altered to suggest the heavy cadences of grief, but intimate details of a special baby's speech and laughter were unfortunately omitted.

55. William S. White to Rev. John S. Watt, December 13, 1860, in H[enry] W. White, ed., *Rev. William S. White, D.D. and His Times* (Richmond: Presbyterian Committee of Publication, 1891), 170.

56. *Richmond Times Dispatch*, April 4, 1859.

57. William M. Willson, quoted in Ollinger Crenshaw's original manuscript before it was pruned to published form as *General Lee's College* 1:464, W&L.

58. JTLP to MJP, December 2, 1859, quoted in *L&L*, 111–14.

59. Susan P. Lee, *Memoirs of William Nelson Pendleton, D.D.* (1893; reprint in Harrisonburg, Virginia: Sprinkle Publications, 1991), 123, 128.

60. Couper 2:62–63.

61. TJJ to "my dear sister" [Laura Arnold], December 29, 1860, Thomas J. Jackson Collection, VMI.

62. JTLP, "Semi-Centenary Anniversary Address," February 1866, in Franklin Society Library, W&L.

63. GJ, quoted in Pope, 28.

64. GJ, "A Voice of a Pennsylvanian in the Heart of Virginia" to Governor-Elect Curtin of Pennsylvania, December 1860, quoted in Pope, 19–20.

65. *March Past*, 115.

66. Ibid, 110.

67. TJJ to "my dear sister" [Laura Arnold], December 29, 1860, Thomas J. Jackson Collection, VMI.

68. *L&L*, 107.

Chapter 5. This Horrid and Senseless War, 1861–1865

1. MJP Diary, April 3, 1862, quoted in *L&L*, 134.

2. William M. Willson, quoted in Crenshaw, 116.

3. GJ, quoted in Pope, 20.

4. Pope, 20.

5. Couper 2:70, 86.

6. H[enry] M. White, ed., *Rev. William S. White, D.D., and His Times (1800–1873): An Autobiography* (Richmond: 1891), 171.

7. Pope, 20; Emily Morrison Bondurant, *Reminiscences* (typed manuscript of original, made in 1962, #2430, UNC), 126.

8. Pope, 20.

9. *March Past*, 118.

10. GJ, *Political Fallacies* (New York: C. Scribner, 1863), 13.

11. DXJ to GJ, May 18, 1863, quoted in *Life of Dr. G. J.*, 551.

12. Professor A. L. Nelson, "Personal Recollections of Washington College," *Ring Tum Phi*, February 11, 1899; 1; William M. Willson, quoted in Ollinger Crenshaw's original manuscript before it was pruned to published form as *General Lee's College* 1:480, W&L.

13. GJ to J. L. Cist, March 22, 1862, Historical Society of Pennsylvania.

14. *L&L*, 131, 134.

15. *March Past*, 129, 136–37.

16. Ibid.

17. JTLP Diary, August 10, 1861.

18. JTLP to MJP, December 5, 1861, quoted in *L&L*, 122–23.

19. JTLP to MJP, December 23, 1861, quoted in *L&L*, 126.

20. JTLP Diary, September 20, 1861; August 15, 1861.

21. JTLP Diary, August 13, 1861; September 13, 1861.

22. JTLP Diary, September 14, 1861.

23. JTLP Diary, August 2, 3, 1861; August 14, 1861; September 13, 1861.

24. JTLP Diary, August 9, 1861.

25. JTLP Diary, August 16, 1861.

26. Ibid.

27. Entry in handwriting of MJP, August 20, 1861, JTLP Diary.

28. *L&L*, 126.

29. JTLP Diary, September 20, 1861.

30. Poem and comment in handwriting of MJP, August 20, 1861, JTLP Diary.

31. TJJ to MJP, November 16, 1861, General Manuscripts [Misc.] CO140, Box JA-JE, Folder "Jackson, Stonewall." Printed

with permission of the Princeton University Libraries. Copy of this letter in Preston Papers, #1543, UNC.

32. *Life of Dr. G. J.*, 554.

33. MJP Diary, December 24, 1862, quoted in *L&L*, 157.

34. MJP Diary, April 3, 1862, quoted in *L&L*, 135.

35. MJP Diary, April 3 and April 14, 1862, quoted in *L&L*, 135, 137.

36. MJP Diary, April 3, 1862, quoted in *L&L*, 134.

37. MJP Diary, April 3 and 10, 1862, quoted in *L&L*, 134–36.

38. MJP Diary, February 23, 1863, quoted in *L&L*, 160.

39. MJP Diary, May 1, 1862, quoted in *L&L*, 138.

40. MJP Diary, May 1, 10, 1862, quoted in *L&L*, 139.

41. William C. Preston to JTLP, August 10, 1862, quoted in *March Past*, 149.

42. MJP Diary, September 4, 1862, quoted in *L&L*, 147.

43. MJP Diary, September 10, 1862, quoted in *L&L*, 149.

44. TJJ to MJP, n.d. [after September 10, 1862], Thomas J. Jackson Collection, VMI.

45. MJP Diary, November 23, 1862, quoted in *L&L*, 155 (misdated in *L&L* as October 23, 1862, but Mary Anna Jackson, in her *Memoirs*, lists November 23 as Julia's birth date. The November date is also given on Julia's gravestone, in Stonewall Jackson Cemetery, Lexington, Virginia).

46. MJP Diary, December 19, 1862, quoted in *L&L*, 156–57.

47. TJJ to JTLP, January 19, 1863, Preston Papers, #1543, UNC.

48. MJP Diary, December 10, 1862, quoted in *L&L*, 156.

49. GJ to "Dear Br" [William Finney of Baltimore], April 15, 1862. In an advertisement for *Political Fallacies*, attached to this letter, Junkin identified himself as "father-in-law of Gen. Stonewall Jackson and Col. Preston" of Virginia.

50. Jedediah Hotchkiss to his wife, Sara, March 27, 1863, Jedediah Hotchkiss Papers, reel 4, Manuscript Division, Library

of Congress.

51. MJP Diary, December 24, 1862, quoted in *L&L*, 157.

52. MJP, "Christmas Carol, for 1862," Scrapbook II:84.

53. MJP Diary, October 27, 1862, quoted in *L&L*, 156–57.

54. MJP Diary, January 9, 1863, quoted in *L&L*, 158–59.

55. *March Past*, 129; MJP Diary, April 3, 1863, quoted in *L&L*, 16; *March Past*, 152–53.

56. Emily Bondurant, *Reminiscences* (typed manuscript of original, made in 1962, #2430, UNC).

57. MJP Diary, April 15, 1863, quoted in *L&L*, 161.

58. MJP Diary, November 24, 1863, quoted in *L&L*, 172.

59. TJJ to JTLP, April 27, 1863, Preston Papers, #1543, UNC.

60. MJP Diary, May 5, 1863, quoted in *L&L*, 163.

61. MJP Diary, May 12, 1863, quoted in *L&L*, 165.

62. Ibid.

63. *March Past*, 126.

64. Ibid, 152.

65. MJP Diary, May 15, 1863, quoted in *L&L*, 166.

66. *March Past*, 154.

67. DXJ to GJ, May 18, 1863, quoted in *Life of Dr. G. J.*, 551–52.

68. MJP Diary, November 10, 1863, quoted in *L&L*, 171.

69. Professor Martin L. Stoever of Pennsylvania, an eyewitness to the extraordinary scene, quoted in *Life of Dr. G. J.*, 550. The cane given by Jackson to Dr. Junkin is now in the Stonewall Jackson House Collection.

70. Editorial in the *Richmond Whig*, July 8, 1863.

71. MJP Diary, December 6, 1863; November 11, 1863, quoted in *L&L*, 173, 171.

72. *March Past*, 173.

73. MJP Diary, April 18, May 10, 1864, quoted in *L&L*, 178–79.

74. MJP Diary, February 10, 1864, quoted in *L&L*, 177.

75. MJP Diary, June 11, 1864, quoted in *L&L*, 188.

76. Recollection of Herbert Preston, Sr., as told to his daughter, Janet Preston.

77. MJ to HD, n.d. [after June 15, 1857].

78. MJP Diary, June 11, 1864, quoted in *L&L*, 189.

79. MJP Diary, June 12, 1864, quoted in *L&L*, 190.

80. Ibid.

81. MJP Diary, June 12, 1864, quoted in *L&L*, 192.

82. MJP Diary, June 14, 1864, quoted in *L&L*, 195.

83. MJP Diary, June 14, 1864, quoted in *L&L*, 196.

84. Ibid.

85. MJP Diary, June 12, 1864, quoted in *L&L*, 192.

86. Susan P. Lee, *Gen. William Nelson Pendleton* (first published in 1893; reprint Harrisonburg, Virginia: Sprinkle Publications, 1991), 348; MJP Diary, June 17, 1864, quoted in *L&L*, 197.

87. A printed copy of "Virginia" is found in Scrapbook II:61; "Hymn to the National Flag" appeared in the *Lexington Gazette*, November 2, 1864 (copy in Scrapbook II:61); "Dirge for Ashby" appeared in the *Lexington Gazette*, August 2, 1862 (copy in Scrapbook II:83); "Christmas Lay for 1864: When the War is Over" appeared in the *Lexington Gazette*, January 4, 1865 (copy in Scrapbook II:63).

88. MJP, "Stonewall Jackson's Grave," inserted at back of 1866 edition of *Beechenbrook*.

89. JTLP to MJP, January 24, 1865, quoted in *March Past*, 174–75.

90. JTLP to MJP, quoted in *L&L*, 199.

91. MJP Diary, n.d. [1865], quoted in *L&L*, 202–3; *March Past*, 182.

92. *Beechenbrook*, 7.

93. Ibid, 14, 15.

94. Ibid, 25.

95. Ibid, 26–27.

96. Ibid, 40.

97. Ibid, 51.

98. Ibid, 59.

99. Ibid, 61.

100. MJP Diary, September 11, 1862, quoted in *L&L*, 149.

101. *Beechenbrook*, 64.

102. MJP Diary, n.d. [1865], quoted in *L&L*, 203.

103. Ibid.

104. *Christian Observer and Presbyterian* 44 (March 30, 1865).

105. Habakkuk 3:27–28.

106. MJP Diary, April 10, 1865, quoted in *L&L*, 207–8.

Chapter 6. Sonnets and Sauces. 1865–1890

1. MJP to W. M. Baskerville, March 21, 1889, Baskerville MSS, Duke.

2. *March Past*, 150.

3. *L&L*, 230.

4. Cornelia Peake McDonald, *A Woman's Civil War: A Diary, with Reminiscences of the War*, ed. Minrose C. Gwin (Madison: The University of Wisconsin Press, 1992), 237; Susan P. Lee, *Memoirs of William Nelson Pendleton, D.D.* (1893; reprint Harrisonburg, Virginia: Sprinkle Publications, 1991), 409.

5. Couper 3:127.

6. *L&L*, 208.

7. MJP to PHH, July 11, 1869, typed copy of letter, Hayne MSS, Duke.

8. John Wesley, "Cleanliness is indeed next to godliness," Sermon 88, "On Dress" (from *The Works of John Wesley*, volume 3, Sermons III:74–114. Copyright 1986 by Abingdon Press. Used by permission.) This was evidently a folk saying by the time

of Wesley, an adage that had derived from Hebrew exegesis.

9. MJP, Postwar Diary, April–May 1868, August–December 1870, quoted in *L&L*, 226–228, 236, 240; MJP to Elizabeth Preston Allan, "Home, Friday. (Waiting for the folks to come to breakfast)," n.d., quoted in *L&L*, 291.

10. *L&L*, 109.

11. Janet Allan Bryan to Herbert Preston, Jr., September 7, 1957, letter in possession of author.

12. MJP Diary, Wednesday, May 13, 1868, quoted in *L&L*, 229.

13. Eleanor Hosie to Herbert Preston, Jr., February 1, n.d., letter in possession of Janet Preston, Baltimore.

14. *L&L*, 212.

15. A. L. Nelson, "Recollections," *Ring Tum Phi*, February 18, 1899, W&L.

16. *Lexington Gazette*, April 18 and 25, 1866, W&L.

17. Leonard Hal Bridges, *Lee's Maverick General: Daniel Harvey Hill* (New York: McGraw-Hill Book Company, Inc., 1961), 274; Gaines M. Foster, *Ghosts of the Confederacy: Defeat, The Lost Cause, and the Emergence of the New South, 1865–1913* (New York: Oxford University Press, 1987), 50.

18. MJP, "Hero's Daughter," "Regulus," *Land We Love* 1 (October 1866): 404, 409.

19. MJP, "Acceptation," *Land We Love* 1 (August 1866): 240.

20. *L&L*, 242.

21. PHH to MJP, December 31, 1867, Preston Papers, #1543, UNC.

22. MJP to PHH, February 14, 1868, typed copy of letter, Hayne MSS, Duke.

23. MJP, Postwar Diary, April 16 and 28, 1868, quoted in *L&L*, 226, 228.

24. *Life of Dr. G. J.*, ix; also Pope, 22.

25. Pope, 23.

26. *Lexington Gazette & Banner*, June 3, 1868.

27. MJP Diary, August 27, 1870, quoted in *L&L*, 236.

28. MJP Diary, January 24, 1870, quoted in *L&L*, 231.

29. MJP Diary, February 15, 1870, quoted in *L&L*, 232.

30. JTLP to PHH, October 8, 1870, typed copy of letter, Hayne MSS, Duke.

31. MJP, "The Dumb Poet," *Old Song*, 126.

32. MJP to PHH, March 26, 1872, Hayne MSS, Duke.

33. Ibid.

34. MJP, Dedication to *Old Song*, 5, 10.

35. MJP Diary, August 27, 1870, quoted in *L&L*, 236.

36. Rayburn S. Moore, *Paul Hamilton Hayne* (New York: Twayne Company, 1972), 56.

37. William Hand Browne, *New Eclectic Magazine* 7 (October 1870): 494–96.

38. Review originally published in *Saturday Review* of London, reprinted in *Southern Magazine* 1 (January 1871): 120.

39. MJP to PHH, May 27, n.d., [1871] typed copy of letter, Hayne MSS, Duke.

40. MJP to Mr. Sargeant, February 10, 1880, Brown University Library, Providence, Rhode Island.

41. JTLP to PHH, October 8, 1870, typed copy of letter, Hayne MSS, Duke.

42. MJP to PHH, November 2, n.d., [1870], Hayne MSS, Duke.

43. MJP to PHH, November 17, 1870, typed copy of letter, Hayne MSS, Duke.

44. MJP Diary, November 7, 1870, quoted in *L&L*, 239.

45. MJP, "Gone Forward," *New Eclectic Magazine* 7 (December 1870): 763; *Cartoons*, 180.

46. MJP to Judge Houston, December 31, n.d., W&L.

47. MJP Diary, August 30, September 17, 1870, quoted in

L&L, 237.

48. MJP to W. M. Baskerville, March 21, 1889, Baskerville MSS, Duke.

49. MJP Diary, October 22, 1870, quoted in *L&L,* 238.

50. MJP, "Smitten," *Cartoons,* 176.

51. MJP to PHH, February 3, 1873, Hayne MSS, Duke.

52. *L&L,* 306.

53. MJP, "Winter Love," Scrapbook IV:91; slightly altered version appears as "Autumn Love" in *Colonial,* 124.

54. MJP to HD, October 20, n.d. [1857].

55. *March Past,* 217.

56. MJP to EPA, June 15, 1875 (original presumed lost), typed copy in William Allan Papers, #2764, UNC.

57. Julia Rush Junkin [Irwin] to Mrs. Ebenezer Junkin, February 7, 1874, letter in possession of Elizabeth Lapsley Pendergrast, granddaughter of Julia Rush Junkin Irwin.

58. MJP, "Georgie and Herbert's Letter," printed version in Scrapbook IV:20; handwritten copy in Scrapbook III:115.

59. MJP to PHH, February 3, 1873, Hayne MSS, Duke.

60. Student Reports, January 1875, in *Washington and Lee Student Reports* (1874–75), W&L.

61. MJP to "My dear Cousin Irvine," November 12, n.d. [1885?], dictated, letter given to the author by Mrs. Herbert Preston, Jr.

62. MJP, quoted in *L&L,* 1.

63. James A. Harrison, "Margaret J. Preston: An Appreciation," Appendix to *L&L,* 363.

64. PHH to MJP, May 12, 1874, Hayne MSS, Duke; quoted in *Man of Letters,* 117–20.

65. Anonymous critic, *Lippincott's Magazine* 17 (May 1876): 647.

66. Anonymous reviewer, *The Critic* 3 (February 17, 1883):

67.

67. MJP to PHH, January 19, 1872, Hayne MSS, Duke.

68. MJP to PHH, March 26, 1872, Hayne MSS, Duke.

69. MJP to PHH, April 3, n.d. [1872], Hayne MSS, Duke.

70. PHH to MJP, April 9, 1872, Hayne MSS, Duke; quoted in *Man of Letters*, 97.

71. MJP, "Sandringham," *Cartoons*, 187–88.

72. MJP to W. M. Baskerville, March 21, 1889, Baskerville MSS, Duke.

73. Ibid.

74. MJP Diary, December 3, 1870, quoted in *L&L*, 240.

75. MJP to Mr. Sargeant, February 10, 1880, Brown University Library, Providence, Rhode Island.

76. MJP Diary, December 3, 1870, quoted in *L&L*, 240.

77. MJP to G. Watson James, June 28, n.d. (BR Box 177 [19]), Huntington Library, San Marino, California.

78. MJP Diary, December 31, 1875, quoted in *L&L*, 290.

79. MJP to PHH, February 3, 1873, Hayne MSS, Duke.

80. MJP, book review of Edward deLeon's *The Khedive's Egypt* (New York: Harper Brothers, 1877), Scrapbook IV:35. The periodical in which MJP review appeared is given wherever the author has been able to discover it.

81. MJP to WTW Barbe, August 20, n.d., Waitman T. Barbe Collection, West Virginia and Regional Historical Collection, West Virginia University Libraries, Morgantown, West Virginia; MJP review of Longfellow's *Ultima Thule* (Boston: Houghton Mifflin, 1880), Scrapbook IV:45; also MJP to PHH, February 29, 1872, Hayne MSS, Duke.

82. MJP, essay, "The New Poet," in Scrapbook IV:69.

83. MJP, review of Abel Stevens, *Madame de Staël: A Study of her Life and Times* (New York: Harper & Brothers, 1880) in "Literary Notes," *Central Presbyterian* [?], Scrapbook IV:74.

84. MJP, November 30, 1881 review of Helen Zimmern's *Maria Edgeworth* (Boston: Roberts Brothers, 1883), Scrapbook

IV:48.

85. MJP, review of the *Life of Mary Russell Mitford: Told by Herself, in Letters to Her Friends,* ed. A. G. K. L'Estrange (New York: Harper & Brothers, 1870) in *New Eclectic Magazine* 7 (May 1870): 518, 520.

86. MJP, review of Harriet Martineau's *Autobiography,* ed. M. Oliphant (Boston: J. R. Osgood, 1877), Scrapbook IV:17.

87. MJP, "Rossetti's New Poems," review, Scrapbook IV:60.

88. MJP, "At Last," poem written for "Festival" of Poe Memorial Society, April 23, 1877, *Colonial,* 138; also MJP review of Edmund Clarence Stedman's "Essay on Edgar Allan Poe" in *Scribner's Monthly* 20 (May 1880), 107–24.

89. MJP, "At Last," *Colonial,* 140.

90. MJP to Thomas Nelson Page, July 25, 1886, TN Page MSS, Duke.

91. MJP review of Cable's *The Grandissimes* (New York: Charles Scribner's Sons, 1880), Scrapbook IV:45; PHH to MJP, December 16, 1884, Hayne MSS, Duke; quoted in *Man of Letters,* 233.

92. MJP, review of *Poems of Henry Timrod,* ed. Paul H. Hayne (New York: E. J. Hale & Sons,1872), in *Southern Magazine* (March, 1872).

93. MJP, essay, "Paul Hamilton Hayne," *Southern Bivouac* 2 (September 1886): 223, 227.

94. MJP to PHH, February 1, 1872, Hayne MSS, Duke; quoted in *Man of Letters,* 18.

95. MJP to W. M. Baskerville, April 26, n.d. [1887], original typed letter, Baskerville MSS, Duke.

96. MJP to G. Watson James of the *Richmond Standard,* June 28, n.d., (BR Box 177 [19]), asking him to reprint notice of John Esten Cooke's *Virginia Bohemians* that had appeared in *Literary World,* original letter (BR Box 177[19]) in Huntington Library, San Marino, California.

97. MJP to PHH, September 13, 1869, typed copy of letter, Hayne MSS, Duke.

98. MJP to PHH, January 19, 1872, Hayne MSS, Duke.

99. MJP, "The Literary Profession in the South," *The Library Magazine of American and Foreign Thought* 8 (1881): 60–74.

100. Ibid.

101. MJP to PHH, February 3, 1873, Hayne MSS, Duke; also *L&L*, 267, 316.

102. MJP to PHH, February 3, 1873, Hayne MSS, Duke.

103. PHH to MJP, July 26, 1878, Hayne MSS, Duke; quoted in *Man of Letters*, 151.

104. PHH to MJP, December 15, 1871, Hayne MSS, Duke; quoted in *Man of Letters*, 91.

105. PHH to MJP, March 22, 1881, Hayne MSS, Duke; quoted in *Man of Letters*, 29.

106. PHH to MJP, February 9, 1884, Hayne MSS, Duke; quoted in *Man of Letters*, 29.

107. PHH to MJP, May 3, 1881, Hayne MSS, Duke.

108. MJP to Mrs. Paul Hamilton Hayne, June 24, 1886, Hayne MSS, Duke.

109. MJP to Mrs. Paul Hamilton Hayne (typed original), July 9, n. d. [1886], Hayne MSS, Duke.

110. JTLP to MJP, August 3, 1882, Preston Papers, #1543, UNC.

111. MJP to PHH, March 1, 1878, Hayne MSS, Duke.

112. MJP, Introduction to *Poems of Paul Hamilton Hayne*, Complete Edition (Boston: D. Lothrop, 1882).

113. MJP to PHH, 11 [December 11, 1882] and MJP to PHH, March 7, 1883, Hayne MSS, Duke.

114. MJP to PHH, September 12, 1883, dictated, Hayne MSS, Duke.

115. JTLP Diary, August 9, 1861, Library of Congress.

116. MJP to PHH, June 28, 1884, typed portion in Hayne

MSS, Duke; longer section in *L&L*, 308–9.

117. MJP, "In Cripplegate Church: A Sonnet," *Monographs*, 219.

118. MJP to PHH, August 20, 1884, Hayne MSS, Duke, quoted in *L&L* 311; *Monographs* 53, 77.

119. MJP to PHH, October 20, 1884, typed copy of letter, Hayne MSS, Duke.

120. Ibid.

121. MJP to W. M. Baskerville, October 15, 1887, and May 11, 1886, dictated, Baskerville MSS, Duke.

122. MJP, "Broidery Work," *FLS*, 75.

123. *The Critic* 6 (December 25, 1886): 315.

124. *The Critic* 7 (March 12, 1887): 135.

125. *The Critic* 8 (July 30, 1887): 53.

126. Julia J to Lizzie Webster, September 15, 1887, W&L.

127. MJP to W. M. Baskerville, March 21, 1889, Baskerville MSS, Duke.

128. Interview, which originally appeared in *Woman's Magazine*, 1883, quoted in *Boston Evening Transcript*, August 7, 1926, Davie Collection, Filson Club, Louisville, Kentucky.

129. Laura C. Holloway, "Margaret Junkin Preston," *Washington Post*, 1888, clipping, with no dateline, given to the author by Mrs. Herbert Preston, Jr. The same article, dated 1888, is found in the Withrow Scrapbooks 19:107, W&L.

130. MJP to Mrs. Paul Hamilton Hayne, March 4, 1890, dictated, Hayne MSS, Duke.

131. MJP to W. M. Baskerville, April 11, 1890, dictated, Baskerville MSS, Duke.

132. Robert F. Hunter, *Lexington Presbyterian Church, 1789–1989* (Lexington, Virginia: Lexington Presbyterian Church, 1991) 99; printed article, 1939, in Withrow scrapbooks 19:100–01, W&L; obituary of JTLP, *Lexington Gazette*, July 24, 1890.

133. James A. Harrison, "Margaret J. Preston: An Appreciation," Appendix to *L&L*, 351.

134. MJP to Mrs. Paul Hamilton Hayne, May 4, 1891, dictated, Hayne MSS, Duke.

Chapter 7. Singing Her Own Song, 1890–1897

1. MJP, "Unconscious Art," *Baldwin's Monthly Magazine* 31 (July 1885): 1.

2. MJP to S.G. [Sophia B. Gilman, of Maine], January 13, 1891, quoted in *L&L*, 323.

3. MJP to Mrs. Paul Hamilton Hayne, July 9, n.d. [1886], dictated, Hayne MSS, Duke.

4. MJP to Mrs. Paul Hamilton Hayne, May 4, 1891, dictated, Hayne MSS, Duke.

5. MJP to Mrs. Paul Hamilton Hayne, July 11, 1886, Hayne MSS, Duke.

6. MJP, "A Letter to Mrs. Myers" [possibly Mrs. Henry H. Myers, president, soon after Maggie, of the Women's Missionary Society of the Lexington Presbyterian Church], August 22, 1866, Scrapbook III:75.

7. MJP, "A Note to Mrs. Pratt" [Mrs. John A Pratt, wife of minister of Lexington Presbyterian Church, 1868–74], February 26, 1869, Scrapbook III:145–46.

8. MJP to S.G. [Sophia B. Gilman], January 15, 1891, quoted in *L&L*, 324.

9. *L&L*, 325.

10. MJP, *Centennial Poem: 1775–1885* (New York: G. P. Putnam's Sons, 1885), 24.

11. MJP, *Semi-Centennial Ode for the Virginia Military Institute: 1839–1889* (New York: G.P. Putnam's Sons, 1889), 22–3.

12. MJP to "my dear Mr. Finney" [John A. Finney], July 3, 1891, Archives, McDonogh School, Baltimore, Maryland.

13. MJP, "Poem, Written for the Unveiling," November 21, 1891.

14. Ibid, footnote at end of poem.

15. Katherine Brown, "Jackson in Lexington," *Proceedings of Rockbridge Historical Society* 9: 207; Chancery file #96, bundle 343, Rockbridge County Court House, Lexington, Virginia; letter of Mary Anna Jackson to Major John W. Graham, January 25, 1907, in appreciation for bill in N.C. legislature to give her a pension (Mrs. Thomas J. Jackson Collection, PC 1157.1, North Carolina Division of Archives & History, Raleigh, North Carolina).

16. Henry M. Field to Messrs. Harper, March 11, 1892, copy in Preston Papers, #1543, UNC.

17. James A. Harrison to MJP, February 25, 1892, Preston Papers, #1543, UNC.

18. James A. Harrison to MJP, March 23, 1892, Preston Papers, #1543, UNC.

19. Henry M. Field to Messrs Harper, March 11, 1892, copy in Preston Papers, #1543, UNC.

20. Harper & Brothers to MJP, March 11, 1892, Preston Papers, #1543, UNC.

21. Preface, vi, to *Memoirs of Stonewall Jackson by His Widow* (Louisville, Kentucky: The Prentice Press, 1895).

22. MJP to "Mrs. Randolph," February 11, 1892, dictated, letter in possession of author.

23. MJP to Mrs. Paul Hayne, May 4, 1891, Hayne MSS, Duke.

24. MJP to "A. deF.," n.d. [1893?], quoted in *L&L*, 327–28.

25. William Porter Kellam, *Episodes in the Life of Charles Francis McCay* (Athens, Georgia: n.p., 1983).

26. Article pasted in Scrapbook IV:66–67.

27. Anonymous reviewer in *The Critic* 15 (January 31, 1890): 54.

28. James A. Harrison, "Margaret J. Preston: An Appreciation," Appendix to *L&L*, 373.

29. MJP to S. G. [Sophia B. Gilman], November 13, 1893, quoted in *L&L*, 329.

30. MJP to Colonel William P. Johnston, December 3, 1894, dictated, Johnston Family Papers, Filson Club, Louisville, Kentucky.

31. MJP to "A. deF.," November 20, 1893, quoted in *L&L*, 331.

32. *L&L*, 337.

33. MJP, "Euthanasia," *The Critic* 30 (April 24, 1894): 291.

34. MJP to "A. deF.," November 20, 1893, and to S. G. [Sophia B. Gilman], October 22, 1894, quoted in *L&L*, 331–32.

35. MJP to Mrs. Mary B. Dodge, of New York City, n.d. [May 1896], *L&L*, 335.

36. *Lexington Gazette*, March 31, 1897.

37. Ibid.

38. Sophia B. Gilman, "Margaret Junkin Preston," *The Outlook* 1 (April 10, 1897): 984–85.

39. Anonymous reviewer in *The Critic* 12 (October 5, 1889): 159, of the book *American Sonnets*, ed. William Sharp (London: Walter Scott, 1889).

40. Edmund C. Stedman to MJP, June 20, 1891, Preston Papers, #1543, UNC. Stedman included in his *Library of American Literature* four of Maggie's poems (Edmund C. Stedman, *Library of American Literature* [New York: Charles L. Webster & Company, 1889], 8:253–58).

41. Maurice Thompson to MJP, December 13, 1887, Preston Papers, #1543, UNC.

42. Laura C. Holloway, "Margaret J. Preston: A Famous American Poet," article in *Washington Post*, 1888, newspaper clipping given to author by Mrs. Elizabeth Preston; quotations from *Boston Evening Traveller* and *Quebec Chronicle* from adver-

tisement for *Colonial Ballads*, dated October 6, 1887, Johnston Family Papers, Filson Club, Louisville, Kentucky.

43. PHH to MJP, May 12, 1874, Hayne MSS, Duke; quoted in *A Man of Letters*, 118.

44. William Gilmore Simms, ed., *War Poetry of the South* (New York: Richardson & Co., 1867), 55, 433; Ida Raymond, ed., *Southland Writers: Biographical and Critical Sketches of the Living Female Writers of the South* (Philadelphia: Claxton Remsen & Haffelfinger, 1870), 735–49.

45. Henry Wadsworth Longfellow, ed., *Poems of Places* (Boston: Osgood, 1876); William Sharp, ed., *The Canterbury Poets: An Anthology of American Sonnets* (London: Walter Scott, [1889].)

46. *Nation* 78 (February 4, 1904): 75.

47. W. P. Trent, ed., *Southern Writers: Selections in Prose and Verse* (New York: The Macmillan Co., 1905), 338.

48. Charles W. Hubner, ed., *Representative Southern Poets* (New York: Neale Publishing Company, 1906), 150.

49. Mildred Lewis Rutherford, *The South in History and Literature* (Atlanta: The Franklin Turner Company, 1906), 431.

50. Armistead C. Gordon, Jr., *Virginia Writers of Fugitive Verse* (New York: James T. White & Co., 1923), 66.

51. MJP to PHH, February 3, 1873, Hayne MSS, Duke.

52. Jay B. Hubbell, *The South in American Literature* (copyright 1954 Duke University Press. Reprinted with permission of the publisher), 619.

53. MJ to HD, March 29, 1840; Elizabeth Preston Allan, "Margaret Junkin Preston," in *Library of Southern Literature*, ed. Edwin Anderson Alderman, Joel Chandler Harris, and Charles William Kent (Atlanta: The Martin Hoyt Company, 1907), 10: 4235.

54. MJP, "Unconscious Art," *Baldwin's Monthly Magazine* 31 (July 1885): 1.

Bibliography

Manuscript Sources

Several hundred manuscript letters, portraits, scrapbooks, and other memorabilia of the Miller, Dickey, Junkin, and Preston families (some dating from the eighteenth century) are in the private collection of Margaret Junkin Preston's granddaughter, Janet Cross Preston, of Baltimore, Maryland.

Additional letters to and from members of the Junkin and Preston families (original or copied) have been given to the author by Elizabeth Preston of Baltimore, Maryland; Anna Brooke Allan of Chapel Hill, North Carolina; Agnes Junkin Peery of Tazewell, Virginia; and Elizabeth Lapsley Pendergrast of Atlanta, Georgia.

Bowdoin College. The Abbot Memorial Collection contains two letters of Margaret Junkin Preston, as well as information concerning a poem of hers entitled "The Mount of Vision."

Brown University. In Special Collection of the John Hay Library is a letter from Margaret Junkin Preston to "Mr. Sargeant."

Duke University. In the Paul Hamilton Hayne Papers, the William Baskerville Papers, and the Marshall McDonald Papers are several hundred letters to and from Margaret Junkin Preston.

The Filson Club, Louisville, Kentucky. Among the Johnston Family Papers are letters of Margaret Junkin Preston; in the Davie Collection there is one folder of her original poems.

Historical Society of Pennsylvania, Philadelphia. In the Gratz Manuscripts and other collections are several letters of George Junkin and Margaret Junkin Preston.

Huntington Library, San Marino, California. Here are four-teen items pertaining to Margaret Junkin Preston: letters, manuscript copies of individual poems, and a handwritten copy of her essay entitled "William C. Preston" (1862).

Lafayette College, Easton, Pennsylvania. In the Skillman Archives of the college are student and faculty letters, letters from George Junkin to a variety of correspondents, pamphlets, newspaper clippings from Easton newspapers, copies of the student newspaper *The Educator*, trustee minutes, alumni records, and other documents relevant to the two tenures of George Junkin as president of the college (1832–1841, 1844–1848). Also in the archives is the unpublished typed manuscript by Earl Pope, "George Junkin and His Eschatological Vision."

Library of Congress. Pertinent material includes microfilm of the handwritten 1861 diary of John Thomas Lewis Preston (written while he was on military duty during the first year of the Civil War); and microfilm of Jedediah Hotchkiss Papers.

Miami University, Oxford, Ohio. In the Havighurst Collection at the university are letters, student records, catalogs, trustees' minutes, and other data relevant to the tenure of George Junkin as president of the college (1841–1844).

Stonewall Jackson House, Historic Lexington Foundation, Lexington, Virginia. Here are court records, newspaper clippings, ledgers, portraits, bank records, and other memorabilia related to Thomas Jonathan Jackson, John Thomas Lewis Preston, Margaret Junkin Preston, and others.

University of North Carolina at Chapel Hill. In the Margaret Junkin Preston Papers, housed in the Southern Historical Collection, are more than 150 items: letters, scrapbooks, and other items pertinent to the life and literary work of Margaret Junkin Preston. Also in the Southern Historical Collection are the Thomas J. Jackson Collection, papers pertaining to the Allan family, and a typed copy of the memoir of Emily Morrison Bondurant (1837–1925), entitled "Reminiscences" (later privately printed, no publisher listed, 1962).

University of West Virginia, Morgantown, West Virginia. In the West Virginia and Regional History Collection, the Waitman Barbe papers contain three letters of Margaret Junkin Preston.

Virginia Military Institute, Lexington, Virginia. In the archives are original letters of Thomas Jonathan Jackson in the Thomas J. Jackson Collection; the manuscript of William Couper (from which *One Hundred Years at V.M.I.* was culled); letters, newspaper clippings, student newspapers, and other manuscript material about Jackson, J. T. L. Preston, Margaret Junkin Preston, and the affairs of the Institute.

Washington and Lee University, Lexington, Virginia. In the Special Collections of the University's library are several notebooks and an "idea" book in Margaret Junkin Preston's handwriting, scrapbooks, and numerous letters of hers written after 1848; letters from Julia Junkin [Fishburn] to Lizzie Webster; minutes and letters of the trustees of Washington College (later Washington and Lee University), student reports, alumni records, student newspapers, and other data about the life of the college and its students; the Daniel Harvey Hill Papers; the Withrow Scrapbooks; minutes of Lexington Presbytery (typed and bound copies 1848–1880); original typed manuscript of Ollinger Crenshaw (before it was pruned to published form as *General Lee's College*); materials from the Franklin Society (a nineteenth-century Lexington debating society); and archives of the Rockbridge Historical Society.

Unpublished Articles

Grey, J. H., Jr. "Margaret Junkin Preston: Virginia's Poetess of the Old South." Master's thesis, Washington and Lee University, 1933, W&L.

Hall, John Augustus Fritchey. "Margaret Junkin Preston: Lexington Poetess." Undergraduate thesis, Washington and Lee University, 1950, W&L.

Pope, Earl A. "George Junkin and his Eschatological Vision." Typed manuscript of Jones Faculty Lecture given at Lafayette College on February 10, 1970, Lafayette.

Preston, John Thomas Lewis. "Address delivered before the Franklin Society, February 1866." Franklin Society Library, W&L.

Quarles, James. "In Review." Typed unpublished manuscript, W&L.

Weaver, Ethan Allen. "Margaret Junkin Preston: An Easton Lass of Long Ago." Memoir read at the meeting of the Northampton County, Pennsylvania Historical and Genealogical Society, September 20, 1921, Lafayette.

Newspapers

Lexington Gazette [in some years called *Lexington Gazette and Banner*], weekly newspaper of Lexington, Virginia, 1848–1897.

Richmond Dispatch, daily newspaper, Richmond, Virginia. April 4, 1859.

Richmond Whig, daily newspaper, Richmond, Virginia. July 8, 1863.

Published Material

Allan, Elizabeth Randolph Preston. *A March Past: Reminiscences of Elizabeth Randolph Preston Allan*. Edited by Janet Allan Bryan. Richmond: Dietz Press, 1938.

————. *The Life and Letters of Margaret Junkin Preston*. Boston: Houghton Mifflin and Company, 1903.

————. "Margaret Junkin Preston." In *Library of Southern Literature*, 10: 4235–54 edited by Edwin A. Alderman, Joel Chandler Harris, Charles William Kent. Atlanta: Martin &

Hoyt Co., 1907.

Arnold, Thomas Jackson. *Early Life and Letters of General Thomas J. Jackson, "Stonewall" Jackson, by His Nephew, Thomas Jackson Arnold.* New York: Fleming H. Revell Company, 1916.

Baird, E. Thompson, ed. *The Voice of Praise, a Selection of Hymns and Tunes for the Sabbath School, Prayer Meeting, and Family Circle.* Richmond: E. Thompson Baird, 1872.

Baym, Nina. *Novels, Readers, and Reviewers: Responses to Fiction in Antebellum America.* Ithaca: Cornell University Press, 1984.

Bridges, Leonard Hal. *Lee's Maverick General, Daniel Harvey Hill.* New York: McGraw-Hill Book Company, Inc., 1961.

Brown, Katherine L. "Stonewall Jackson in Lexington." In *Proceedings of Rockbridge Historical Society,* 9 (1982): 197–210, edited by Sharon Ritenour and Larry I. Bland. Lexington, Virginia: Rockbridge Historical Society.

Burgess, Hugh F., Jr. and Robert C. Smoot III. *McDonogh School: An Interpretive Chronology.* Columbus, Ohio: Charles E. Merrill Publishing Company, 1973.

Burke, William Jeremiah and Will D. Howe. *American Authors and Books, 1640–1940.* New York: Gramercy Publishing, 1943.

Chambers, Lenoir. *Stonewall Jackson.* Wilmington, North Carolina: Broadfoot Publishing Company, 1958.

Cocks, Robert S. *One Hundred and Fifty Years of Evangelism, 1811–1961.* Northumberland County Historical Society,

Sunbury, Pennsylvania, 1961.

Coffin, Selden Jennings. *The Men of Lafayette, 1829–1893: Lafayette College, its History, its Men, Their Record*. Easton, Pennsylvania: G. W. West, 1891.

Cogan, Frances B. *All-American Girl: The Ideal of Real Womanhood in Mid-Nineteenth Century America*. Athens: University of Georgia Press, 1989.

Conrad, Susan Phinney. *Perish the Thought: Intellectual Women in Romantic America, 1830–1860*. New York: Oxford University Press, 1976.

Constitution of the Presbyterian Church. Confession of Faith, Section IV of Chapter XXIV: *Of Marriage and Divorce*. Philadelphia: Presbyterian Board of Publication, 1853, 1859.

Couper, William. *One Hundred Years at V. M. I.* Richmond: Garrett and Massie, 1939.

Crenshaw, Ollinger. *General Lee's College: The Rise and Growth of Washington and Lee University*. New York: Random House, 1969.

Curran, Stuart. *Shelley's Cenci: Scorpions Ringed with Fire*. Princeton, New Jersey: Princeton University Press, 1970.

Dooley, Edwin L. "Lexington in the 1860 Census." In *Proceedings of the Rockbridge Historical Society*, 9 (1982): 189–96, edited by Sharon R. Ritenour and Larry I. Bland. Lexington, Virginia: Rockbridge Historical Society.

Eliot, George. "Silly Novels by Lady Novelists." In *Essays of George Eliot*, edited by Thomas Pinney. New York: Columbia University Press, 1963.

Faris, John Thomson. *Old Roads out of Philadelphia*. Philadelphia: J. B. Lippincott, 1917.

Foster, Gaines M. *Ghosts of the Confederacy: Defeat, the Lost Cause, and the Emergence of the New South, 1865–1913*. New York: Oxford University Press, 1987.

Fox-Genovese, Elizabeth. *Within the Plantation Household: Black and White Women of the Old South*. Chapel Hill: University of North Carolina Press, 1988.

Friedman, Jean. *The Enclosed Garden: Women and Community in the Evangelical South, 1830–1900*. Chapel Hill: University of North Carolina Press, 1985.

Gilman, Sophia B. "Margaret Junkin Preston." *The Outlook* 1 (April 10, 1897): 984–85.

Godcharles, Frederic A. "Margaret Junkin Preston." *Proceedings of the Northumberland County Historical Society* 12 (March 1, 1942): 132–51.

Gordon, Armistead C., Jr. *Virginia Writers of Fugitive Verse*. New York: James T. White & Co., 1923.

Harrison, James A. "Margaret Junkin Preston: An Appreciation." Appendix to Elizabeth Preston Allan, *Life and Letters of Margaret Junkin Preston*. Boston: Houghton, Mifflin, and Company, 1903.

Hatch, David Arthur, ed. *Biographical Record of the Men of Lafayette*. Easton, Pennsylvania: Lafayette College, 1948.

Havighurst, Walter. *The Miami Years: 1809–1969*. New York: G. P. Putnam's Sons, 1969.

Hawke, David Freeman. *Benjamin Rush: Revolutionary Gadfly*. Indianapolis: Bobbs-Merrill, 1971.

Hawks, Joanne V. and Sheila L. Skemp, editors. *Sex, Race, and the Role of Women in the South*. Jackson: University Press of Mississippi, 1983.

Hayne, Paul Hamilton. *Poems of Paul Hamilton Hayne*. Boston: D. Lothrop and Company, 1882.

Heilbrun, Carolyn G. *Writing a Woman's Life*. New York: Ballantine Books, 1988.

Heron, John W. "George Junkin, DD., LL.D." In *The Diamond Anniversary Volume*, edited by Walter Lawrence Toby and William Oxley Thompson. Oxford, Ohio: Miami University, 1899.

Hill, Daniel H. "The Real Stonewall Jackson." *The Century Magazine* 47 (February 1894): 623–28.

History of Northampton County, Pennsylvania. Under supervision of William T. Heller. Boston: American Historical Society, 1920.

Holloway, Laura C. "Margaret Junkin Preston." *Washington Post*, 1888.

Hubbell, Jay B. *The South in American Literature, 1607–1900.* Durham: Duke University Press, 1954.

Hubner, Charles W., ed. *Representative Southern Poets.* New York: Neale Publishing Company, 1906.

Hunter, Robert F. *Lexington Presbyterian Church, 1789–1989.* Lexington, Virginia: Lexington Presbyterian Church, 1991.

Jackson, Mary Anna. *Life and Letters of General Thomas J. Jackson (Stonewall Jackson), by His Wife, Mary Anna Jackson.* New York: Harper & Brothers, 1892; rev. ed., *Memoirs of Stonewall Jackson by His Widow.* Louisville, Kentucky: The Prentice Press, 1895.

————. "With Stonewall Jackson in Camp." *Hearst's Magazine* 24 (1913): 386–94.

Junkin, David Xavier. *The Reverend George Junkin: A Historical Biography.* Philadelphia: J. B. Lippincott & Co., 1871.

Junkin, George. *Political Fallacies: An Examination of the False Assumptions, and Refutations of the Sophistical Reasonings, which Have Brought on this Civil War.* New York: C. Scribner, 1863.

Junkin, Margaret. "Magazine Literature." *Christian Parlor Magazine* 9 (1852): 27–30.

[Junkin, Margaret.] *Silverwood: A Book of Memories.* New York: Derby & Jackson, 1856.

Kellam, William Porter. *Episodes in the Life of Charles Francis McCay.* Athens, Georgia: n.p., 1983.

Kelley, Mary. *Private Woman, Public Stage: Literary Domesticity in Nineteenth Century America.* New York: Oxford University Press, 1984.

Lane, Maggie. *Literary Daughters.* New York: St. Martin's Press, 1989.

Leavitt, Judith Walzer. *Brought to Bed: Birthing Women and their Physicians in America, 1750–1950.* New York: Oxford University Press, 1986.

Lee, Susan P. *Gen. William Nelson Pendleton.* Harrisonburg, Virginia: Sprinkle Publications, 1991; first published as *Memoirs of William Nelson Pendleton, D.D.* Philadelphia: J. B. Lippincott Company, 1893.

MacLeod, Norman. *Wee Davie.* Richmond: Presbyterian Committee of Publication, 1864.

Mathews, Donald G. *Religion in the Old South.* Chicago: University of Chicago Press, 1977.

McDonald, Cornelia Peake. *A Woman's Civil War.* Madison: University of Wisconsin Press, 1992.

McElroy, Janice H., ed. *Pennsylvania Women in History: Our Hidden Heritage.* Washington, D. C.: Pennsylvania Division of American Association of University Women, 1983.

McKeithan, D. M., ed. *A Collection of Hayne Letters.* Austin: University of Texas Press, 1944.

McMillen, Sally G. *Motherhood in the Old South: Pregnancy, Child-*

birth, and Infant Rearing. Baton Rouge: Louisiana State University Press, 1989.

Moers, Ellen. *Literary Women.* Garden City, New York: Doubleday, 1976.

Moore, Rayburn S., ed. " 'Courtesies of the Guild and More': Paul Hamilton Hayne and Margaret Junkin Preston." *The Mississippi Quarterly* 43 (Fall 1990): 485–93.

————, ed. *Man of Letters in the Nineteenth-Century South: Selected Letters of Paul Hamilton Hayne.* Baton Rouge: Lousiana State University Press, 1982.

————. *Paul Hamilton Hayne.* New York: Twayne Publishers, Inc., 1972.

Moore, Sally Alexander. *Memoirs of a Long Life in Virginia.* Staunton, Virginia: McClure Company, 1920.

Painter, F. V. N. *Poets of the South: A Series of Biographical and Critical Studies with Typical Poems.* New York: American Book Company, 1903.

Pickett, LaSalle Corbell. *Literary Hearthstones of Dixie.* Philadelphia: J. P. Lippincott Company, 1912.

Preston, Margaret Junkin. *Aunt Dorothy: An Old Virginia Plantation Story.* New York: A. D. F. Randolph and Co., 1890; Black Heritage Library Collection Series, reprint of 1890 ed., Salem, New Hampshire: Ayer Company Publications, n.d.

————. *Beechenbrook: A Rhyme of the War.* Richmond: J. W.

Randolph, 1865.

———. *Cartoons.* Boston: Roberts Brothers, 1875.

———. *Centennial Poem for Washington and Lee: 1775–1885.* New York: G. P. Putnam's Sons, 1885.

———. *Chimes for Church Children.* Philadelphia: Presbyterian Board of Publication and Sabbath-School Work, 1889.

———. *Colonial Ballads, Sonnets, and Other Verse.* Boston: Houghton, Mifflin and Company, 1887.

———. *For Love's Sake: Poems of Faith and Comfort.* New York: Anson D. F. Randolph and Company, 1886.

———. "General Lee After the War." *The Century Magazine* 38 (1889): 271–76.

———. "The General's Colored Sunday School," *Sunday School Times* 29 (December 3, 1887): 771–72.

———. "Giving Children Right Impressions of Death." *Sunday School Times* 33 (November 7, 1891): 707–8.

———. *A Handful of Monographs: Continental and English.* New York: A. D. F. Randolph and Company, 1886.

———. "The Literary Profession in the South," *Library Magazine of American and Foreign Thought* 8 (1881): 60–74.

———. *Old Song and New.* Philadelphia: J. B. Lippincott & Co., 1870.

———. *Poem: At Unveiling of Marble Bust of Col. William Allan, McDonogh School.* Printed pamphlet, 1891.

———. "Paul Hamilton Hayne." *Southern Bivouac* 2 (September 1886): 222–29.

———. "Personal Reminiscences of Stonewall Jackson." *The Century Magazine* 32 (1886): 927–36.

———. "President George Junkin, D.D., 1848–1861." In "The Presidency of Washington College," edited by Henry A. White. *Proceedings of the Scotch-Irish Congress 1895.* Nashville, Tennessee. n.p., 1895.

———. *Semi-Centennial Ode for the Virginia Military Institute.* New York: G. P. Putnam's Sons, 1889.

Pusey, William W. III. "Junius M. Fishburn (1830–1858): Professor of Latin." In *Proceedings of the Rockbridge Historical Society* 9 (1982): 139–56. Edited by Sharon R. Ritenour and Larry I. Bland. Lexington, Virginia: Rockbridge Historical Society.

Raymond, Ida. *Southland Writers: Biographical and Critical Sketches of the Living Female Writers of the South.* Philadelphia: Claxton, Remson & Haffelfinger, 1870.

Reidenbaugh, Lowell. "Introduction to Morningside Edition." In *Memoirs of Stonewall Jackson by His Widow, Mary Anna Jackson.* Dayton, Ohio: Morningside Press, 1976.

Robinson, Richard D. and Elisabeth C. *Repassing at My Side: A Story of the Junkins.* Blacksburg, Virginia: The Southern Printing Company, 1975.

Rutherford, Mildred Lewis. *The South in History and Literature: A Handbook of Southern Authors*. Atlanta: The Franklin-Turner Company, 1906.

Scott, Anne Firor. *Making the Invisible Woman Visible*. Urbana: University of Illinois Press, 1984.

———. *The Southern Lady: 1830–1930*. Chicago: University of Chicago Press, 1970.

———. "Women, Religion, and Social Change in the South." In *Religion and the Solid South*, edited by Samuel S. Hill, Jr. Nashville: Abingdon Press, 1972.

Sharp, William, ed. *Canterbury Poets: An Anthology of American Sonnets*. London: Walter Scott, 1889.

Shoop, Michael I., comp. *Genealogies of the Jackson, Junkin, & Morrison Families*. Lexington, Virginia: Garland Gray Memorial Research Center, Stonewall Jackson House, Historic Lexington Foundation, 1981.

Simms, William Gilmore, ed. *War Poetry of the South*. New York: Richardson & Company, 1867.

Skillman, David Bishop. *The Biography of a College: Being the History of the First Century of the Life of Lafayette College*. Easton, Pennsylvania: Lafayette College, 1932.

Smith-Rosenberg, Carroll. "The Female World of Love and

Ritual: Relations between Women in Nineteenth-Century America." *Signs* 1 (Autumn 1975): 11–22.

Stedman, Edmund Clarence and Ellen M. Hutchinson, eds. *Library of American Literature.* 8: 253–58. New York: Charles L. Webster & Company, 1889.

Stowe, Steven. *Intimacy and Power in the Old South.* Baltimore: The Johns Hopkins Press, 1987.

Trent, William Peterfield, ed. *Southern Writers: Selections in Prose and Verse.* New York: The Macmillan Company, 1905.

Vandiver, Frank E. *Mighty Stonewall.* New York: McGraw-Hill, 1957.

Wamsley, James S. *Idols, Victims, Pioneers: Virginia's Women from 1607.* Richmond: Dietz Company, 1976.

Washington and Lee Historical Papers 4 (1893). Baltimore: John Murphy and Company, 1893.

Watts, Emily Stipes. *The Poetry of American Women 1632–1945.* Austin: University of Texas Press, 1977.

Weaver, Ethan Allen. *Local Historical and Biographical Notes.* Germantown, Pennsylvania: n.p., 1906.

———. *Poets and Poetry of the Forks of the Delaware.* Germantown, Pennsylvania: n.p., 1906.

Weber, William Lander, ed. *Selections from the Southern Poets.* New York: The Macmillan Company, 1901.

Welter, Barbara. *Dimity Convictions: The American Woman in the Nineteenth Century.* Athens: Ohio University Press, 1976.

White, H[enry] M., ed. *Rev. William S. White, D.D. and His Times.* Richmond: Presbyterian Committee of Publication, 1891.

Woolf, Virginia. "Women and Fiction." In *Collected Essays.* London: Hogarth Press, 1966.

Wood, Ann D. "The 'Scribbling Women' & Fanny Fern: Why Women Wrote." *American Quarterly* 23 (1971): 3–24.

Index

Finney, William: 9n, 23
Fishburn, George Junkin: 103, 104, 105, 107, 156n, 200, 208
Fishburn, Julia Rush Junkin (Julia J): childhood, 30, 32, 33, 36, 46; gravesite, 156n; mention of, 9n, 74, 104n, 122, 208; poems written about, 28, 33-34, 36; relationship with MJP, 33, 46, 61, 87, 88, 103, 104 and n, 105, 118, 122, 151, 160, 163, 181, 183, 184; years in Lexington, 59, 61, 63, 72, 76, 77, 78, 86, 87, 88, 103, 104, 105, 107; years in Philadelphia, 116, 122, 129
Fishburn, Junius: 63, 82, 87, 88, 104, 105, 156n, 200, 208
Florida: 58, 60, 61, 82, 84
For Love's Sake: see Preston, Margaret Junkin, books
Fort Sumter, South Carolina: 114
France: 93, 181, 182
Franklin Society: 91, 105, 108
Fredericksburg, Virginia: 58, 129, 131
Fuller, Jacob: 91n, 194
Fuller, Margaret: 173

Galileo: 46
General Assembly of Virginia: 91
"General Lee After the War:" see Preston, Margaret Junkin, prose articles and stories
Geneva, Switzerland: 182
George III of England: 101
Georgia: 41, 108, 175, 197, 202
Georgia, University of: 41
Germantown, Pennsylvania: 8, 19, 20, 21, 23, 26, 27, 31, 71
Germantown Manual School (Manual Academy): 19, 20, 21, 22, 23, 26, 31, 197
Germany: 87, 156, 181
Gettysburg, battle of: 134
Gilham, William: 91n, 194
Gilman, Sophia: 177, 201
"Giving Children Right Impressions of Death:" see Preston, Margaret Junkin, prose articles and stories
Gladstone, William Ewart: 169
Goethe, von, Johann Wolfgang: 182
Gordon, Armistead C., Jr.: 202

Gordonsville, Virginia: 58
Graham's Magazine: 62

Hampden-Sydney College, Virginia: 166
Hampton Roads, Virginia: 118
Handful of Monographs: see Preston, Margaret Junkin, books
Hangchow, China: 177
Hannah (servant): see Junkin slaves/ servants
Hanover, Presbytery of: 190n
Harper's Ferry, Virginia: 107, 122
Harper's Magazine: 166, 182, 198
Harrisburg, Pennsylvania: 7
Harrison, James: 186, 195, 198
Harrisonburg, Virginia: 136
Hawthorne, Nathaniel: 50n
Hayne, Paul Hamilton (PHH): 153, 154, 155, 158, 159, 160n, 162, 165, 167 and n, 168, 169, 175, 177, 178, 179, 180, 182, 201 and n
Hayne, Mrs. Paul Hamilton: 178, 185, 188, 189
Hetty (slave): see Jackson slaves
Highland folklore: see Scottish folklore/ legends
Hill, Daniel H.: 59, 63, 65, 66, 68, 77, 97, 153
Hill, Isabella (Mrs. Daniel): 63, 68, 97
Holmes, Oliver Wendell: 185, 202n
Home Journal: 167n
Hooker, General Joseph (USA): 130
Hotchkiss, Jedediah: 130
Hubbell, Jay B: 203
Hubner, Charles W.: 202
Hunt, Leigh: 157
Hunter, General David (USA): 138n, 143

Iliad: 179
Illinois: 116n
Indiana: 91n, 93, 116n, 201
Ingelow, Jean: 177
Iris: 62
Irving family (fictional): see Preston, Margaret Junkin, books, *Silverwood*
Irwin, Julia Rush Junkin: 164, 186
Italy: 93

Jackson, Eleanor [Elinor] "Ellie" Junkin (EJ[J]): characteristics, 8, 36;

courtship, marriage to MJP, 89, 94-97, 99-100, 102-4, 107-8, 109-11, 137, 204, 205; description of John Brown's hanging, 107; founder of VMI, 91, 186; last illness, death and burial, 185-86, 187, 197, 198, 200, 205; letters to MJP, 119 and n, 120-21; loyalty to Virginia, 107-8; marriage to Sally Caruthers, 92-93; mention of, 63, 64, 84, 88, 90, 91 and n, 92, 93, 109, 113, 129, 131, 132, 135, 144, 179-80, 185, 210; opposition to secession, 106, 108; poems written about, 157-59, 163; property, 90, 91 and n, 115 and n, 116, 139 and n, 148, 188n, 189n, 194; silver wedding anniversary, 179 and n; slaves, see Preston slaves/servants; wartime activities, 116, 118, 123, 124, 125, 127-28, 135, 136, 139, 140, 141; wartime diary, 93, 119-21, 180; years after war, 148-49, 151, 153, 156, 162, 163, 164, 171, 179, 180, 185, 190; will of, 188n

Preston, Julia Christian: 193 and n, 196n, 211

Preston, Margaret (MJP's granddaughter): 196n, 197

Preston, Margaret Junkin: appearance, xiii, xiv, 35, 62, 95, 100, 185; birth, 3-4, 9, 200n, 201n; childhood, 4-6, 8-12, 13-24; children's births, 104, 110; courtship and marriage to JTLP, 40, 94-104, 109-11, 119, 204, 205; death and burial, 199 and n; diaries, 124 and n, 127, 145, 149, 155, 157, 158, 162; education, 10, 14, 31-32, 49; evaluation of abilities, 201-6; fear of death, 16-19, 53, 60, 73-74, 128, 144, 197 and n, 199, 204; first years in Lexington, 58-68, 71-76, 84-86, 87-89, 113; formative years at Lafayette & Miami, 25, 27-41, 43-45, 46-54, 56; friendship with TJJ, xiii, xiv, 77-79, 84-86, 88, 98, 122, 127, 132, 192-93, 195 and n, 204; friendship with PHH, 154-55, 167, 169, 175, 177-78, 182; health, xiv, 12, 49 and n, 50-51, 74 and n, 78, 103, 135, 155, 168-69, 180, 182-83, 184, 188, 199-200, 204; mention of, xiv, 9n, 17n, 41, 57,

81 and n, 82-84, 85, 90, 91, 93, 94 and n, 100n, 104n, 105, 107, 109, 119, 128n, 152n, 211; opposition to TJJ, 65-69, 70, 72, 82, 193, 205; "Poetess of South," xiv, 5, 201; relationship with EJ[J], 11, 13, 28, 36, 51, 57, 62, 65, 67-68, 69 and n, 71-72, 76-77, 204-5; relationship with GJ, 4-6, 10, 15, 32, 43-44, 51, 109, 115, 116, 155-56, 204-5; relationship with JRJ, 27, 51-52, 63, 72-74, 204; relationship with Julia J, 86-88, 103, 104n, 105, 183; relationship with sons, 164-66; view of slavery, 52-53, 63-65; view of war, 112, 124, 127, 130, 134, 144, 145, 146, 204; war years, 112, 115-19, 120-33, 135-41, 142, 143-46; years after war, 148-86, 187-93, 194-200

_____books: *Aunt Dorothy*, 198;. *Beechenbrook*, 127, 141-46, 152, 154, 159, 192, 203; *Cartoons*, 167-69; *Chimes for Church Children*, 184; *Colonial Ballads*, 183-85; *For Love's Sake*, 182-83; *A Handful of Monographs*, 17n, 20n, 182-83; *Old Song and New*, 158, 1159, 161, 168, 176, 180; *Silverwood*, 69n, 80, 81 and n, 82-84

_____poetry: "Acceptation," 153-54; "All's Well," 121; "Attainment," 157; "Ballad in Reply to Tupper's Ballad to Columbia," 52-53; "The birth of the Flowers," 37-38; "Boy Van Dyck," 21; "Centennial Poem" [W&L], 190 and n; "Christ-crotch," 22; "Christmas Carol for 1862," 130, 139, 142; "Christmas Lay for 1864," 139; "A Cloud is on my heart, darling," 81-82, 83; "Comforted," 18-19; "Cripplegate Church," 181-82; "A Dirge for Ashby," 139, 140n; "Dumb Poet," 157-58; "Euthanasia," 198-99; "Evening," 25, 33; "The Fairies' Tablecloth," 22; "Georgie and Herbert's Letter," 164-65; "Gone Forward," 160-61; "Hawthorn Bower," 37, 38; "Hero's Daughter," 153; "A Hymn to the National Flag," 139; "I, too, shall die," 47;